EFFECTS OF MISTAKE AND OTHER DEFECTS ON THE PASSAGE OF LEGAL TITLE

EFFECTS OF MISTAKE AND OTHER DEFECTS ON THE PASSAGE OF LEGAL TITLE

Samuel Zogg

intersentia
Cambridge – Antwerp – Chicago

Intersentia Ltd
8 Wellington Street | Cambridge
CB1 1HW | United Kingdom
Tel.: +44 1223 736 170
Email: mail@intersentia.co.uk
www.intersentia.com | www.intersentia.co.uk

Distribution for the UK and Ireland:
NBN International
Airport Business Centre, 10 Thornbury Road
Plymouth, PL6 7PP
United Kingdom
Tel.: +44 1752 202 301 | Fax: +44 1752 202 331
Email: orders@nbninternational.com

Distribution for Europe and all other countries:
Intersentia Publishing nv
Groenstraat 31
2640 Mortsel
Belgium
Tel.: +32 3 680 15 50 | Fax: +32 3 658 71 21
Email: mail@intersentia.be

Distribution for the USA and Canada:
Independent Publishers Group
Order Department
814 North Franklin Street
Chicago, IL 60610
USA
Tel.: +1 800 888 4741 (toll free) | Fax: +1 312 337 5985
Email: orders@ipgbook.com

ISBN 978-1-78068-831-2
D/2019/7849/74
NUR 822

British Library Cataloguing in Publication Data. A catalogue record for this book is available from the British Library.

This book is dedicated to my parents, Thomas and Regula Zogg,
who have always provided every imaginable kind of support,
during this project and far beyond that.

PREFACE*

This book analyses the question of how legal ownership in tangible movable property – goods and corporeal money[1] – is transferred from one person to another and of how certain kinds of defects, particularly mistakes, affect the passage of legal title in that regard. Take the simple case that A, the beneficial legal owner of a car, transfers that car to B – for example by way of sale, barter or gift – and that A is in some manner mistaken about certain facts relevant to the transaction. A might, for example, wrongly believe that there is a contract between him and B, or that the relevant contract is valid, or he might believe that B is in fact someone else. In such cases, a broad variety of issues may arise. This book's scope, however, is limited to the question of whether and in what circumstances *legal* ownership passes to B or whether it remains vested in A. We shall not – or only peripherally – deal with the question of whether A might claim the transferred property's value from B by a *personal* restitutionary claim or whether A might assert *equitable* property rights by way of proprietary restitution (for example under a constructive or a resulting trust). We shall neither consider whether A might – once legal ownership has passed to B – *revest* property (legal or equitable) by way of rescission.[2] Our analysis furthermore presupposes that the very asset transferred from A to B might still be found in B's hands in an unchanged form. We shall not insofar deal with questions of *mixture* or *tracing* (i.e. whether A might assert rights in relation to mixtures or traceable substitutes of the asset transferred to B) or *following* (i.e. whether A might assert rights against third-party recipients of the transferred asset).[3]

Though this area of the law may well be regarded as a core area of private law, it has not yet received much attention in academic literature. It is the object of this book to set out the current state of the law and to offer – based on the existing case law – a coherent and rationalised explanation of how legal ownership is

* This is an updated version of the author's doctoral thesis ("Transfer of legal ownership in tangible movable property: The effects of mistake and other defects on the passage of title"), which has been accepted by the University of Zurich, Faculty of Law, in 2016 with the distinction *summa cum laude*.

1 This book's scope is confined to goods and corporeal money; it does not deal with transfers of real property, choses in action or incorporeal bank money.

2 Those issues are discussed by the author in detail in another book; ZOGG, Proprietary Consequences.

3 A profound analysis of tracing and following may be found in the monumental work of L. SMITH, Tracing; see also ZOGG, Proprietary Consequences, Chapter 1 sections 3 and 4.

transferred from one person to another and of how mistakes and other defects operate in that regard.

The book will be divided into three main parts. In a first step, some basic principles applying in the context of defective transfers of ownership shall be delineated at a somewhat abstract level (chapter 1). This will be an essential prerequisite to our analysis of the respective impacts of any particular defect on the passage of property.

Second, we shall examine the mechanics of how legal title is transferred from one person to another (chapter 2). It will be seen that there are basically three different modes of transfer at common law which may effect the passage of legal title, namely *delivery*, *sale* and *deed*. The respective requirements and the scope of those modes of transfer will be scrutinised in some detail. In particular, the question shall be raised whether and to what extent a valid contractual (or other) obligation is needed to transfer legal ownership and whether those three modes of transfer are, accordingly, governed by a *principle of causality* (a valid obligation is required) or *abstraction* (no obligation is required).

In a third step, we shall examine various kinds of defects with regard to the question of whether and in what circumstances they might prevent the passage of legal ownership (chapters 3 and 4). Our focus will clearly lie on the most difficult type of defect, namely mistake. It will be seen that the question of whether and under what conditions mistakes may prevent the passage of property *ab initio* is a delicate one which is not clearly settled by the case law.

ACKNOWLEDGEMENTS

My sincerest thanks go to Professor Wolfgang Ernst, my PhD supervisor and mentor, who has inflamed my passion for private law, and the law in general, by his brilliant and inspiring way of thinking and sense for legal reasoning. For this, and for many other things, I will always be indebted to him.

My further thanks go to Professor Andrew Burrows who has kindly reviewed my PhD thesis and who has provided valuable remarks on the subject.

CONTENTS

LIST OF CASES

LIST OF ABBREVIATIONS

A-G	Attorney General
A&E	Adolphus & Ellis' Queen's Bench Reports
ABCA	Alberta Court of Appeal
ABGB	Allgemeines Bürgerliches Gesetzbuch (Austria)
AC	Law Reports, Appeal Cases (3rd Series)
affd	affirmed
AG	Aktiengesellschaft
AlbLR	Alberta Law Review
All ER	All England Law Reports
All ER (Comm)	All England Law Reports (Commercial Cases)
All ER (D)	All England Direct Law Reports (Digests)
All ER Rep Ext	All England Law Reports Reprint, Australian Extension Volumes
App Cas	Law Reports, Appeal Cases (2nd Series)
B	Baron
B&A	Barnewall & Alderson's King's Bench Reports
B&C	Barnewall & Cresswell's King's Bench Reports
BC	Borough Council
BCC	British Company Law Cases
BGB	Bürgerliches Gesetzbuch (Germany)
BGE	Bundesgerichtsentscheid (decision of the Federal Court of Switzerland)
BingNC	Bingham's New Cases, English Common Pleas
Bros	Brothers
Burr	Burrow's King's Bench Reports tempore Mansfield
C	Chancellor
CA	Court of Appeal
Cal App 2d	California Appellate Reports, 2nd Series
CanLII	Canadian Legal Information Institute
Car & P	Carrington & Payne's Nisi Prius Reports
CB	Common Bench Reports/Chief Baron of the Exchequer
CBNS	Common Bench Reports, New Series
CBR (NS)	Canadian Bankruptcy Reports, New Series
CC	County/City Council
CCC (2d)	Canadian Criminal Cases, 2nd Series

Ch	Law Reports, Chancery Division (3rd Series)
ChD	Chancery Division/Law Reports, Chancery Division (2nd Series)
CJ	(Lord) Chief Justice
CJM	Chief Justice of Manitoba
CLC	Commercial Law Cases
CLJ	Cambridge Law Journal
CLP	Current Legal Problems
CLR	Commonwealth Law Reports, Australia
Co Rep	Coke's King's Bench Reports
Cox	Cox's Criminal Cases
CPL	Conveyancer and Property Lawyer
CR	Criminal Reports, Canada
Crim LR	Criminal Law Review
De G F&J	De Gex, Fisher & Jones' Chancery Reports
Dears	Dearsley's Crown Cases Reserved
Dist CA	District Court of Appeal
Div Ct	Divisional Court
DLR	Dominion Law Reports
DPP	Director of Public Prosecutions
East	East's Term Reports, King's Bench
EdinLR	Edinburgh Law Review
EMLR	Entertainment and Media Law Reports
ER	English Reports
EWCA Civ	England & Wales Court of Appeal (Civil Division)
EWCA Crim	England & Wales Court of Appeal (Criminal Division)
EWHC (Admlty)	England & Wales High Court (Admiralty Court)
EWHC (Ch)	England & Wales High Court (Chancery Division)
EWHC (Comm)	England & Wales High Court (Commercial Court)
EWHC (QB)	England & Wales High Court (Queen's Bench Division)
EWHC (TCC)	England & Wales High Court (Technology and Construction Court)
Ex	Exchequer Reports
ex p	*ex parte*
ExD	Law Reports, Exchequer Division
FC	Federal Court
FCAFC	Federal Court of Australia: Full Court
H&C	Hurlstone & Coltman's Exchequer Reports
H&N	Hurlstone & Norman's Exchequer Reports
HC	High Court
Hil	Hilary term

HL	House of Lords
HL Cas	Clark & Finnelly's House of Lords Reports New Series
HLR	Housing Law Reports
IR	Irish Reports
IRC	Inland Revenue Commissioners
J	Justice
JA	Justice of Appeal
JBL	Journal of Business Law
JCL	Journal of Contract Law
(J)JSC	Justice(s) of the Supreme Court of the United Kingdom
KB	Law Reports, King's Bench
KBD	King's Bench Division
LBC	London Borough Council
LC	Lord Chancellor
LJ(J)	Lord Justice(s)
LLC	Limited liability company
Lloyd's Rep	Lloyd's Law Reports
Lloyd's Rep Bank	Lloyd's Law Reports Banking
LMCLQ	Lloyd's Maritime & Commercial Law Quarterly
LQR	Law Quarterly Review
LR A&E	Law Reports, Admiralty and Ecclesiastical
LR App Cas	Law Reports, Appeal Cases (2nd Series)
LR CCR	Law Reports, Crown Cases Reserved
LR Ch App	Law Reports, Chancery Appeal Cases
LR Ex	Law Reports, Exchequer Cases
LR HL	Law Reports, English & Irish Appeals
LR PC	Law Reports, Privy Council Appeal Cases
LR QB	Law Reports, Queen's Bench (1st Series)
LS	Legal Studies
LT	Law Times Reports
m	million
M&G	Manning & Granger's Common Pleas Reports
M&W	Meeson & Welsby's Exchequer Reports
Mich	Michigan Reports
MLR	Modern Law Review
Mood CC	Moody's Crown Cases Reserved
MR	Master of the Rolls
NA	National association
NIQB	High Court of Justice Northern Ireland: Queen's Bench Division
NZ L Rev	New Zealand Law Review

NZLJ	New Zealand Law Journal
NZLR	New Zealand Law Reports
OJLS	Oxford Journal of Legal Studies
Ottawa LR	Ottawa Law Review
OUCLJ	Oxford University Commonwealth Law Journal
P	President
P&CR	Property & Compensation Reports
PC	Privy Council
Pty Ltd	Proprietary limited company
QB	Law Reports, Queen's Bench (3rd Series)
QBD	Queen's Bench Division/Law Reports, Queen's Bench Division
QC	Queen's Counsel
R	The King/Queen *(Rex/Regina)* = The Crown
revd	reversed
RLR	Restitution Law Review
SA	société anonyme
SASR	South Australian State Reports
SC	Supreme Court
sch(s)	schedule(s)
SCR	Supreme Court Reports, Canada
SGA	Sale of Goods Act
SI	statutory instrument
Str	Strange's King's Bench Reports
sub nom	under the name *(sub nomine)*
TLR	Times Law Reports
Trin	Trinity term
TruLI	Trust Law International
UKHL	United Kingdom House of Lords
UKPC	United Kingdom Privy Council
UKSC	United Kingdom Supreme Court
UWALR	University of Western Australia Law Review
V-C	Vice-Chancellor
Ves Jr	Vesey Junior's Chancery Reports
WLR	Weekly Law Reports
YB	Yearbook
ZEuP	Zeitschrift für Europäisches Privatrecht
ZGB	Zivilgesetzbuch (Switzerland)

CHAPTER 1

AN INTRODUCTION TO DEFECTIVE TRANSFERS OF PROPERTY

This chapter is preliminary to our actual inquiry. It shall offer a general introduction to the law of defective transfers of ownership, setting out the basic doctrinal framework which is essential to understand the following chapters of this book.[1] It is crucial to note that the principles set forth here have rarely, if ever, been properly spelled out by the courts. They are rather the product of a careful analysis and a process of rationalisation of the extensive case law existing in this area of the law.

1. THREE DISTINCT LEVELS WHERE A DEFECT MIGHT OPERATE: PROPERTY, CONTRACT AND UNJUST FACTORS

If one is concerned with a (potentially) defective transfer of property, it is inevitable to strictly distinguish between three different "levels" where any particular defect – for example a mistake – might operate. In fact, it might do so on one, two, all three or on none of those levels.

The first level, with which this book is primarily concerned, is the *proprietary level*. A defect may be strong enough to prevent the passage of ownership – legal or equitable – or it might operate to impose some new proprietary rights (proprietary restitution). If the effect of a certain defect is to completely negative a transferor's intention to transfer away a certain proprietary interest – such as legal or equitable ownership – those property rights will generally be retained *ab initio*. By contrast, if a certain defect does not entirely eradicate a transferor's relevant intention, ownership will generally pass to the transferee; yet, if the defect is still severe enough, it may lead to the conclusion that the proprietary transfer is voidable, which means that it may be rescinded (set aside), or that some other mechanism of (equitable) proprietary restitution confers some new restitutionary property rights on the claimant.

---

1 See further ZOGG, Proprietary Consequences, passim, esp Chapter 2.

The second level is the *contractual level*. A defect might – also or only – affect a contract which has (supposedly) been concluded between the transferor and the transferee. It is of paramount importance to note that the contractual and the proprietary levels are *distinct*.[2] It would be a fundamental error to believe that these levels are inextricably linked or even unified. The conclusion of a contract is different from the transfer of property. Very obviously, property may be retained even though a contract has been concluded.[3] Conversely, property may pass – if and as far as a principle of abstraction applies[4] – even in the absence of an underlying contract; the most evident examples are gifts. This is not to say that the passage of property and a contract's existence *cannot* or *do not* interrelate altogether; it merely means that they are *distinct* and that they *need not* depend on each other – but they *may*.

Different kinds of defects may have different effects on contracts. They may prevent a contract from coming into existence *ab initio* (rendering it void) or – if not being as serious but still serious enough – they may render it voidable. A voidable contract is entirely valid in a first step but may be avoided by rescission in a second instance. Conceptually, this is realised by conferring a *power in personam* to rescind the contract on the aggrieved party.[5] Other defects may render contracts merely unenforceable or terminable or they may leave them unaffected altogether.

On the third level, the *level of unjust enrichment*, a defect might trigger a so-called unjust factor.[6] If such an unjust factor applies and if the other requirements of the unjust enrichment cause of action are met, this event's response is generally a personal right to restitution of the value received (though unjust enrichment might also create new proprietary rights[7]). The range of unjust factors inter alia includes lack of consent or authority, mistake, duress, undue

2 It will be argued that contract and conveyance (transfer of property) are distinct even within the law of sales of goods (principle of separation); see Chapter 2 section 2.2.

3 For example, due to lack of ascertainment and appropriation of the contract goods; see (e.g.) *Re Goldcorp Exchange Ltd* [1995] 1 AC 74 (PC).

4 See Chapter 2 section 1.4. (transfer of legal title by delivery), Chapter 2 section 2.3. (transfer of legal title by sale) and Chapter 2 section 4.5. (transfer of legal title by deed).

5 See Häcker, Impaired Consent, 198–202; Häcker, CLJ 2009, 339 (fn 85); Birks, Unjust Enrichment, 173, 176; see generally on the law of rescission: O'Sullivan et al, Rescission, chs 10–12; Cartwright, Misrepresentation, ch 4; Zogg, Proprietary Consequences, Chapter 4.

6 This book follows (a hybrid version of) the so-called "unjust factor regime"; see Chapter 1 section 2.1.1.1.

7 See Birks, Unjust Enrichment, 28–38, ch 8; Birks, NZ L Rev 1997; Birks, UWALR 1999, 54–63; Birks, CLP 2001; Burrows, Restitution, ch 8; Goff/Jones, Unjust Enrichment, chs 37–40; Chambers, Resulting Trusts, esp chs 4–7; Häcker, Impaired Consent, 125–59; Häcker, CLJ 2009; contra: Virgo, Restitution, 7–17, 559–65; Virgo, Looking Glass, 100–1; Millett, Proprietary Restitution, 312–13; Swadling, Property and Unjust Enrichment, 130. That the event of unjust enrichment may at least create proprietary rights in the context of subrogation was recognised in *Banque Financiere de la Cité v Parc (Battersea) Ltd* [1999] 1 AC 221 (HL); *Bank of Cyprus UK Ltd v Menelaou* [2015] UKSC 66.

influence or failure of consideration.[8] A defect which triggers such an unjust factor, for example mistake, *may* also operate on the level of property and/or the level of contract but that *need not* be so. The level of unjust enrichment clearly inheres the lowest threshold, whereas the level of property generally yields to the highest. A defect which is operative on the level of property or contract will usually – if not inevitably – also operate on the level of unjust enrichment; but the converse is not true.

If one is analysing the effects of mistake or of various types of mistakes, it is inevitable to strictly distinguish between the three levels set out above. A mistake which operates as an unjust factor *may* but *need not* also affect a contract and it *may* but *need not* have proprietary consequences. These basic principles have rarely, if ever, been explicitly spelled out by courts[9] until Goff J's landmark decision in *Barclays Bank Ltd v WJ Simms Son & Cooke (Southern) Ltd.*[10] In that case, Goff J ground-breakingly established the "but for causation test" – as still applied today[11] – which is required to make out an unjust enrichment claim based on mistake. In his discussion of the relevant authorities, particularly *Chambers v Miller*[12] (where the court was mainly concerned with the transfer of legal property rather than personal restitution), he very helpfully explained that there are, in fact, different levels (in that case: property and unjust enrichment) which must be strictly distinguished and which may impose different thresholds for a defect (mistake) to be operative:

> "[*Chambers v Miller*] was not concerned with recovery of money paid under a mistake of fact, but with an action for assault and false imprisonment. [...] The crucial question

---

8 See only GOFF/JONES, Unjust Enrichment, chs 8–26; BURROWS, Restitution, chs 9–20.

9 Lord Wright's dictum in *Norwich Union Fire Insurance Society Ltd v WMH Price Ltd* [1934] AC 455 (PC), 461–63, is certainly no longer good law (if it has ever been); his Lordship was concerned with an unjust enrichment claim based on mistake and – by completely intermingling the three mentioned levels – appeared to require a "fundamental mistake" on all three levels, including unjust enrichment: "The mistake, being of the character that it was, prevented there being that intention which the common law regards as essential to the making of an agreement or the transfer of money or property. [...] It is true that in general the test of intention in the formation of contracts and the transfer of property is objective; that is, intention is to be ascertained from what the parties said or did. But proof of mistake affirmatively excludes intention. It is, however, essential that the mistake relied on should be of such a nature that it can be properly described as a mistake in respect of the underlying assumption of the contract or transaction or as being fundamental or basic"; cf also *Morgan v Ashcroft* [1938] 1 KB 49 (CA), 65–67 (Greene MR), 70–71, 77 (Scott LJ).

10 *Barclays Bank Ltd v WJ Simms Son & Cooke (Southern) Ltd* [1980] QB 677 (QBD).

11 *Rover International Ltd v Cannon Film Sales Ltd* [1989] 1 WLR 912 (CA), 933 (Dillon LJ); *Kleinwort Benson Ltd v Lincoln CC* [1999] 2 AC 349 (HL), esp 407–8 (Lord Hope); *Dextra Bank & Trust Co Ltd v Bank of Jamaica* [2002] 1 All ER (Comm) 193 (PC), [28]; *Deutsche Morgan Grenfell Group plc v IRC* [2006] UKHL 49, [2007] 1 AC 558, [59]–[62] (Lord Hope), [84]–[87] (Lord Scott), 143 (Lord Walker).

12 *Chambers v Miller* [1862] 13 CBR (NS) 125, 143 ER 50; see discussion in Chapter 4 section 2.1.1.

> in the case was whether, in these circumstances, the property in the money had passed to the [transferee]. [...] It was part of the [transferor's] argument that the money was recoverable, as having been paid under a mistake of fact. *However that was [...] irrelevant to the question whether the property had passed*; indeed, where an action is brought to recover money paid under a mistake of fact, property will almost invariably have passed to the defendant, the effect of the action, if successful, being simply to impose on the defendant a personal obligation to repay the money. *Furthermore, the kind of mistake that will ground recovery is [...] far wider than the kind of mistake which will vitiate an intention to transfer property.*"[13]

The distinction between the level of unjust enrichment and the level of contract was further emphasised by Waller J in *Citibank NA v Brown Shipley & Co Ltd* (though he was actually concerned with the question of whether title had passed on the level of property):

> "[T]he type of mistake necessary to give rise to a right to recover under the restitutionary remedy of money paid under a mistake of fact need not necessarily be of the same fundamental character that makes a contract totally void. Thus to point to a case where the plaintiff has succeeded on a restitutionary remedy, would not establish that the plaintiff would also have established a mistake fundamental enough to avoid any contract altogether."[14]

1.1. INTERRELATION BETWEEN THE THREE LEVELS

Even though a strict distinction between the three levels is absolutely crucial, it must equally be emphasised that there are various ways of how those levels might – and to some extent do – interrelate. The most obvious impacts emanate from the contractual level. It will be seen that contracts unfold what may be called "curing effects" in relation to both other levels: On the one hand, the existence of a valid contractual (or other) obligation justifies an enrichment which would otherwise have been "unjust".[15] On the other hand, the fact that a contract has not been affected by the existence of a certain defect strongly suggests, if not necessitates, that that same defect may neither affect the transfer of property.[16]

---

13 *Barclays Bank v Simms* [1980] QB 677, 688–89 (Goff J) (emphases added); see also *Ilich v R* [1987] 162 CLR 110 (HC of Australia), 126–27 (Wilson, Dawson JJ); Swadling, Unjust Delivery; Fox, Property Rights, 3.99–101, 4.118; Virgo, Restitution, 574–76; Häcker, Impaired Consent, 115–16, 137–38; Burrows, Restitution, 219; cf also Williams, CLJ 1977.

14 *Citibank NA v Brown Shipley & Co Ltd* [1991] 2 All ER 690 (QBD), 700–1 (Waller J) (sub nom *Midland Bank plc v Brown Shipley Co & Ltd*).

15 Chapter 1 section 2.1.1.1.

16 Chapter 2 section 2.1.1.2.

Apart from that, it *could* be concluded – though such a view will not be adopted in this book[17] – that a valid contract is required to effect a transfer of property (particularly if this happens by sale).

1.2. MISTAKE AS AN EXAMPLE

Mistake is perhaps the best example to illustrate, on the one hand, the distinctness of the three levels and, on the other hand, the fact that these levels have not, unfortunately, always been strictly kept apart by courts and commentators. Confusion of those levels is well reflected in the usage of language in relation to mistake.

In modern terms, a mistake must be "fundamental" in order to prevent legal ownership from passing;[18] this may, according to the orthodox view, only be the case in three closed and narrow categories (mistakes as to the transferee's identity, mistakes as to the identity of the transferred goods and mistakes as to the goods' quantity).[19] These types of mistakes may equally render a contract void *ab initio*. Applying the general amalgam of the objective and the subjective principle as applying in the law of contract formation,[20] a contract cannot come into existence if a mistake puts the parties so much at cross-purposes that an agreement is simply not reached. It is often said that this requires that the relevant mistake has been "fundamental". The concurrent usage of the term "fundamental mistake" in the proprietary and the contractual context would perhaps not be too disturbing if it were limited to those kinds of mistakes which may prevent both, the passage of property and the coming into existence of a contract. However, the range of mistakes which may negative a contract is, in fact, broader than the range of mistakes which may prevent the passage of property. An example is the disagreement of the parties (mutual mistake) about the contract price or other consideration.[21] Furthermore, so-called "common mistakes" – which

17 See Chapter 2 section 1.4. (transfer of legal title by delivery), Chapter 2 section 2.3. (transfer of legal title by sale) and Chapter 2 section 4.5. (transfer of legal title by deed).

18 *Ilich v R* [1987] 162 CLR 110, 126–27 (Wilson, Dawson JJ); Williams, Crim LR 1958, 222–23; Williams, CLJ 1977; Williams, Criminal Law, 32.133–34; J. Smith, Crim LR 1972, 586–88; Virgo, Restitution, 574–76; Fox, Property Rights, 3.99–102, 4.116–46; Fox, RLR 1996, 64–67; Pollock/Wright, Possession, 100–14, 205–12; Grantham/Rickett, RLR 1997, 88–89; Häcker, Impaired Consent, 119–20, 138; critically: Swadling, Unjust Delivery (but cf still Swadling, RLR 1994, 82; Swadling, LQR 2005, 152).

19 See Chapter 4 section 2.; it will be argued that there is an additional fourth category of proprietarily fundamental mistakes, namely if the parties are in disagreement about the kind of legal interest – ownership or possession – to be transferred.

20 Cf Chapter 4 section 1.1.

21 See Chapter 4 sections 1.1. and 2.5.

must relate to some "fundamental" exterior facts – may equally render a contract void, though not by negativing the parties' consent but by nullifying it. The term "fundamental" is also used to denote this type of mistake (or at least one of its requirements[22]). It will be argued, however, that such mistakes are insufficient to prevent the passage of property.[23]

In so far, the term "fundamental" has evidently a broader meaning in the contractual context than in the proprietary one. To render things worse, Lord Wright in *Norwich Union Fire Insurance Society v WMH Price*[24] has used the term "fundamental" to denote the type of mistake required to establish a personal claim in unjust enrichment. Though this is certainly no longer good law,[25] if it has ever been, it reveals the confusion and the insecure usage of language in that regard.

Terminology should be cleared up in order to avoid misunderstandings. Unless unambiguous from the context, it is preferable to refer to *proprietarily fundamental mistakes*, denoting mistakes which prevent the passage of property, and to *contractually fundamental mistakes*, denoting mistakes which render a contract void. In any event, the term "fundamental" should be completely abandoned in the context of unjust enrichment yielding mistakes. In order to establish an unjust factor, a *causative mistake* is sufficient.

2. CONTRACTUAL AND NON-CONTRACTUAL TRANSFERS OF PROPERTY

A profound analysis of the effects – proprietary or personal – of mistakes and other defects in transfers of ownership requires a distinction between transfers of property which occur in the context of a contractual (or other) obligation and transfers which occur outside the contractual setting. This is for two main reasons: First, a contractual (or other) obligation may justify an enrichment which would otherwise have been unjust. Second, a defect which is not even serious enough to affect a contract may not, as such, have any (greater) impact on the proprietary plane.

22 As established in *Bell v Lever Bros Ltd* [1932] AC 161 (HL) and *Great Peace Shipping Ltd v Tsavliris Salvage (International) Ltd (The Great Peace)* [2002] EWCA Civ 1407, [2003] QB 679.

23 See Chapter 4 section 2.1.2.

24 *Norwich Union Fire Insurance Society v WMH Price* [1934] AC 455, 461–63 (Lord Wright) (see fn 9); see also *Morgan v Ashcroft* [1938] 1 KB 49, 65–67 (Greene MR), 70–71, 77 (Scott LJ); *Ilich v R* [1987] 162 CLR 110, 118 (Gibbs CJ); *Porter v Latec Finance (Qld) Pty Ltd* [1964] 111 CLR 177 (HC of Australia); *Australia and New Zealand Banking Group Ltd v Westpac Banking Co* [1988] 164 CLR 662 (HC of Australia).

25 See fn 11.

The relevant criterion, which decides about whether a transfer is contractual or non-contractual, is not just whether there is *some* contract (or other legal obligation) in the factual context between the parties but rather whether the *actual transfer in question* is *covered* by some obligation. In other words, there must be an obligation which precisely relates to the relevant transfer of property in question. If A owes 100 kilograms of soybeans under a contract of sale to B and if he transfers such an amount twice over, only the first but not the second delivery is covered by the contractual obligation. Double or overpayments (or -deliveries) are non-contractual transfers to the extent of their excessive conferment, just as in the case where A delivers the soybeans to the wrong person.[26] If an insurer pays out an amount of money, it is simply irrelevant whether there is a valid contract of insurance between the parties if, on the facts of the case, the insured event has not occurred and if there is, accordingly, no valid contractual obligation covering the payment as such.

2.1. CONTRACTUAL TRANSFERS OF PROPERTY

2.1.1. Valid Contracts: "Curing Effects"

2.1.1.1. Unjust Factor Regime: Contract as a Justifying Factor

Traditionally, the law of unjust enrichment has followed a so-called unjust factor regime according to which a claimant must show a positive reason for restitution (unjust factor). There is a long list of unjust factors, including mistake, duress, undue influence, failure of consideration, ignorance and others; the list is not a strictly closed one.[27] In his last book, Peter Birks – following a suggestion of Sonja Meier[28] – has fundamentally changed his view in that regard, advocating the view that the so-called swaps litigation[29] had (implicitly) adopted a civilian

26 Cf the four examples given by Goff J in *Barclays Bank v Simms* [1980] QB 677, 697 (though relating to gifts).

27 For example, a new category of unlawful tax demands has been established in *Woolwich Equitable Building Society v IRC* [1993] AC 70 (HL); similarly, the unjust factor mistake was extended to mistakes of law in *Kleinwort Benson v Lincoln CC* [1999] 2 AC 349; see also *CTN Cash and Carry Ltd v Gallaher Ltd* [1994] 4 All ER 714 (CA).

28 Meier/Zimmermann, LQR 1999; Meier, Void Contracts; Meier, Unjust factors; see Birks, Unjust Enrichment, xii–xiii.

29 See esp *Westdeutsche Landesbank Girozentrale v Islington LBC* and *Kleinwort Benson Ltd v Sandwell BC* [1994] 4 All ER 890 (QBD) (reported together); the former case was affd in [1994] 1 WLR 938 (CA) but revd (on grounds not strictly relevant here) in [1996] AC 669 (HL); there was no appeal in the latter case; see also *Guinness Mahon & Co Ltd v Kensington and Chelsea Royal LBC* [1999] QB 215 (CA); *Kleinwort Benson v Lincoln CC* [1999] 2 AC 349.

"absence of basis" or "*sine causa*" approach.[30] According to this view, any enrichment is unjust unless some explanatory basis may be found which justifies the enrichment. Without expressing a final view on this basic question, it is here, however, assumed that the law has not – at least not yet – adopted an absence of basis approach but apparently still follows the traditional unjust factor regime.[31] Whatever may happen in the future, the unjust factor regime is adhered to in this book.

The unjust factor regime, however, is certainly not – and has never been – a pure one but has rather always embodied a *hybrid approach* which requires, on the one hand, the establishment of an *unjust factor* (rendering the enrichment prima facie unjust) and, on the other hand, the *absence of a justifying legal ground*.[32] To that extent, it essentially shares the main feature of the absence of basis regime. One of those justifying grounds is, at least in principle,[33] the

---

30 Birks, Unjust Enrichment, chs 5–6 (but cf still Birks, UWALR 1993); see also Stevens, Unjust Enrichment. The absence of basis approach may derive some support from Lord Walker's speech in *Deutsche Morgan Grenfell Group plc v IRC* [2006] UKHL 49, [2007] 1 AC 558, [150]–[158], indicating his tentative inclination to it (but cf [21]–[22] (Lord Hoffmann) and [59] (Lord Hope)).

31 See esp *Woolwich Equitable Building Society v IRC* [1993] AC 70, 172 (Lord Goff): "[The structure of our law of restitution] might have developed so as to recognise a condictio indebiti – an action for the recovery of money on the ground that it was not due. But it did not do so"; *Kleinwort Benson v Lincoln CC* [1999] 2 AC 349, 407–9 (Lord Hope): "The approach of the common law is to look for an unjust factor, something which makes it unjust to allow the payee to retain the benefit [Birks, Introduction, 140 ff]. It is the mistake by the payer which, as in the case of failure of consideration and compulsion, renders the enrichment of the payee unjust. The common law accepts that the payee is enriched where the sum was not due to be paid to him, but it requires the payer to show that this was unjust. Whereas in civilian systems proof of knowledge that there was no legal obligation to pay is a defence which may be invoked by the payee, under the common law it is for the payer to show that he paid under a mistake. My impression is that the common law tends to place more emphasis on the need for proof of a mistake"; see also: *Banque Financiere v Parc* [1999] 1 AC 221, 227 (Lord Steyn); *Foskett v McKeown* [2001] 1 AC 102 (HL), 127 (Lord Millett); *Uren v First National Home Finance Ltd* [2005] EWHC 2529 (Ch), [16], [18] (Mann J); *Sempra Metals v IRC* [2007] UKHL 34, [23] (Lord Hope); *Chief Constable of Greater Manchester v Wigan Athletic AFC Ltd* [2008] EWCA Civ 1449, [2009] 1 WLR 1580, [50] (Morritt C), [67] (Kay LJ); *Marine Trade SA v Pioneer Freight Futures Co Ltd BVI* [2009] EWHC 2656 (Comm), [2009] 2 CLC 657, [62]–[65] (Flaux J); *Haugesund Kommune v Depfa ACS Bank* [2009] EWHC 2227 (Comm), [142] (Tomlinson J) (affd in [2010] EWCA Civ 579, [2012] QB 549); *Test Claimants in the FII Group Litigation v Revenue and Customs Commissioners* [2012] UKSC 19, [2012] 2 AC 337, [81] (Lord Walker), [162], [188]–[190] (Lord Sumption); *Patel v Mirza* [2016] UKSC 42, [246] (Lord Sumption; in dissent, though on other points); *Lowick Rose LLP v Swynson Ltd* [2017] UKSC 32, [22] (Lord Sumption), [69] (Lord Mance); Goff/Jones, Unjust Enrichment, 1.12, 1.21–27; Burrows, Restitution, ch 5; Burrows, Absence of Basis; Virgo, Restitution, 127–32; cf also Krebs, Restitution; Krebs, Unjust factors.

32 See now convincingly Virgo, Restitution, ch 7.

33 There might perhaps be exceptions: Burrows, Restitution, 90–91; cf also Goodwin, RLR 2013.

existence of a valid contractual (or other) obligation. It suffices to cite the clear words of Lord Scott[34] in *Deutsche Morgan Grenfell v IRC*:

> "[M]oney paid, or property transferred, under a mistake of law is [not] *necessarily* recoverable, just as money paid, or property transferred, under a mistake of fact is not *necessarily* recoverable. It surely all depends on the part played by the mistake, whether of fact or law, in the sequence of events that has led to the payment or transfer. If A and B enter into a contract with one another for the sale by A to B of a horse and B pays the price and takes delivery of the horse, B cannot, absent some causative misrepresentation on A's part, claim his money back, proffering the horse in return, on the ground that he was mistaken as to the horse's breeding. The money once paid would be irrecoverable unless there were some ground for invalidating the contract. It cannot be enough for the buyer to assert and prove that but for his mistake about the horse's breeding he would not have entered into the contract and so would not have paid the money. [...] If a contract has been entered into that would not have been entered into but for a mistake, but the contract is then completed by a payment of the price for the goods or services that the payee has supplied, the payment cannot be recovered unless the contract can be set aside. The proposition seems such an obviously correct one that it may seem pointless to ask why it is that it is correct. But I think the question does need to be asked for the answer casts, in my opinion, valuable light on the nature of the restitutionary remedy for the recovery of money paid under a mistake. The reason, it seems to me, why the proposition is correct is that the mistake does not necessarily undermine the legal obligation which required the payment of the money or for the discharge of which the money was paid. If the mistake does enable the contract to be set aside then, subject to a change of position defence, the money should be recoverable. If the contract was void from the outset (as in the 'swaps' cases) or had been avoided before the payment was made, the money should be recoverable. *But if the legal obligation under which the money was paid cannot be, or has not been, invalidated, then, in my opinion, whether or not it can be shown that 'but for' the mistake in question the money would not have been paid, a restitutionary remedy for the recovery of the money would not be available.*"[35]

---

34 Lord Scott gave a dissenting judgment but the majority did not disagree on that point; rather, their Lordships apparently believed that the relevant statutory tax obligation had been destroyed by EU law.

35 *Deutsche Morgan Grenfell v IRC* [2006] UKHL 49, [84]–[85] (Lord Scott) (last emphasis added); see also *Steam Saw Mills Co Ltd v Baring Bros & Co Ltd* [1922] 1 Ch 244 (CA), 250–51 (Lord Sterndale MR), 253–54 (Warrington LJ); *Bell v Lever Bros* [1932] AC 161; *Barclays Bank v Simms* [1980] QB 677, 695 (Goff J); *Portman Building Society v Hamlyn Taylor Neck* [1998] 4 All ER 202 (CA), 208 (Millett LJ); *Kleinwort Benson v Lincoln CC* [1999] 2 AC 349, 407–9 (Lord Hope); *Harrison v Madejski* [2014] EWCA Civ 361, esp [39] (Etherton C); *DD Growth Premium 2X Fund v RMF Market Neutral Strategies (Master) Ltd* [2017] UKPC 36, [62] (Lord Sumption and Lord Briggs); *David Securities Pty Ltd v Commonwealth Bank of Australia* [1992] 175 CLR 353 (HC of Australia), 376, 392; Virgo, Restitution, 133–44; Goff/Jones, Unjust Enrichment, 1.12, chs 2–3, 9.93–97; Burrows, Restitution, 88–90; Meier, Irrtum, 99–103; Meier, Unjust factors, 39–40, 53–54; Stevens, Unjust Enrichment, 17–30; Stevens, OUCLJ 2005; L. Smith, Unjust Enrichment, 48–49; Häcker, Impaired Consent, 105–6; Tang, JCL 2007; Tettenborn, Restitution, 1.43; contra: Krebs, Restitution, 71–72 (but cf ch 14); cf also S. Smith, LQR 1999; Tettenborn, RLR 2002.

It becomes apparent that a contract (more exactly: a contractual obligation covering the relevant transfer) may unfold a somewhat "curing effect" on a transfer of an enrichment (value) which would otherwise – but for the contract's existence – have been "unjust". Hence, if a transfer of value is covered by a contractual obligation, defects may only be operative on the level of unjust enrichment if they are serious enough to have *also* effects on the level of contract.

2.1.1.2. If a Defect Cannot Affect a Contract, it Can Neither Affect the Passage of Property

A contract may furthermore have a somewhat *indirect* curative effect with regard to the level of property. Though it is clear that a valid contract's existence *alone* may not cause a transfer of ownership – whether governed by the principle of abstraction or causality – unless there is an equally valid intention of the transferor to transfer property, the fact that a certain defect cannot or does not affect a contract must almost inevitably mean that that same defect may neither affect the proprietary transfer.[36] If a particular mistake is not even capable (serious enough) to render a contract void, it cannot still prevent ownership from passing. The range of defects operating on the level of property is certainly *narrower* than that which operates on the level of contract. Hence, the fact that a contract is not rendered void or voidable on the basis of a certain defect must *indirectly* mean that a corresponding transfer of property is neither rendered void or voidable by that same defect. This was apparently borne out by Waller J in *Citibank v Brown Shipley*: "[I]n the bilateral contract context for no title to pass it must be established that there is no contract under which such a title can pass".[37]

2.1.2. Terminated (Discharged) Contracts

A valid contract can be terminated (or discharged) for repudiatory breach and is automatically discharged by frustration.[38] As opposed to rescission, termination operates with *prospective* effects and only brings a contract to an end *de futuro*.[39]

---

36 An apparent (though not an actual) exception applies if the contract has not been affected by any defect in the *formation stage* but if a subsequent – proprietarily relevant – defect occurs in the *execution stage*; cf Chapter 1 section 3.

37 *Citibank v Brown Shipley* [1991] 2 All ER 690, 700 (Waller J).

38 The consequences of frustration are today governed by s 1 of the Law Reform (Frustrated Contracts) Act 1943 where particularly the total failure requirement has been removed.

39 *Johnson v Agnew* [1980] AC 367 (HL); *Photo Production Ltd v Securicor Transport Ltd* [1980] AC 827 (HL), 844–45 (Lord Wilberforce), 848–50 (Lord Diplock); *Hurst v Bryk* [2002] 1 AC 185 (HL), 193–94 (Lord Millett); *McDonald v Dennys Lascelles Ltd* [1933] 48 CLR 457 (HC of Australia), 469–70 (Starke J), 476–77 (Dixon J); O'Sullivan et al, Rescission, 1.6–34; see generally Stannard/Capper, Termination.

The theoretical foundations and the exact consequences of termination, particularly with regard to unjust enrichment, are convoluted and not entirely clear.[40] They need not, however, be considered within the confines of this book. Though there is a debate as to whether and to what extent *equitable* proprietary restitution might be available on the ground of "failure of consideration",[41] there can be no doubt that neither a defect which allows termination of a contract (i.e. frustration or fundamental breach of contract) nor "failure of consideration" (i.e. failure of a condition in the transferor's intention to carry out the relevant transfer) may, as such, prevent the passage of legal ownership.

2.1.3. Unenforceable and Voidable Contracts

Unenforceable contracts are contracts which are, in principle, entirely valid but which cannot (at least not by one of the parties) be judicially enforced against the other party's will.[42] The best example is a contractual obligation which is time-barred. If such an unenforceable obligation has been executed, however, it generally unfolds the ordinary "curing effects" of a valid contractual obligation. Once executed, it justifies an enrichment transferred under it.[43] Furthermore, a defect which merely renders a contract unenforceable (rather than void or voidable) cannot generally prevent the passage of legal ownership.

Voidable contracts are contracts which are initially valid and which initially unfold all effects of valid contracts; they are valid until set aside and remain valid if not set aside. Yet, rescission of a voidable contract largely operates with *retrospective* effects. The exact interrelations between voidable contracts and transfers of property (and unjust enrichment) are fiendishly complex; they cannot be considered within the confines of this book.[44] It may be noted, however, that a voidable contract justifies an enrichment until it has been set

---

40 A detailed account may be found in Stannard/Capper, Termination, esp chs 9, 11; see also Virgo, Restitution, 133–44, ch 13; Treitel, Contract, 18.15–22; Burrows, Restitution, 90, 327–30; Goodwin, RLR 2013.

41 Broadly in favour of equitable proprietary restitution based on failure of consideration: Chambers, Resulting Trusts, ch 6; Chambers, AlbLR 1999, 207–18; Chambers, Mapping the Law, 261–62; Birks, Unjust Enrichment, 181–98; Birks, Tied Money; cf already Birks, Restitution and Resulting Trusts, 356–59, 362; cf also Burrows, Restitution, 399–402; contra: Swadling, LS 1996, 117–25; Swadling, RLR 2004, 279–83; Millett, Proprietary Restitution, esp 317–22; Zogg, Proprietary Consequences, Chapter 5.

42 See Goode, Commercial Law, 3.33; Beatson et al, Anson's Law of Contract, 23–25.

43 *Moses v Macferlan* [1760] 2 Burr 1005, 97 ER 676, 680–81 (Lord Mansfield); *Kleinwort Benson v Lincoln CC* [1999] 2 AC 349, 408 (Lord Hope); Virgo, Restitution, 144; Goff/Jones, Unjust Enrichment, 2.41–44; Burrows, Restitution, 88 (fn 15); Meier, Unjust factors, 42–43, 55–56; Stevens, Unjust Enrichment, 20–23.

44 A detailed account of this complex area of law may be found in the specialist literature; see esp Zogg, Proprietary Consequences, Chapter 4; O'Sullivan et al, Rescission; Cartwright, Misrepresentation, ch 4; Worthington, RLR 2002; Häcker, Third Party Rights; Fox, Property Rights, ch 6.

aside and that the fact that a certain defect has merely rendered a contract voidable – rather than void – must inevitably mean that that same defect cannot render a proprietary transfer void either. It follows that ownership – legal or equitable – is not, in voidable transactions, retained by the transferor but passes to the transferee (pending rescission).

2.2. NON-CONTRACTUAL TRANSFERS OF PROPERTY

2.2.1. Gifts

Gifts[45] are non-contractual transactions; this follows from the doctrine of consideration.[46] This does not, however, mean that executed gifts can always and without more be recovered by a claim in unjust enrichment. The absolute minimum requirement would be that there is an unjust factor, for example a causative mistake. Yet, it is arguable that gifts, whether informal or by deed, cannot be recovered on the basis of non-induced causative mistakes – whether by personal or proprietary restitution – unless the mistake has been "serious".[47] According to a preferred analysis, gifts constitute *legal bases* – similar to but still different from contracts – which justify enrichments respectively received.[48]

Hence, voluntary transfers are not just "transfers without bases", such as mistaken payments or mistaken deliveries under void contracts. Rather, gifts have – as long as subsisting – similar curing effects as contracts (though gifts may be avoided more easily): On the one hand, an executed gift arguably justifies – pending rescission – an enrichment received under it (i.e. in accordance with the *animus donandi*).[49] On the other hand, a defect which may not render a

---

45 In this book, we are exclusively concerned with *inter vivos* gifts.

46 This is not only true with regard to *informal* gratuitous promises (which cannot be enforced if unexecuted) but also with regard to gifts *by deed*. Though a deed may create a legally enforceable obligation even in the absence of consideration, a voluntary transfer of property under a unilateral obligation created by deed is still not "contractual" in nature; such an obligation may be effective even if the creditor has not assented to or even known of it; see *Macedo v Stroud* [1922] 2 AC 330 (PC); Treitel, Contract, 3.170. Crucially, voluntary (non-contractual) deeds can – just as informal gifts – be rescinded in broader circumstances than contracts; cf *Great Peace Shipping v Tsavliris Salvage* [2002] EWCA Civ 1407 (contract); *Pitt v Holt* [2013] UKSC 26, [2013] 2 AC 108 (voluntary transactions).

47 Cf *Pitt v Holt* [2013] UKSC 26.

48 See Zogg, Proprietary Consequences, Chapter 5 section 7.2.2; Meier, Irrtum, 49–53, 85–91, 105–9; Meier, Unjust factors, 41–54; Meier/Zimmermann, LQR 1999, 561–63; Tang, JCL 2004, 22–23; Virgo, Restitution, 148–49, 181–83; cf also Bell, Personal Property, 223; Birks, Unjust Enrichment, chs 5–6, 148–52; Goff/Jones, Unjust Enrichment, 9.98–99, 9.146–47 (but cf the 8th edn, 9.110, where this idea has been described as a "rather civilian way of putting the point, which may not be consistent with English law").

49 Certainly, gifts – just as contracts – may not justify enrichments which *exceed* the envisaged amount, as for example if a gift is overpaid or executed twice. This is a simple over- or double payment without any legal basis which is recoverable for *any* causative mistake; this is plainly

gift (legal basis) entirely void can neither render a corresponding transfer of property void (preventing the passage of legal ownership).

2.2.2. Transfers without (Any) Basis

Transfers of property which occur *without any basis whatsoever*, i.e. such which are neither covered by a contractual or other obligation nor by a gift, may arise in various circumstances. Examples include overpayments or -deliveries, double payments or double deliveries, payments or deliveries to the wrong person or cases where a transferor for some reason (self-induced or not) believes that he owes the respective payment or delivery to the transferee even though the parties had never had any dealings before. In such cases, the full range of personal or proprietary restitution is *potentially* available. There is no contract or other legal basis which might justify the enrichment received by the transferee. A personal restitutionary unjust enrichment claim arises without more if the claimant may establish an unjust factor, for example a causative mistake (whether induced or not and whether serious or not).

Similarly, there is no contract, gift or other legal basis which could unfold any "indirect curative effects" onto the proprietary level. However, it seems quite impossible that a defect, which would not have had the effect of rendering a contract void, had the transfer been made in a contractual setting, can still have the effect of preventing the passage of property in a non-contractual setting. It would be difficult to understand how a transfer of property could be affected more easily – or how proprietary restitution could be available in a broader range of circumstances[50] – only because the transfer is executed in a non-contractual setting as compared with the case – all other facts remaining unchanged – that it is executed on a contractual or other legal basis.

It follows that non-contractual transfers of property without basis, such as mistaken double or overpayments, can only be void at the proprietary level

borne out by the four examples offered by Goff J in *Barclays Bank v Simms* [1980] QB 677, 697; see also *Larner v London CC* [1949] 2 KB 683 (CA) (concerned with an overpaid gift); Meier, Irrtum, 49–53, 84–91, 105–9; Meier, Unjust factors, 41–54; Meier/Zimmermann, LQR 1999, 561–63; this was overlooked by Etherton, TruLI 2013, 167–68; see further Zogg, Proprietary Consequences, Chapter 5 section 7.2.2.2(b).

50 According to one academic view – which is, however, not shared by the author of this book – equitable proprietary restitution (by rescission or by an immediate equitable interest) is (or should be) available on the ground of *non-induced* (non-fundamental) mistakes if the transfer of property has been a non-contractual one but not if it was covered by a contract; cf Birks, Restitution and Resulting Trusts; Birks, RLR 1996; Birks, NZ L Rev 1997, 640–42; Birks, Unjust Enrichment, 181–98; Chambers, Resulting Trusts, esp chs 4–5; Chambers, AlbLR 1999, 207–18; Chambers, AlbLR 2000; Chambers, Mapping the Law; Häcker, Impaired Consent, 125–59, esp 151–53 (left open in Häcker, CLJ 2009, 354–57); see also Goff/Jones, Unjust Enrichment, esp 37.15–35; Burrows, Restitution, ch 8; contra: Millett, Proprietary Restitution, 317–22; Swadling, LS 1996, esp 126–28; Swadling, Property and Unjust Enrichment, 139–45; Zogg, Proprietary Consequences, esp Chapter 5 section 7.

(title remaining vested in the transferor) if and as far as such a transfer had equally – *hypothetically* – been void had it – all other facts remaining unchanged – been made in a (void) contractual or similar environment. Though this is not strictly a logical truism, it still follows from a principled analysis of the available case law and inevitably from the conclusion reached in this book that transfers of legal ownership – whether by delivery, by sale or by deed – are notionally *distinct* and *independent* from an underlying obligatory transaction's (particularly a contract's) existence or validity and thus governed by a *principle of abstraction*.[51]

2.2.3. *Void Contracts*

Transfers of property carried out under void contracts (or void gifts) are largely similar to non-contractual transfers without any basis. On the one hand, a void contract (or a void gift) cannot serve as a justifying basis on the level of unjust enrichment; a transferor who transferred property under a void contract may, without more, claim personal restitution based on unjust enrichment if he may establish an unjust factor.[52] On the other hand, a void contract cannot unfold any "indirect curative effects" onto the proprietary level. The reason which rendered a contract void *may* – but *need not* (since the range of defects operating on the proprietary level is narrower than that operating on the contractual one) – also render a corresponding transfer of property void (at law and/or in equity).

There may, however, be one exception from the principle that transfers of property carried out under void contracts (or void gifts) are subject to the same rules as transfers of property made without any basis whatsoever, such as mistaken double or overpayments: It will be argued that the strict *delivery requirement* to transfer legal title (otherwise than by deed) is tied to the criterion of *consideration* and that actual counter-performance may, in some cases, count as consideration (exempting from the delivery requirement) even though the

---

51 See Chapter 2 section 1.4. (transfer of legal title by delivery), Chapter 2 section 2.3. (transfer of legal title by sale) and Chapter 2 section 4.5. (transfer of legal title by deed).

52 Particularly mistake or failure of consideration. However, it is a difficult question whether – under the unjust factor regime – personal restitution should be available if the claimant has *known* that the contract was void (there being no mistake) and if the void transaction has still been *fully executed*. The crucial question is whether "failure of consideration" may only involve failure of a condition that counter-*performance* will be made or also failure of a condition that the claimant will receive a valid contractual *obligation* in return. In favour of the broader notion: *Westdeutsche Landesbank v Islington* [1994] 4 All ER 890, 924 (Hobhouse J), [1996] AC 669, 710–11 (Lord Browne-Wilkinson); *Guinness Mahon v Kensington and Chelsea Royal LBC* [1999] QB 215; *Re Goldcorp Exchange* [1995] 1 AC 74, 103–4 (Lord Mustill); *Patel v Mirza* [2016] UKSC 42, [246]–[249] (Lord Sumption; in dissent, though on other points); Goff/Jones, Unjust Enrichment, 13.25–32; Treitel, Contract, 22.13–18; contra: Burrows, Restitution, 319–20, 385–86, 395–97; cf also *Fibrosa Spolka Akcyjna v Fairbairn Lawson Combe Barbour* [1943] AC 32, esp 48–49 (Viscount Simon LC), 56 (Lord Russell).

underlying contract has been void.[53] In so far, a "void contract" might still have – though this might look like a contradiction in terms – some (very) minimal residual effects. It might, in some cases, at least preserve what may be called the "nexus of reciprocity" between the two performances of the parties' void bargain; if one of the void promises is actually executed, it might still count as consideration for the other. At any rate, this is inconceivable with regard to "transfers without any basis" which always and inevitably require delivery for legal title to pass (just as gifts do).

3. DEFECTS IN THE FORMATION STAGE AND DEFECTS IN THE EXECUTION STAGE

It is uncommon for courts and commentators to distinguish between defects which (only or also) occur in the stage of *formation* of a transaction and defects which (only or also) occur in the stage of its *execution*.[54] In the broad majority of cases concerned with defective transfers of ownership, the defect in question has operated in both, the formation *and* the execution stage. For example, if A concludes a contract with B in the fundamentally mistaken belief that B is C (mistake of identity), he will almost always still labour under that same mistake when he later delivers the supposedly owed goods or money to B. As far as this *is* the case, it is not quite crucial to strictly distinguish between defects occurring in the formation stage and defects occurring in the execution stage.

However, it is conceivable that a transferor labours under such a mistake only in the formation stage or only in the execution stage. If A – having concluded a contract with B under a contractually fundamental identity mistake – later learns about B's true identity but then still delivers the supposedly owed goods or money to B, legal ownership does pass to B since A makes delivery without suffering from a proprietarily fundamental mistake. At the time of conveyance (in the execution stage), there is no longer any relevant defect. It could at most be asked whether A has thereby affirmed the contract[55] (or executed a gift) and whether, if not, at least a personal restitutionary unjust enrichment claim might

---

53 See Chapter 2 section 3.2.

54 But see MEIER, Unjust factors, 43–46 (only concerned with personal restitution).

55 Affirmation is *not* generally possible in relation to void contracts; see CARTWRIGHT, Misrepresentation, 14.11; *Matthews v Baxter* [1873] LR 8 Ex 132 (Ct of Exchequer); *Fawcett v Star Car Sales Ltd* [1960] NZLR 406 (CA of New Zealand), 412 (Gresson P). However, B might be *estopped* from denying the contract's existence if he had made inaccurate representations; see CARTWRIGHT, Misrepresentation, 14.11. Alternatively, the fact that A has executed the "contract" notwithstanding his identity mistake might also be taken as an *indication* that B's identity had never actually been fundamental to the transaction; furthermore, A's act of execution might also be considered as a *new offer* to contract with B.

be available; this would at least require that A has still acted under some (other) causative mistake, for example as to the contract's validity, or that some other unjust factor had come into play, for example failure of consideration.

Similarly, a defect might also occur exclusively in the execution stage.[56] What is the position if there is an entirely valid contract between the parties (covering the transfer in question) but if the transferor has still executed the proprietary transfer under a proprietarily fundamental mistake or other defect? Suppose that buyer A has concluded two entirely valid executory contracts of sale, one with Mr Blenkarn (whom he had met face-to-face) for the purchase of 100 kilograms of mandarins for £100, and the other with Mr Blenkiron (who lived in same town as Blenkarn) for the purchase of 100 kilograms of oranges for £100.[57] Suppose further that A, having received the oranges from Blenkiron, takes out £100 from his wallet and puts them – together with a short letter thanking "Blenkiron" for the oranges – into an envelope which he intends to send over to "Blenkiron" in order to pay the oranges but that the postman – by some strange blunder or because A has not written very nicely – then delivers the envelope to Blenkarn. Would legal ownership in the money still pass to Blenkarn? The latter must have noticed the fact that the money was actually intended for Blenkiron. According to the view adopted in this book, this is a proprietarily fundamental identity mistake[58] which, at least in principle, prevents legal ownership from passing even if it exclusively occurred in the execution stage and even though the transferor was under an entirely valid contractual (or other) obligation to carry out the very transfer in question. Hence, legal ownership in the £100 delivered to Blenkarn would not pass to the latter even though A still owed payment of exactly such a sum of money. A contract's valid existence may not, at least in principle, cure a proprietarily fundamental defect occurring in the execution stage.[59]

There are more extreme examples where this principle might become more obvious. Suppose that Blenkarn, having concluded an entirely valid contract of sale with A, knocks at A's door, holds a gun at A's head and forces him to hand

---

56 This is inevitably the case as far as "transfers without any basis" are concerned, such as double or overpayments; in such cases, there is – apart from the transferor's unilateral decision-making-process – no "formation stage" at all.

57 This fictitious case is obviously inspired by *Cundy v Lindsay* [1878] LR 3 App Cas 459 (HL); see further Chapter 4 section 2.2. However, the case here is very different in that A and Blenkarn had supposedly met in person, that A actually wanted to contract (also) with Blenkarn and that Blenkarn had in no way acted fraudulently.

58 Fundamental mistakes will be discussed in detail in Chapter 4.

59 This is *not* a true exception to the principle that contracts have "indirect curative effects" on proprietary transfers (cf Chapter 1 section 2.1.1.2.) but rather results from the fact that the defect in question (mistake) had only occurred at the time of the proprietary conveyance but had not yet existed at the time of conclusion of the obligatory contract; had the defect (identity mistake) already existed by that time, it would equally have negatived (rendered void) the contract.

over the envelope containing the money intended for Blenkiron (or to pay over another £100). If A thereupon hands over the money, legal ownership does not pass by reason of Blenkarn's fundamental duress.[60] The same would obviously apply if Blenkarn breaks into A's premises and simply steals the envelope or other money. The fact that A still owes £100 to Blenkarn does not alter anything.[61]

A similar problem may occur on the level of unjust enrichment. Suppose that A, owing £100 under an existing contractual or other obligation to B, transfers such an amount to B under a defect – for example a non-fundamental causative mistake – which has only occurred in the execution stage but which is not proprietarily relevant. But for the obligation to carry out the transfer, A could have claimed personal restitution on the basis of the unjust factor mistake. However, it appears to be settled law that the existence of a contractual or other obligation *still justifies* an enrichment transferred under it even if the defect in question (unjust factor) has only occurred in the execution stage. This stands in marked contrast with the just described position on the proprietary level where a contract cannot justify a proprietarily fundamental defect occurring in the execution stage.

A good example is *Steam Saw Mills v Baring Bros*.[62] The claimant exported timber from Russia to England under a licence from the Russian Government under which he was obliged to pay the received sterling amount into an account of the Russian Government held with London bankers; the Russian Government, in turn, undertook to pay the equivalent amount in roubles at a fixed rate of exchange in Petrograd. On November 7, 1917, the Russian Government was displaced in the course of the Bolshevist revolution. That information, however, had not yet arrived in England when the claimant paid a sterling amount to the defendant bank on November 9. The Court of Appeal held that the claimant had not known of the revolution at the time of payment and that he would not otherwise have paid the money. Yet, it was also held that the claimant's contractual obligation to pay the money into the account held with the defendant

---

60 See Chapter 3 section 3.

61 However, it is not inconceivable that there might be cases where a court could eventually still refuse to enforce A's retained property rights on the basis that it would be *entirely pointless* to recognise, in a first step, A's existing property rights and to compel him, in a second step, to transfer the very same item of property (or other items of the same kind) back to the defendant ("dolo facit, qui petit quod redditurus est"; *Paulus*, Dig. 50, 17, 173, §3). But it appears that this should, if at all, only be so in very limited circumstances where A (or his trustee in bankruptcy) has *absolutely no real interest* in asserting such proprietary rights. Particularly, A might have an interest in claiming proprietary rights in the £100 transferred to Blenkarn if the latter has profitably invested them (A being entitled to trace and claim the profits) or if Blenkarn has become insolvent. Similarly, if A has become insolvent, A's trustee in bankruptcy might have an interest in claiming back the money and in compelling Blenkarn to queue with other unsecured creditors.

62 *Steam Saw Mills v Baring Bros* [1922] 1 Ch 244.

was still subsisting, not being frustrated by the events in Russia. That was fatal to the claim. Since the claimant was *obliged* to pay the money, he could not have claimed in unjust enrichment based on his causative mistake; the existing legal obligation justified the enrichment.[63]

It may be concluded that the effects of a valid contractual (or other) obligation on defects occurring exclusively in the execution stage are very different on the level of property as they are on the level of unjust enrichment. With regard to the latter, an existing contractual obligation is, at least in principle, capable of curing defects (unjust factors) which have occurred in the execution stage. As far as proprietarily fundamental defects are concerned, however, this is not the case. Fundamental mistakes, fundamental duress or other fundamental defects do prevent property from passing, at least in principle, even if there is an entirely valid contractual (or other) obligation covering the transfer. The conceptual reason for this discrepancy lies in the fact that a contract's curing effects are *direct* on the level of unjust enrichment but only *indirect* on the proprietary plane. Regarding the former, the absence of a justifying legal basis is an actual (negative) requirement of the very unjust enrichment cause of action. Regarding the latter, however, the proprietary transfer is independent (abstract) from the underlying transaction. The indirect interrelation between the contractual and the proprietary levels only operates inasmuch as the range of defects capable of affecting proprietary transfers is arguably narrower than the range of defects capable of affecting contracts. If, however, a defect does not exist by the time of the contract's conclusion but only by the time of the property's conveyance, that logical correlation becomes irrelevant; it is then fairly possible that a contract exists but that the proprietary transfer is void.

---

63 Ibid, 250–51 (Lord Sterndale MR), 253–54 (Warrington LJ); see also *David Securities v Commonwealth Bank of Australia* [1992] 175 CLR 353, 376, 392; Goff/Jones, Unjust Enrichment, 1.12, chs 2–3, 9.93–97; Burrows, Restitution, 88–91; Meier, Unjust factors, 39–40, 53–54; Stevens, Unjust Enrichment, 17–30.

CHAPTER 2

TRANSFER OF LEGAL OWNERSHIP IN TANGIBLE MOVABLE PROPERTY

The previous chapter has offered a brief introduction to the law of defective transfers of ownership at a somewhat abstract level. Before considering the question of how certain kinds of defects (particularly mistakes) affect the passage of legal title, we must examine the mechanics of how precisely legal ownership is transferred from one person to another. Our analysis will be broadly confined to consensual inter vivos transfers of legal title in tangible movable property (goods and corporeal money). Involuntary transfers by operation of law, for example upon execution or bankruptcy or as a result of accession, specification, mixture or tracing, or transfers of title in contemplation of or upon death are beyond the scope of this book.

It is surprisingly difficult to state the rules governing such consensual inter vivos transfers of legal ownership. In contrast to transfers of land, this branch of the law is still largely underdeveloped.[1] Modern common law basically recognises three[2] different modes of how legal title in tangible personal property may be transferred,[3] namely transfers *by delivery*, *by sale* (i.e. by mere intention) and *by deed*.[4,5]

---

1 Cf the remarks of Bridge, Property Law, 29; Baker, English Legal History, 379; Fox, Property Rights, 3.32–33. The law has recently received a significant doctrinal "face-lift" by the critical and inspiring analyses of Swadling, LQR 2005; Swadling, Unjust Delivery; Häcker, Impaired Consent and Fox, Property Rights.

2 There is a fourth, statutory mode of transfer, namely by registration, which applies in relation to British ships; see Chapter 2 section 5.2.

3 This stands in contrast to most civil law jurisdictions which usually only know *one* general mode of transfer for all kinds of transactions and for all kinds of tangible movable property (perhaps providing for special requirements, such as registration, in relation to certain kinds of chattels, such as ships, aircrafts or cattle).

4 It should be borne in mind that transfers effected *prior to delivery*, i.e. without possession, may be subject to the Bills of Sale Act 1878. Under this Act, a written document (deed or otherwise) which effects or records a transfer of property without possession may be void in the event of insolvency (i.e. against a trustee in bankruptcy, an assignee for the benefit of creditors or executing persons), unless certain formalities have been observed and unless registration has been made (s 8 and s 10). However, the scope and effects of the Act are limited. It only applies to very few sales (almost only to written, non-commercial ones) and even if it applies, the voidness only strikes against the document but property may still pass orally (by sale or by delivery); see Bridge et al, Benjamin's Sale of Goods, 1.16–17. In so far, the Act has only practical effects regarding transfers effected by deed.

5 Until the transfer of property takes effect at law, an *equitable* interest may only pass if an express trust has been declared with sufficient certainty. Regarding sale transactions, this is

Deeds may be used to transfer any kind of personal property (goods or corporeal money) in any kind of transaction (gratuitous or commercial). Transfers by deed apart, delivery is *required* to transfer corporeal money or to transfer legal title voluntarily (i.e. by an informal gift); however, the mode of transfer by delivery *may* also be used for any other transfer of legal title in personal property. Transfers by sale are governed by the Sale of Goods Act (SGA) 1979. Strictly speaking, this mode of transfer only applies to proper sales, i.e. transfers of legal title in goods for money consideration (but not to the corresponding transfer of legal title in the money). Though this is not finally settled by authority, it will be argued that the mode of transfer *by sale*, i.e. a transfer *by mere intention*, is equally available – though based on the common law rather than the SGA 1979 – outside the strict sale context, namely with regard to transfers of legal title in goods (other than money) for non-money consideration, for example barters.[6] It follows that the availability of a transfer by mere intention depends on the nature of the transaction (gratuitous or for consideration) and the nature of the chattel transferred (goods or money).

This has not always been the position. Historically, delivery was the only and original mode of transfer.[7] Probably until the 13th or 14th century, chattels could neither be transferred by deed nor by mere intention but only by delivery, i.e. by a transfer of possession. It appears that transfers by deed and transfers by sale have emerged from the original transfer by delivery as *two exceptions* which dispensed from the strict delivery requirement. Fry LJ has helpfully reviewed the history of those developments in the well-known case of *Cochrane v Moore*:

> "In Bracton's day [13th century], [...] [t]he law recognised seisin as the common incident of all property in corporeal things, and tradition or the delivery of that seisin from one man to another as essential to the transfer of the property in that thing, whether it were land or a horse, and whether by way of sale or of gift, and whether by word of mouth or by deed under seal. This necessity for delivery of seisin has disappeared from a large part of the transactions known to our law [...]. In the reign of Edward IV. [second half of the 15th century[8]] a step seems to have been taken in the law relative to gifts which

---

an implication of the SGA 1979; see *Re Wait* [1927] 1 Ch 606 (CA), 636 (Atkin LJ); *Leigh & Sillivan Ltd v Aliakmon Shipping Co Ltd (The Aliakmon)* [1986] AC 785 (HL), 812–13 (Lord Brandon); *Re Goldcorp Exchange Ltd* [1995] 1 AC 74 (PC); yet, the same must apply regarding any other transfer for consideration; see Goode, Commercial Law, 2.49 (fn 147). In relation to gifts, this follows from the maxim that equity will not assist a volunteer and that it does not perfect imperfect gifts; see Newman, Halsbury's Laws of England, vol 52(2), paras 267–70 (with references).

6 See Chapter 2 section 3.1.

7 See Baker, Oxford History, vol 6, 738–44; Baker, English Legal History, 383–85; Holdsworth, History of English Law, vol 3, 353–58.

8 The development of the deed exception may perhaps even be traced into the late 14th century; see Baker, English Legal History, 383–84.

> resulted in this modification: that whereas under the old law a gift of chattels by deed was not good without the delivery of the chattel given, it was now held that the gift by deed was good and operative until dissented from by the donee. [...] It was in the reigns of the early Tudors [late 15th century[9]] that the action on the case on indebitatus assumpsit obtained a firm foothold in our law; and the effect of it seems to have been to give a greatly increased importance to merely consensual contracts. It was probably a natural result of this that, in time, the question whether and when property passed by the contract came to depend, in cases in which there was a value consideration, upon the mind and consent of the parties, and that it was thus gradually established that in the case of bargain and sale of personal chattels, the property passed according to that mind and intention, and a new exception was thus made to the necessity of delivery."[10]

Cochrane v Moore concerned an oral gift, purportedly made without delivery, of a 25% co-ownership share in a horse. Prior to delivery, the horse was sold to a third party and the question arose whether an oral gift could transfer property without delivery. The Court of Appeal unanimously rejected such a proposition and firmly held that a gift of legal title could only be perfected by delivery or by deed.[11] Having set out the above historical analysis, Fry LJ concluded:

> "This review of the authorities leads us to conclude that according to the old law no gift or grant of a chattel was effectual to pass it whether by parol or by deed, and whether with or without consideration unless accompanied by delivery: that on that law two exceptions have been grafted, one in the case of deeds, and the other in that of contracts of sale where the intention of the parties is that the property shall pass before delivery."[12]

Those remarks reveal that a transfer of possession (delivery) was originally required for any transfer of property and that the two exceptions, sale and deed, emerged to overcome the strict delivery requirement. It appears that the development of the sale exception went hand in hand with the development of binding executory obligations in the 13th century. In those times, a sale did not impose binding obligations on the parties unless one of the parties had performed its part of the bargain; this was extended to the giving of an "earnest money" by the buyer.[13] It furthermore appears that (part) payment or the giving of an earnest money resulted in a fiction that "possession" had passed to

9 The first developments of the sale exception may apparently equally be traced into the 14th century (or even earlier); see esp Ibbetson, LQR 1991; see also Milsom, LQR 1961, 273–76, 282–84; Baker, English Legal History, 384–85.

10 *Cochrane v Moore* [1890] 25 QBD 57 (CA), 65–71 (Fry LJ).

11 Affirming *Irons v Smallpiece* [1819] 2 B&A 551, 106 ER 467; see also Holdsworth, History of English Law, vol 7, 503–9; but cf still Pollock, LQR 1890.

12 *Cochrane v Moore* [1890] 25 QBD 57, 72–73 (Fry LJ).

13 See generally Ibbetson, LQR 1991; Milsom, LQR 1961.

the buyer; this could be regarded as a form of constructive delivery which might, at least in an early stage, have satisfied the delivery requirement as such.[14] As a matter of fact, buyers started to successfully sue sellers in possession in detinue, rather than debt, to count on a bailment.[15] Eventually, the fiction of constructive delivery – comparable with some implied attornment by the seller or with some form of a *constitutum possessorium*[16] – was given up when it came to be recognised that property could simply pass by mere intention.[17]

This reveals that the transfer of legal title by sale (i.e. by mere intention) gradually emancipated from the transfer by delivery with the result that the strict delivery requirement was eventually wholly exempted from in sale transactions. Since the modern transfer by sale is, accordingly, a genuine descendant from the original transfer by delivery, it is arguable that these two modes of transfer only differ in one single respect, namely the delivery requirement as such. In particular, it will later be argued that the transfer by sale (and the transfer by deed) still essentially embodies – apart from the exempted delivery requirement – the same "type of transfer" as the original transfer by delivery.[18] The underlying structure and the constituent parts of those modes of transfer are still – the delivery requirement apart – broadly identical. It will furthermore be argued that transfers by sale (and transfers by deed) do equally require – just as transfers by delivery do – an intention of the transferor to transfer ownership and an intention of the transferee to receive ownership[19] and, crucially, that transfers by sale and transfers by deed are equally governed by the principles of separation (i.e. the contract is distinct from the conveyance) and abstraction (i.e. the conveyance's effectiveness is independent from an underlying transaction's validity or existence).

A transfer by delivery requires three elements, namely (i) an (abstract) intention of the transferor to transfer ownership, (ii) an (abstract) intention of the transferee to receive ownership and (iii) delivery. In the sale context, the last of those requirements has been entirely exempted from but (i) and (ii) are arguably still equally required. In the context of deeds, the delivery requirement has been replaced by a requirement to deliver (execute) a deed but (i) and (ii) are

---

14 Milsom, LQR 1961, 273–78, 282–84; Ibbetson, LQR 1991, 480, 490–91 (citing a case in the Chester Portmote of 1306); Baker, Oxford History, vol 6, 740–44; cf also van Vliet, Transfer of movables, 116–18.

15 Ibid.

16 Cf Zwalve/Sirks, Privatrechtsgeschichte, 368.

17 Eventually, the common law position was codified in the SGA 1893 and later in the SGA 1979 (both statutes intended to reflect the common law).

18 See Chapter 2 section 2. (sale) and Chapter 2 section 4. (deed).

19 The transferee's acceptance is not, however, necessarily a constituent element *ab initio* to transfer legal title but the transferee might still later reject the transfer with retrospective effects; see Chapter 2 section 1.3.

arguably still equally required. Such a view might have underlain the following observation of Erle CJ in *Chambers v Miller*:

> "The ordinary rule of law is, that the property in a chattel passes according to the intention of the parties. In an ordinary transaction of sale, where the proposed seller says to the proposed buyer, 'I will sell you such and such goods at such a price,' the assent of the buyer signified by the word 'done' is enough to fix the right of property. In the case of a gift, the property passes by delivery."[20]

1. TRANSFER OF LEGAL TITLE BY DELIVERY

The historically original mode of transfer by delivery still applies today. Transfers by deed apart, it is the only method to transfer legal title in corporeal money and to transfer legal title in personal property by way of gift.[21] As just mentioned, a transfer by delivery requires three things, namely (i) a voluntary transfer of possession (delivery), (ii) an intention of the transferor to transfer ownership and (iii) an intention of the transferee to receive ownership.

1.1. VOLUNTARY TRANSFER OF POSSESSION

Delivery is the voluntary – in the sense of "executed by free will" – transfer of possession.[22] On the one hand, this obviously requires that the transferee has somehow obtained *possession* of the relevant chattel. Possession has two requirements, namely physical control over a chattel and a concomitant intention to exercise such control (*animus possidendi*).[23] It follows that a transfer – particularly a gift – by delivery is impossible without the transferee's knowledge. A transfer by delivery cannot become effective before the transferee has formed some positive intention to possess the chattel in question.[24]

---

20 *Chambers v Miller* [1862] 13 CBR (NS) 125, 143 ER 50, 53.

21 As to the scope of the delivery requirement, see Chapter 2 section 3.

22 This notion closely resembles the Roman (civilian) requirement of a *traditio*; cf Fox, Property Rights, 3.33–34.

23 See only Pollock/Wright, Possession, esp 11–16; Bridge, Property Law, 33; *JA Pye (Oxford) Ltd v Graham* [2002] UKHL 30, [2003] 1 AC 419, [32] (Lord Browne-Wilkinson).

24 Lord Hobhouse's remark in *R v Hinks* [2001] 2 AC 241 (HL), 266–67, that "[i]t is not necessary for the donee to know of the gift" is not strictly inconsistent with the proposition that a transfer by delivery may only ever be completed if the transferee has knowledge of and an intention to exercise *possession*; see *Cochrane v Moore* [1890] 25 QBD 57, 75–76 (Lord Esher MR). In fact, the transferee does not need to know of or accept the transfer of *ownership* for it to become effective – subject to rejection – and it is arguable that this was what Lord Hobhouse has had in mind; see Chapter 2 section 1.3.

On the other hand, delivery requires that the transferor has played some active role in the procurement of possession. Delivery is not perfected if the transferee, for example upon an oral promise of a gift, simply unilaterally takes possession of the chattel. Delivery is a bilateral consensual act by which not only the transferee must have formed an intention to receive and exercise possession but by which the transferor must equally have formed (and acted upon) an intention to give up and transfer possession to the transferee.[25] This may be called a *possessory agreement*.

Such a voluntary transfer of possession can either be executed by an *actual delivery*, i.e. by physically handing over the chattel itself[26] or the means to exercise control over it (for example a key),[27] or by *constructive delivery*.[28] In English law, there are various forms of constructive delivery which are recognised as substitutes for an actual delivery. This includes cases where the transferee is already in possession of the chattel prior to the transaction (*brevi manu traditio*),[29] where the transferor, who has himself lost possession, discloses the (probable) whereabouts of the chattel and the transferee subsequently takes possession of it,[30] and – in exceptional circumstances – perhaps even where a symbolic or representative delivery of bulky chattels is made.[31] Furthermore, an undertaking (*attornment*) of a physically possessing third-party bailee, for example a carrier or warehouseman, to only surrender possession to the transferee equally amounts to constructive delivery. This is essentially what happens if a document of title is transferred, for example a bill of lading, which contains an undertaking of the bailee to only deliver to the respective lawful holder.[32] However, a so-called *constitutum possessorium*, where the transferor and the transferee merely agree that the former shall remain in possession in

---

25 *Cochrane v Moore* [1890] 25 QBD 57, 75–76 (Lord Esher MR); *R v Hinks* [2001] 2 AC 241, 266–67 (Lord Hobhouse); Fox, Property Rights, 3.39–42; Bridge, Property Law, 74–75; cf also Pollock/Wright, Possession, 43–47; but cf Pollock, LQR 1890, 446–47.

26 See (e.g.) *Chambers v Miller* [1862] 13 CBR (NS) 125 where a bank clerk put corporeal money on the counter and the claimant took it; the clerk immediately demanded it back when the claimant was still counting it; an argument that the transaction (delivery) had been incomplete was rejected.

27 *Wrightson v McArthur and Hutchinsons (1919) Ltd* [1921] 2 KB 807 (KBD).

28 See Pollock/Wright, Possession, 57–75; Holdsworth, History of English Law, vol 7, 503–4; Bridge, Property Law, 74–78, 172–74; R. Smith, Property Law, 118–22; Swadling, English Private Law, 4.462–68; van Vliet, Transfer of movables, 121–30.

29 *Re Stoneham* [1919] 1 Ch 149 (ChD).

30 *Thomas v The Times Book Co Ltd* [1966] 2 All ER 241 (ChD).

31 *Lock v Heath* [1892] 8 TLR 295 (gift of furniture in an inventory by handing over one chair); *Rawlinson v Mort* [1905] 93 LT 555 (KBD) (transfer of a church organ); but cf Swadling, English Private Law, 4.466–68 (treating it as a case of actual delivery); cf also *Re Cole* [1964] Ch 175 (CA).

32 See Bridge, Property Law, 75–78; Goode, Commercial Law, 2.45.

the capacity of a bailee, holding possession for the transferee, does not seem to amount to constructive delivery in English law.[33]

1.2. INTENTION OF THE TRANSFEROR TO TRANSFER OWNERSHIP

Evidently, a voluntary transfer of possession (delivery) cannot alone be sufficient to transfer *ownership* to the transferee. If this were otherwise, any transfer of *possession* for mere bailment, for example on terms of hire, lending or deposit, would effect a transfer of ownership. Indubitably, a transferor must – to effect a transfer of legal ownership by delivery – transfer possession with the intention to transfer legal ownership too.[34]

In the context of transfers by sale, it is well known that property may not pass prior to the point in time and prior to the conditions being satisfied as intended by the parties (ss 17 and 18 of the SGA 1979). A seller may, for example, reserve a right of disposal by inserting a retention of title clause[35] in the contract or in his act of appropriation which has the effect of preventing the passage of legal ownership until the respective conditions (usually payment) have been fulfilled. This was already the position at common law prior to the codification of the sales law in 1893 and is, it is submitted, still equally the position with regard to transfers by delivery. If a donor or transferor of money intends that property shall not pass upon and by delivery, but only at some later point in time, perhaps upon some conditions being fulfilled, legal ownership will not pass prior to that.[36] If this were otherwise, delivery would – assuming that the mode of transfer by delivery is cumulatively available in sale transactions[37] – routinely outflank Romalpa clauses in transfers by sale. On the other hand, if one

---

33 Cf *Michael Gerson (Leasing) Ltd v Wilkinson* [2001] QB 514 (CA) (concerning s 24 of the SGA 1979 in a sale and lease back agreement); cf also *Dublin City Distillery Ltd v Doherty* [1914] AC 823 (HL), 843–49 (Lord Atkinson) (concerning the creation of a pledge). As far as the transfer of legal title is concerned, this question is only relevant outside transfers by sale or by deed, thus particularly in relation to gifts and money. At least as far as gifts are concerned, it appears that the donor must relinquish possession; see Häcker, Impaired Consent, 47 (fn 153); van Vliet, Transfer of movables, 127–28; Bell, Personal Property, 222–23; this apparently emerges from *Cochrane v Moore* [1890] 25 QBD 57; but cf more liberally R. Smith, Property Law, 121.

34 See *R v Hinks* [2001] 2 AC 241, 266–67 (Lord Hobhouse); *Cochrane v Moore* [1890] 25 QBD 57, 75–76 (Lord Esher MR); Swadling, Unjust Delivery, 287–90; Swadling, English Private Law, 4.459–61; Fox, Property Rights, 3.40; Bell, Personal Property, 223–24.

35 "Romalpa clause"; see s 19 of the SGA 1979; *Aluminium Industrie Vaassen BV v Romalpa Aluminium Ltd* [1976] 1 WLR 676 (CA).

36 See *R v Hinks* [2001] 2 AC 241, 266–67 (Lord Hobhouse).

37 See esp Swadling, LQR 2005, 126–27, 141–42, 152; Häcker, Impaired Consent, 136–37, 194–96; Häcker, Causality and abstraction, 210–12; cf already Diamond, MLR 1960, 453.

assumed – contrary to the view adopted in this book[38] – that in barters or other transfers for non-money consideration property could only pass by delivery, Romalpa clauses would otherwise be virtually impossible in such transactions.

1.3. INTENTION OF THE TRANSFEREE TO RECEIVE OWNERSHIP

No one can be forced to accept legal ownership against his will. Ownership can be burdensome and may bring along potential liabilities, for example in the laws of tort, taxation or environment; legal title may also be encumbered with equitable interests which would render the transferee a trustee. A transfer by delivery therefore requires that the transferee somehow accepts the receipt of legal title.[39]

However, it appears that the transferee's acceptance is not *initially* a constitutive element to effect the transfer of legal ownership. Though a transfer by delivery certainly presupposes that the transferee has formed an intention to exercise *possession*,[40] it is not strictly required that he has also formed an intention to accept legal *ownership*. If a transferee merely accepts possession but not (yet) ownership, for example because he believes that the transfer is made on terms of a deposit, lending or hire, rather than being an outright gift, legal ownership still passes immediately upon delivery.[41] However, the transferee, upon becoming aware that ownership has in fact been transferred, is still entitled to *reject* the transfer of ownership *with retrospective effects*.[42] Rejection of the transfer retrospectively revests ownership in the transferor and relieves

---

38 See Chapter 2 section 3.1.

39 *Hill v Wilson* [1873] LR 8 Ch App 888 (CA in Chancery), 896 (Mellish LJ); *Cochrane v Moore* [1890] 25 QBD 57, 75–76 (Lord Esher MR); *R v Hinks* [2001] 2 AC 241, 266–67 (Lord Hobhouse); NEWMAN, Halsbury's Laws of England, vol 52(2), paras 201, 249–50; CRAGO, UWALR 1999; HILL, LQR 2001; SWADLING, English Private Law, 4.469; HÄCKER, Impaired Consent, 47, 193; R. SMITH, Property Law, 117; BELL, Personal Property, 224; KERSLEY, Goodeve's Modern Law of Personal Property, 144; POLLOCK/WRIGHT, Possession, 100–2; cf also *Townson v Tickell* [1819] 3 B&A 31, 106 ER 575; *Standing v Bowring* [1885] 31 ChD 282 (CA); contra: Fox, Property Rights, 3.41–42, 3.72–75.

40 See fn 24 and text to it.

41 *Standing v Bowring* [1885] 31 ChD 282, 286 (Lord Halsbury LC), 288 (Cotton LJ), 289–90 (Lindley LJ); *Dewar v Dewar* [1975] 1 WLR 1532 (ChD), 1537–39 (Goff J); *R v Hinks* [2001] 2 AC 241, 266–67 (Lord Hobhouse); NEWMAN, Halsbury's Laws of England, vol 52(2), paras 201, 249–50; SWADLING, English Private Law, 4.469; LAWSON/RUDDEN, Law of Property, 55; but cf *Hill v Wilson* [1873] LR 8 Ch App 888, 896 (Mellish LJ); HILL, LQR 2001, 127–33, 148–49.

42 *Butler and Baker's Case* [1591] 3 Co Rep 25, 76 ER 684; *Townson v Tickell* [1819] 3 B&A 31; *Standing v Bowring* [1885] 31 ChD 282, 286 (Lord Halsbury LC), 288 (Cotton LJ), 289–90 (Lindley LJ); *Re Paradise Motor Co Ltd* [1968] 1 WLR 1125 (CA); *R v Hinks* [2001] 2 AC 241, 266–67 (Lord Hobhouse); NEWMAN, Halsbury's Laws of England, vol 52(2), paras 201, 249–50; O'SULLIVAN et al, Rescission, 29.13; CRAGO, UWALR 1999; SWADLING, English Private Law, 4.469.

the transferee from any burdens or liabilities in connection with the chattel. This is apparently what Lord Hobhouse had in mind in *R v Hinks*:

> "The making of a gift is the act of the donor. It involves the donor in forming the intention to give and then acting on that intention by doing whatever it is necessary for him to do to transfer the relevant property to the donee. Where the gift is the gift of a chattel, the act required to complete the gift will normally be [...] delivery to the donee [...]. Unless the gift was conditional, in which case the condition must be satisfied before the gift can take effect, the making of the gift is complete once the donor has carried out this step. The gift has become the property of the donee. *It is not necessary for the donee to know of the gift. The donee, on becoming aware of the gift, has the right to refuse (or reject) the gift in which case it revests in the donor with resolutive effect [...].*"[43]

Though the transfer of legal ownership by delivery might – apart from the requirement that the transferee must at least accept possession – be conceived as an initially unilateral transaction,[44] it is in fact essentially a *bilateral* act which requires (sooner or later) both, the transferor's intention to transfer ownership and the transferee's intention to receive ownership.[45] This requirement of a mutual intention directed at the transfer and the receipt of ownership may be compared with an *offer* and an *acceptance* to transfer and receive ownership or with the civilian notion of a *real agreement.*[46] Though it must of course always be borne in mind that the analogy might be a loose one and that, in English law, legal ownership may provisionally pass even without the transferee's knowledge or acceptance, the two requirements that the transferor must intend to transfer ownership and that the transferee must (at some point) accept to receive it, may – taken together – conveniently be called the requirement of a real agreement.

1.4. THE PRINCIPLES OF SEPARATION AND ABSTRACTION IN TRANSFERS BY DELIVERY

The so-called principle of separation, which is well known in civil laws, refers to the notion that a certain mode of transfer distinguishes between an

---

43 *R v Hinks* [2001] 2 AC 241, 266–67 (Lord Hobhouse) (emphasis added).

44 Fox, Property Rights, 3.41–42, 3.72–75.

45 Hill, LQR 2001; R. Smith, Property Law, 117.

46 Cf §929 of the German BGB; see also Häcker, ZEuP 2011, 340–42, 357; Häcker, Impaired Consent, 193; van Vliet, Transfer of movables, 120–21; cf already Pollock, Principles of contract, 3: "[The definition of 'agreement'] includes every kind of transaction which affects the rights of the parties and to which the consent of more than one of them is necessary. Not only contract, but every sort of conveyance is covered by it; even a conveyance by way of absolute and immediate gift. [...] [T]o say that a conveyance by way of gift imports an agreement is only to say that ownership cannot be thrust on a man against his will, and in this form there is nothing strange in the proposition"; cf fn (a): "[E]very conveyance includes an agreement".

underlying personal obligation to effect a transfer (usually based on a contract) and the real conveyance which effects the proprietary transfer. The principle of abstraction and the principle of causality, which are mutually exclusive, refer to the question whether a certain mode of transfer *may*, in principle, be effective even if an underlying transaction is ineffective, void or inexistent (the mode of transfer being "abstract") or not (the mode of transfer being "causal"). The principle of abstraction can only come along in combination with the principle of separation[47] but the principle of causality can exist with[48] or without[49] a principle of separation.

These concepts are creatures of and belong to the legal vocabulary of the continental civil laws; the common law is not familiar with them. However, the use of and reference to those principles may evidently enhance the understanding of this area of the law.[50] As a matter of legal logic, the common law must be able (and is able) to give an answer to the question of whether and in how far it follows either of those principles. The answer must not be the same for all modes of transfer; but it must be possible to classify any one mode of transfer as being abstract or causal.

As far as transfers by delivery are concerned, the answer is straightforward: Delivery is governed by the principles of *separation* and *abstraction*.[51] This is most obvious with regard to gratuitous transfers. Gifts are not contracts (lack of consideration) and do not, unless contained in a deed, impose any enforceable legal obligations on the promisor. Notwithstanding the absence of a personal obligation to execute the transfer, however, a donor might of course pass legal ownership by delivery. This reveals that the effectiveness of a transfer by delivery is independent (abstract) from a contract or other underlying obligation.

---

47 Abstraction and separation is the position in Germany; see §929 BGB.

48 Causality and separation is the position in Austria (see §§380 and 424 ABGB), the Netherlands (see article 84 of book 3 (3:84) of the Burgerlijk Wetboek) and Switzerland (BGE 55 II 302, interpreting article 714 paragraph 1 ZGB).

49 Causality without separation is apparently (still) the position in France; see article 1196 (in general; basically similar to the old article 1138), article 938 (gifts), 1583 (sales) and 1703 (barters) of the new Code Civil.

50 See (e.g.) Swadling, LQR 2005, 139–42; Häcker, ZEuP 2011; Häcker, Impaired Consent, 46–50, 191–202; Häcker, Causality and abstraction; Fox, Property Rights, 3.48–67, 4.3–16; van Vliet, Transfer of movables; van Vliet, EdinLR 2008; Stadler, Gestaltungsfreiheit (concerning US law).

51 Fox, Property Rights, 3.48–67, 4.3–16; Fox, RLR 1996, 69–70; Häcker, Impaired Consent, 50, 191–97; Häcker, ZEuP 2011, 346–51; Häcker, Causality and abstraction, 205–8, 221; Swadling, LQR 2005; Swadling, RLR 1994, 81–82; Sheehan, Personal Property, 153–56; cf also Virgo, Restitution, 570–80; McCormack, JBL 1997, 57–58; ambiguous: van Vliet, Transfer of movables, 130–32; not considered in van Vliet, EdinLR 2008; apparently contra: *Fawcett v Star Car Sales Ltd* [1960] NZLR 406 (CA of New Zealand), 423–24 (Gresson P) (but cf the majority judgment of North and Cleary JJ).

It could be objected that this, to some extent, misconceives the true nature of gifts and that gratuitous promises in fact produce at least "unenforceable" obligations.[52] There may be force in this objection. But however that may be, there is still ample evidence outside the law of gifts that the mode of transfer by delivery is abstract rather than causal: Corporeal money may only be transferred by delivery (or by deed) and it is clearly established that legal title in money may pass irrespective of whether there is an underlying obligation or not.[53] In *R v Prince*,[54] for example, a fraudulent wife, intending to leave her husband, presented a forged order for payment of her husband's deposit whereupon the bank's clerk paid out the money. It was held that – notwithstanding the clerk's fraudulently induced motivational mistake and notwithstanding the fact that there had been no obligation entitling the wife to the money whatsoever – legal ownership in the money had passed to her.[55,56] The same principles must apply with regard to transfers of goods without basis. Suppose that the wife had presented a forged request to deliver an amount of gold bullions standing to her husband's credit. If the clerk had thereupon handed over such an amount of gold bullions, property in them would equally have passed from the bank to the wife notwithstanding the absence of any contractual or other obligation entitling the wife to the gold. Furthermore, it is well settled that legal ownership may pass at least upon and by delivery in transfers made under void contracts.[57]

It can be concluded that delivery is an abstract mode of transfer. A perhaps existing underlying contract or other obligation must be strictly distinguished from conveyance (principle of separation). Three clarificatory remarks must be added: First, the relevant conveyance, which is distinct from an underlying obligation, itself consists of two elements, namely delivery (including a *possessory*

---

52 At any rate, an executed gift at least provides a legal basis (similar to a contract) which justifies an enrichment transferred under it; see Chapter 1 section 2.2.1.; cf VAN VLIET, Transfer of movables, 130–31 (assuming that a gift is a *causa traditionis*).

53 See only Fox, Property Rights, 3.48–67.

54 *R v Prince* [1868] LR 1 CCR 150 (Ct for Crown Cases Reserved).

55 See also *Chambers v Miller* [1862] 13 CBR (NS) 125; *Moynes v Coopper* [1956] 1 QB 439 (QBD); *Barclays Bank Ltd v WJ Simms Son & Cooke (Southern) Ltd* [1980] QB 677 (QBD), 688–89 (Goff J); cf also *Westdeutsche Landesbank Girozentrale v Islington LBC* [1996] AC 669 (HL), 689 (Lord Goff): "[T]here is no general rule that the property in money paid under a void contract does not pass to the payee" (though *Westdeutsche* itself apparently concerned a transfer of incorporeal money).

56 The money would have been recoverable by a personal unjust enrichment claim. Furthermore, the bank would have received – based on the fraud – a power in rem to revest ownership in the money; cf *Moynes v Coopper* [1956] 1 QB 439, 445 (Lord Goddard CJ). But this does not alter the fact that the transfer of legal title as such was still abstract; had there been no misrepresentation, the bank could not have revested property.

57 It will furthermore be argued that legal ownership might, in some cases of transfers made under void contracts, even pass prior to delivery and by mere intention; see Chapter 2 sections 2.3. and 3.2.

agreement) and a *real agreement*.[58] Second, it is of course not delivery which is independent (abstract) from the real agreement but rather the conveyance (as a whole) which is independent (abstract) from an underlying obligation. Third, even though a transfer by delivery does not *require* a valid underlying obligation and even though the fact that a certain defect renders a contract void is not in and of itself a reason which affects the abstract conveyance's effectiveness, it is of course *possible* that the very same defect – for example a fundamental mistake – also and independently affects the conveyance, namely the transferor's (or the transferee's) intention to transfer (or receive) ownership.[59] In other words, defects which render contracts void *may* – but need not – also affect the real agreement. Defects which render contracts void may be called *obligatory defects*. Defects which render the real agreement void may be called *real defects*. Defects which affect both, the contract and the real agreement, may be called *dual*, *twofold* or *double defects*. This can be compared with the similar German doctrine of "Fehleridentität" (identity of defect) or "Doppelmangel" (dual defect).[60]

2. TRANSFER OF LEGAL TITLE BY SALE

2.1. THE REQUIREMENT OF SPECIFIC OR ASCERTAINED GOODS

Transfers of legal ownership by sale are today governed by the SGA 1979.[61] Section 16 contains a mandatory requirement for property to pass, namely that the transferred goods have either been *specifically* identified in the contract of sale or, if not, that they have been *ascertained* by an unconditional appropriation to the contract.[62] As long as the contract goods remain unascertained (generic), legal ownership may not pass.[63] Today, a limited statutory exception to this rule is contained in s 20A which provides that pre-paying buyers may acquire co-ownership in a bulk if the bulk has been identified in the contract as

---

58 Cf Chapter 2 section 1.3.

59 McCormack, JBL 1997, 57–58; Fox, Property Rights, 3.58–67, 3.99–109, ch 4.

60 Cf Häcker, Impaired Consent, 60–63, 191–202; Häcker, ZEuP 2011, 338, 353–54.

61 Previously, they were governed by the SGA 1893 and, prior to that, by the common law. Both, the SGA 1893 and the SGA 1979 have largely codified the former common law position.

62 Appropriation fixes the contract goods and "attaches" them to the contract. It requires the assent of both parties, given in advance or subsequent to the contract formation, and must be unconditional; usually, the seller appropriates the goods with the buyer's assent given in advance. As a consequence, the source from which the seller might perform may no longer be altered unilaterally; see generally Bridge et al, Benjamin's Sale of Goods, 5.67–108; Goode, Commercial Law, 8.19–22.

63 This was the problem of the non-allocated claimants in *Re Goldcorp Exchange* [1995] 1 AC 74, 89–95 (Lord Mustill).

the only source from which the seller might perform (quasi-specific goods) or if the bulk has been unconditionally appropriated to the contract (quasi-ascertained goods).[64]

Section 20A apart, the rule of s 16 is of very general application in English property law. Property rights can only attach to specific goods but not to a genus. This is not only a requirement in transfers of legal title by sale but applies equally, at least in theory, with regard to transfers by delivery (though ascertainment will rarely be a problem in delivery cases[65]) and transfers by deed. Furthermore, this requirement equally applies with regard to declarations of trust and other transfers of equitable interests.[66]

2.2. INTENTION OF THE PARTIES TO TRANSFER OWNERSHIP: CONTRACTUAL INTENTION OR PRINCIPLE OF SEPARATION?

Delivery was originally required to transfer legal title even in sale transactions; but this requirement has been gradually exempted from since the 13th or 14th century.[67] Section 17 of the SGA 1979 today provides that legal ownership passes "at such time as the parties to the contract intend it to be transferred" and s 19 acknowledges the possibility that the transfer of property may be deferred (expressly or impliedly) until after delivery and until certain conditions have been fulfilled, for example payment. Sections 18, 19(2) and 19(3) provide rebuttable presumptions (rules) to determine the parties' intention in that regard; yet, it is always the parties' *actual* intention which is, if proved, ultimately relevant.

A transfer of legal title by sale accordingly requires two basic elements: First, the parties must have intended that ownership shall be transferred from the seller to the buyer *at all*. Section 17 refers to "parties" – in the plural – which means that the *seller* must have intended to transfer property to the buyer and that the *buyer* must have intended to receive property. This resembles the real agreement requirement in transfers by delivery.[68] Second, the conditions which the parties have imposed on their intentions must be fulfilled. If the parties intended to pass ownership immediately upon conclusion of the contract or automatically on day X, nothing or no more than passage of time will be required. If the parties agree that

64 See generally Bridge et al, Benjamin's Sale of Goods, 5.109–30.

65 If delivery has been made, the goods will almost always be ascertained, perhaps except where the transferor has explicitly delivered a bulk larger than agreed (subject to future appropriation) or where the transferee is in possession of a larger bulk from which the transferor has agreed to transfer a portion.

66 See *Re Goldcorp Exchange* [1995] 1 AC 74, esp 89–95 (Lord Mustill).

67 See fn 9 and introductory remarks of Chapter 2.

68 Cf Chapter 2 section 1.3. (though with the difference that the buyer will always have agreed to the transfer at the inception).

property shall pass immediately upon appropriation (or if s 16 applies) or if they agree that property shall pass upon delivery or payment, property will only pass if those conditions are met. The SGA accordingly confers a great autonomy and flexibility on the parties; they may essentially tailor their own mode of transfer.

The exact doctrinal analysis of this apparently straightforward position is not, however, quite easy. In fact, the reference to the parties' intention in s 17 is ambiguous: Does this exclusively refer to the parties' *contractual* intention, i.e. to the parties' intention to conclude a contract of sale on certain terms, or does it rather refer to a *real* intention which is distinct from the parties' strictly contractual intention? Are there two different kinds of intentions (real and contractual) or is there only one (contractual)? This bears the question whether the transfer by sale is governed by a principle of separation and whether it distinguishes between contract and conveyance or whether there is exclusively a contract and no distinct conveyance.

It is very generally assumed that property passes *by the force of the contract alone*;[69] this apparently suggests that there is – similarly as in French law[70] – no principle of separation in transfers by sale.[71] Swadling has observed that "[t]he distinction between contract and conveyance has unfortunately been obscured in the area of the sale of goods, where [...] it is possible for property to pass by virtue of the contract alone".[72] Bridge has noted that "[s]ale of goods law deals with a hybrid transaction that consists of contract and conveyance. [...] [T]he sequence of contract and conveyance is not as clearly differentiated as it is in the case of sale of land."[73] These remarks reveal the uncertainties and

69 See (e.g.) *Cundy v Lindsay* [1878] LR 3 App Cas 459 (HL), 464 (Lord Cairns): "[I]f the property in the goods in question passed, it could only pass by way of contract; there is nothing else which could have passed the property"; *Fawcett v Star Car Sales* [1960] NZLR 406, 423–24 (Gresson P) (but cf the majority judgment of North and Cleary JJ who apparently conceived the passage of property as somewhat more independent from the contract); HÄCKER, Impaired Consent, 191–92; HÄCKER, ZEuP, 339–40; HÄCKER, Causality and abstraction, 202–3; SWADLING, LQR 2005, 141; FOX, Property Rights, 3.51, 3.63–64, 4.26 ("simply by force of a contract of sale"); GOODE, Commercial Law, 8.37 ("by virtue of the contract itself"); TWIGG-FLESNER et al, Atiyah and Adams' Sale of Goods, 35; MATTEI, Property law, 106; DROBNIG, Transfer of Property, 1014–15.

70 See fn 49.

71 Explicitly: HÄCKER, Impaired Consent, 191–92 (considering but rejecting a separate notion of a real agreement); HÄCKER, Causality and abstraction, 202–3; HÄCKER, ZEuP 2011, 339–40; but cf HÄCKER, Third Party Rights, 36–37 (adopted by O'SULLIVAN et al, Rescission, 20.19–20), arguing that the "bargain aspect of the contract of sale can be successfully decoupled from its proprietary effect" and that "there is no inherently necessary link between these two aspects"; see also HÄCKER, Impaired Consent, 272. Conceptually, this argument (designed to enable the much-needed abolition of the third-party rights bar in the law of rescission) would be much more easily feasible if the principles of separation and abstraction were adopted.

72 SWADLING, LQR 2005, 141.

73 BRIDGE, Sale of Goods, 3.1; see also 3.6 (speaking of a "fusion of the contract and the conveyance").

ambiguities coming along with the assertion that there is nothing but a contract in a sale transaction and that it is the contract alone and nothing else which operates as a vehicle to transfer property. Though this received orthodoxy has apparently never been seriously challenged,[74] it cannot withstand closer scrutiny. It is submitted that the analytical uncertainties in this regard are a direct result of the failure to strictly distinguish between the contract and the conveyance in sale transactions.

The orthodox analysis of transfers of property by sale encounters particular difficulties if property is agreed to pass not immediately upon conclusion of the contract but by some later act of the parties, for example by delivery. In such cases, the distinction between contract and conveyance becomes particularly evident. In fact, such a distinction is already inherent in the SGA 1979 itself: Section 2(4) provides that where property passes immediately upon conclusion, the transaction is called a "sale"; s 2(5) provides that where property is agreed to pass at a future date or subject to some conditions to be fulfilled, it is an "agreement to sell"; s 2(6) provides that an agreement to sell becomes a sale if such time has passed or if such conditions have been fulfilled. In that regard, it is often said that an agreement to sell is only an (executory) "contract" whereas a sale is "a contract *plus* a conveyance".[75] If this means anything, it must be that an executed sale in fact contains two different things, namely a contract *and* a (distinct) conveyance. This would acknowledge the principle of separation. Property would not in fact be transferred by the contract *alone* but – also or only – by the conveyance. By contrast, it would be impossible to see how this could meaningfully denote a conception that there is, even in cases of executed agreements to sell, still only one thing, namely a contract, which upon its execution became (or now also serves as) a conveyance. If an unexecuted agreement to sell is initially *only* a

---

74 See only van Vliet, Transfer of movables, 104–14, 203–4; van Vliet, EdinLR 2008; cf also Montrose, Canadian Bar Review 1937, 760: "[Section 1 of the SGA 1893] exhibits an unhappy confusion of the concepts of contract and conveyance. [...] [T]he transfer though part of the entire transaction which includes the contract is not part of the contract; it is a conveyance."

75 See *Colley v Overseas Exporters (1919) Ltd* [1921] 3 KB 302 (KBD), 310 (McCardie J): "A sale or, as it is called for distinction, an executed contract of sale is a contract plus a conveyance"; Bell, Personal Property, 236: "The sale of goods involves both a conveyance and a contract"; Bridge et al, Benjamin's Sale of Goods, 1.26–28: "[A] sale involves not only a contract, but also a conveyance of the property in the goods"; Twigg-Flesner et al, Atiyah and Adams' Sale of Goods, 35: "[The actual contract] may operate both as a conveyance and a contract"; McKendrick, English Private Law, 10.8: "A sale is, however, more than a contract. It is both a contract and a conveyance"; Häcker, Third Party Rights, 36: "the same agreement contains both the bargain and the conveyance"; Häcker, Impaired Consent, 272: "For contracts of sale, English law has chosen to combine both the bargain and the conveyancing aspect in the same agreement. [...] Bargain and conveyance, though notionally distinct, are to be found in the same transaction"; Merrett, Chitty on Contracts, vol 2, 44.21; Goode, Commercial Law, 3.161, 7.16–17, 7.25; cf also Stadler, Gestaltungsfreiheit, 37.

contract, how could that same contract – without being altered or modified – all at once also become a conveyance? Evidently, there must be something else which constitutes – or partially constitutes – the conveyance in such a case. Where the parties agree that property shall pass upon certain acts to be executed by them, for example delivery or payment, it would obviously be inaccurate to say that it is the contract *alone* which transfers ownership. If at all, it could at most be the contract coupled with delivery or payment or some other act which constitutes conveyance and which effects the transfer of property. Such acts must be regarded as an integrating part of the conveyance itself.

This point may perhaps best be made by the example that the parties agree that property shall pass upon delivery. In such a case, property may not pass by the contract *alone*; delivery rather becomes part of the conveyance. Effectively, such an agreement would simply reinstate the pre-15th century common law position when delivery was still required to transfer property in sale transactions.[76] In fact, there is no fundamental difference between this case and a case where property actually passes by the genuine mode of transfer by delivery. In neither case would property pass "by the contract alone" and in both cases is the contract separate and distinct from the conveyance. Suppose that the parties concluded an entirely valid agreement to sell whereby property was agreed to pass upon delivery and that a fundamental defect occurs in the execution stage: The buyer knocks at the seller's door, holds a gun at his head and forces him to "deliver" the goods. If it were indeed "the contract *alone*" which effects the transfer of property, the defect in the execution stage would not be relevant at all. It could be objected that the parties' intended condition "delivery" would not actually be fulfilled in such a case. This might be right. But the preferable analysis still seems to be that delivery is genuinely part of the conveyance itself. Suppose that the buyer has merely defrauded the seller in the execution stage by fraudulently inducing him to deliver the goods which he would not otherwise have done. Would the parties' intended condition "delivery" neither be met in such a case? If not, why should property be retained rather than passing subject to rescission? If yes, the seller would still not be able to rescind the contract since the defect has not affected the *contract*; and if it were the contract *alone* that transferred property, property would apparently pass non-voidably. That would not seem right.[77]

According to the view adopted in this book, it is preferable to analyse transfers by sale broadly in accordance with the underlying structure of transfers by delivery. A transfer by sale basically requires two elements: First, a *real agreement*

---

[76] See the introductory remarks of Chapter 2.

[77] Cf Chapter 1 section 3.

is needed by which the transferor (seller) intends to transfer ownership to the transferee (buyer) and by which the latter intends to receive ownership.[78] There is some difference compared with the actual mode of transfer by delivery in that the problem of a "provisional" transfer of legal title, subject to a retrospective rejection, does not occur in sale transactions.[79] The real agreement is concluded at the same time – *uno actu* – as the obligatory contract; most usually, these two things will be contained in one and the same piece of document or one and the same oral expression.[80] However, the real agreement is still *separate* and *notionally distinct* from the obligatory contract. In sale transactions, the real agreement contains, apart from the parties' intention that property shall pass *at all*, a further element, namely the *definition* – explicit, implicit or by an application of the statutory presumptions – of the *exact mode of how and when property is to pass* (immediately, upon appropriation, payment, delivery or something else). This is part of the real agreement. There is no conceptual problem with this. Even in transfers by delivery, the parties may agree that property shall not pass until some conditions have been fulfilled, for example that counter-performance is made.[81] The only difference is that the parties may here effectively agree that property shall pass prior to delivery.

The second element which is required for property to pass by sale is the fulfilment of those conditions which the parties have (explicitly or implicitly) imposed on their real agreement. If they agree that property shall pass upon delivery, delivery is needed. If they agree that property shall pass upon appropriation (or if s 16 applies), appropriation is needed. Such acts, which must be wilfully executed by the parties in order to effect the transfer of property,

---

78 The fact that the transferee (buyer) must *accept* the receipt of ownership may be illustrated by the case of *Hardman v Booth* [1863] All ER Rep Ext 1847, 158 ER 1107. The seller intended to sell and transfer goods to "Gandell & Co" when he concluded a (void) contract with and handed over the goods to Edward Gandell, a clerk without authority. It was held that there had been no contract with Edward Gandell because the seller had not intended to contract with him and that no property had passed to him because the seller had not intended to transfer property to him. It was also held that the seller had retained legal title which – at least implicitly – meant that property had neither passed to Gandell & Co. Since the seller had clearly formed an intention to transfer property to Gandell & Co, this may be taken to mean that property had not passed *due to the lack of acceptance of ownership by the transferee*. Edward Gandell's "acceptance", at any rate, was void since he had no authority.

79 Cf Chapter 2 section 1.3.

80 See also van Vliet, Transfer of movables, 104–14, 203–4: "In a consensual system, it is true, the real agreement may coincide with the contract obliging to make the transfer, but it should nonetheless be seen as a distinct element. If the contract itself passed ownership the transfer would inevitably be causal. Yet, it is not the contract that passes ownership; it is the real agreement. Therefore the transfer might be abstract even in a consensual system"; cf also Häcker, Impaired Consent, 191–92 (considering but apparently rejecting such a proposition as "highly artificial"); Häcker, ZEuP 2011, 339–40.

81 See Chapter 2 section 1.2.

must be regarded as *part of the conveyance* – together with the real agreement as initially concluded. If the transfer of property is agreed to occur automatically at some specific date or upon a condition which does not require the act of a party, conveyance is arguably completed at the time of the real agreement; yet, conveyance is then still *conditional*. It will, upon the passage of time or fulfilment of the condition, automatically become effective.

If the parties agree that property in specific goods shall pass immediately upon conclusion of the contract, no such second step is needed. The real agreement – but not the obligatory one! – is then conveyance in itself. In this case, the distinction between the real agreement and the obligatory contract may become blurred. They are concluded at the same time, *uno actu*, and potentially within and by one and the same document or oral expression. However, they must still be strictly distinguished. There is a "sale" at the inception (s 2(4) of the SGA 1979) which contains two things, the obligatory contract *and* the real agreement, and it is the latter – and only the latter! – which effects the transfer of property.

This analysis is consistent with the historical observation that the transfer by sale organically emerged from the transfer by delivery.[82] This new mode of transfer in fact *only* exempted from the delivery requirement but did not, besides that, alter the fundamental structure of the original mode of transfer itself. Particularly, the requirement of a distinct and separate real agreement is still the same.

It may furthermore be noted that the proposed analysis is not inconsistent with the wording of the SGA 1979. Section 17(1) provides that property passes "at such time as the parties to the contract intend it to be transferred". It does not say that "it is the *contract* and nothing else which is the vehicle to transfer property"; it only says that it is the parties' "intention". This may equally be taken to refer to a real intention or a real agreement. Neither is s 17(2) inconsistent with this. Though it refers to the "terms of the contract" which are, amongst other factors, relevant to ascertain "the intention of the parties", the relevant intention may still be a *real* one. It is obvious that the obligatory contract (or the document in which that obligatory contract is contained) will serve as *evidence* to prove the parties' distinct *real* intention. But this does still not mean that they are one and the same thing.

Finally, it may be added that the principle of abstraction, which will be defended in the next sub-section, logically presupposes the existence of a distinction between contract and conveyance (principle of separation). In so far, any argument in favour of abstraction is equally an argument in favour of separation.

---

[82] See the introductory remarks of Chapter 2.

2.3. TRANSFER BY SALE: PRINCIPLE OF CAUSALITY OR ABSTRACTION?

Clear distinction between the obligatory contract and the real conveyance in sale transactions paves the way for the recognition of a principle of abstraction. Abstraction is impossible without separation. However, the mere fact that contract and conveyance are notionally distinct does not decide or prejudice the question whether the transfer is *causal* (the conveyance's effectiveness depending on the contract's validity)[83] or *abstract* (the conveyance's effectiveness being independent from the contract's validity).[84]

Courts have never directly considered the question whether transfers by sale are causal or abstract; this is unsurprising in light of the general failure to strictly distinguish between contract and conveyance. Commentators have, until quite recently, similarly amalgamated contract and conveyance which seems to favour, at least implicitly, some notion of causality;[85] yet, this was rarely the product of a proper examination of the issue but rather simply resulted from a lack of distinction. Van Vliet – apparently the only commentator who strictly distinguished between contract and conveyance – advocated a principle of causality.[86] Note may furthermore be taken of the sometimes expressed (undifferentiated) blanket assertion that the law follows a principle of causality very generally.[87] With respect, this is certainly inaccurate at least with regards to transfers by delivery. Evidently, the question of causality or abstraction cannot be answered by a single blanket response; the issue must rather be analysed separately for each mode of transfer (delivery, sale and deed).

The preferable view is that transfers by sale, today governed by the SGA 1979, follow the principle of abstraction.[88] The available case law in this area, which has not explicitly considered the issue but which may still provide an implicit answer by their respective outcomes, seems to be somewhat inconsistent at first sight: On the one hand, there are cases where the relevant contract was void but where property was still held to have passed. Those cases may best be explained

---

83 This is the position in Austria, the Netherlands and Switzerland; see fn 48.

84 This is the position in Germany; see fn 47.

85 See the references in fn 69.

86 VAN VLIET, Transfer of movables, 104–14; VAN VLIET, EdinLR 2008.

87 BRIDGE et al, Personal Property, 8.38–46 (esp fn 130), 10.28; L. SMITH, Unjust Enrichment, 43–44; DROBNIG, Transfer of Property, 1014–19; MATTEI, Property law, 106; cf also *Fawcett v Star Car Sales* [1960] NZLR 406, 423–24 (Gresson P) (but cf the majority judgment of North and Cleary JJ); BEATSON et al, Anson's Law of Contract, 24, 27–28.

88 Perhaps in favour of abstraction: BRIDGE, Property Law, 154, stating – in the context of transfers by sale – that "[...] the validity of the conveyance is not inexorably tied to the validity of the contract"; cf also (though not explicitly regarding transfers by sale): WATTS, RLR 1995, 53; MCCORMACK, JBL 1997, 57–58.

by the principle of abstraction. On the other hand, there are cases where the contract was void and where it was held that property had not passed. Though those cases could be explained by a principle of causality, they may equally well be explained under a doctrine of abstraction, namely on the basis of *dual defects* operating on the contractual *and* the proprietary level.

2.3.1. Cases where the Relevant Contract was Void and where Property had Not Passed: The Doctrine of Dual Defects

There are various cases, particularly in the context of identity mistakes, where the underlying contract of sale was found to be void and where it was held that legal ownership had not passed to the buyer.[89] It has been assumed that those cases "form an unequivocal proof that the transfer system of the Sale of Goods Act is causal and certainly not abstract".[90] With respect, this is to read far too much into those cases. It is correct that the judges have apparently somewhat automatically and naturally inferred that property had not passed *because* they had found that the underlying contract was void. This is perhaps most obvious in Lord Cairns' dictum in *Cundy v Lindsay* where a defrauded seller had sent handkerchiefs to a fraudster whom he had never met in person and about whose identity he had been fundamentally mistaken. The House of Lords unanimously held that the contract was void.[91] Regarding the transfer of property, Lord Cairns said this:

> "[I]f the property in the goods in question passed, it could only pass by way of contract; there is nothing else which could have passed the property. […] [His Lordship then concluded that the contract was void and continued:] [T]hat being so [i.e. the contract being void], it is idle to talk of the property passing. The property remained, as it originally had been, the property of the [seller]."[92]

---

89 See esp *Cundy v Lindsay* [1878] LR 3 App Cas 459 and *Ingram v Little* [1961] 1 QB 31 (CA) where it was held that the contract of sale was void by reason of an identity mistake and that property had not passed. In *Lewis v Averay (No 1)* [1972] 1 QB 198 (CA), a contract of sale was found to be merely voidable but Lord Denning MR stated obiter (205–6) that property would not have passed had the contract been void. In *Hardman v Booth* [1863] All ER Rep Ext 1847, the seller intended to transfer goods to a firm but handed them over to an "agent" acting without authority; in relation to the firm, there was no contract due to lack of authority; in relation to the agent, there was no contract because the seller had not intended to contract with him; it was held that property had not passed. *Shogun Finance Ltd v Hudson* [2003] UKHL 62, [2004] 1 AC 919, finally resolved the question whether *contracts* are void or voidable for identity mistakes but did not (directly) deal with the question of property passing in such cases; see further Chapter 4 section 2.2.

90 van Vliet, Transfer of movables, 111–12; van Vliet, EdinLR 2008, 178–79.

91 This ratio was affd in *Shogun Finance v Hudson* [2003] UKHL 62; see further Chapter 4 section 2.2.1.

92 *Cundy v Lindsay* [1878] LR 3 App Cas 459, 464–66 (Lord Cairns); their other Lordships did not, at least not as clearly as Lord Cairns, tie the ineffectiveness of the proprietary transfer

The first part of his Lordship's statement that "there is nothing else which *could* have passed the property" is not entirely accurate, at least from today's perspective. Certainly, there was "nothing in this case" which could have *successfully* passed the property to the fraudster since the seller's real intention to transfer ownership was completely absent by reason of his proprietarily fundamental identity mistake.[93] But still, property *could potentially* have passed *by delivery* which is an abstract mode of transfer and which might arguably operate *cumulatively*, even in void sale transactions.[94] Whatever the position regarding the mode of transfer by sale, delivery could – had the seller's real intention been effective – have operated to transfer property abstractly.

The second part of his Lordship's dictum that it was, by reason of the contract's voidness, "idle to talk of the property passing" and that the seller's retention of legal ownership was somehow an automatic product of the contract's voidness, is flawed in two respects. First, this is certainly no answer to the argument that property could at least have passed upon and by delivery. Delivery is abstract. The true reason why property did not, in fact, pass to the fraudster by delivery has not lain in the *contract's* but rather in the *real agreement's* voidness. The seller had not formed a sufficient real intention to transfer ownership to the fraudster. Second, his Lordship's utterly brief reasoning is – with regard to the question whether property was transferred *by sale* – clearly the result of a failure to distinguish between contract and conveyance. The few words "idle to talk of the property passing" are not the product of a proper consideration whether the law of sales of goods should follow the principle of causality or abstraction. His Lordship was simply unaware of the fact that the contract was different from the conveyance or that this question could have arisen at all.

to the contract's invalidity; Lord Hatherley (468): "But no contract was made with [the fraudster], nor any contract was made with [the seller], because [the seller] knew nothing at all about it, and therefore there could be no delivery of the goods with the intent to pass the property"; Lord Penzance (470–71): "I am not aware, my Lords, that there is any decided case in which a sale and delivery intended to be made to one man, has been held to be a sale and delivery so as to pass the property to another, against the intent and will of the vendor." In other cases, the failure of the proprietary transfer was neither as clearly tied to the contract's voidness: *Ingram v Little* [1961] 1 QB 31, 56 (Pearce LJ): "[If there was an identity mistake], there was no contract and the property did not pass"; 63 (Devlin LJ): "If, however, mistake as to identity prevented the contract being made at all, the property in the car did not pass"; *Lewis v Averay (No 1)* [1972] 1 QB 198, 205–6 (Lord Denning MR): "[I]f there was no contract of sale [...], then no property would pass from [the seller] to the [buyer]"; *Hardman v Booth* [1863] All ER Rep Ext 1847, 1850 (Wilde B): "The result is, there was no contract. The property in the goods still remained in the [seller]". Equally merely assuming that it is simply a logical and natural consequence of a contract's voidness that property does not pass: Whittaker, Chitty on Contracts, vol 1, 1.115 (but cf 1.116); Beale, Chitty on Contracts, vol 1, 3.9, 3.36; Bridge et al, Benjamin's Sale of Goods, 7.23; Cartwright, Misrepresentation, 14.10–11.

93 See further Chapter 4 section 2.2.2.

94 See esp Swadling, LQR 2005, 126–27, 139–42; Häcker, Impaired Consent, 136–38, 191–202; Häcker, Causality and abstraction, 211–12; cf also Fox, Property Rights, 4.6–8.

It must be emphasised that the theory of abstraction in the law of sales does in no way suggest that *Cundy v Lindsay* and other cases[95] have been wrongly decided. Quite to the contrary, their *outcomes* were clearly correct. It is only suggested that their *reasonings* why property did not pass – as far as there was a proper reasoning at all – should have been different. In fact, the results of those cases are perfectly explainable even if transfers by sale are regarded as abstract. Abstraction does in no way infer that a transfer of property must always be effective if an underlying contract is void;[96] that would be quite absurd. Quite to the contrary, a proprietary transfer may well be infected by the very same defect which has also rendered a corresponding contract void (*dual defect*);[97] fundamental mistake as to the transferee's identity is such an example.[98] But there may be defects which *only* infect the contract but which leave unaffected the parties' intention to transfer and receive ownership (real agreement). In such cases, the principle of abstraction dictates that ownership will pass.

2.3.2. *Cases where the Contract was Void but where Property did Pass: Abstraction as the Best Explanation*

It has been pointed out that *Cundy v Lindsay* and other cases *may* be interpreted in terms of abstraction and that they do not positively prove that transfers by sale are governed by a principle of causality. But those cases are neither, of course, positive proof in favour of abstraction. However, there is another group of cases, mainly in the context of incapacity and illegality, where the underlying contract of sale was held to be void but where property was still held to have passed.

In *Stocks v Wilson*,[99] a seller sold and delivered furniture to an infant under a contract of sale which was "absolutely void" (and not merely voidable or unenforceable) under s 1 of the old Infants Relief Act 1874 (as then in force[100]). Lush J held that legal ownership in the goods had nonetheless passed to the infant.[101] In the headnote of the case, it is noted that:

> "[N]otwithstanding the Infants Relief Act, 1874, the delivery of the goods to the [infant buyer] with intent to pass the property therein operated to vest the property in him, and [...] [the buyer] was not liable for conversion of the goods."[102]

---

95 The only case which was, in fact, wrongly decided is *Ingram v Little* [1961] 1 QB 31; this case was overruled in *Shogun Finance v Hudson* [2003] UKHL 62; see Chapter 4 section 2.2.1.

96 See esp Fox, Property Rights, 3.58–67, 3.99–109, ch 4; cf also McCormack, JBL 1997, 57–58.

97 Cf Chapter 2 section 1.4.

98 See Chapter 4 section 2.2.

99 *Stocks v Wilson* [1913] 2 KB 235 (KBD), see esp 246–47 (Lush J).

100 Repealed by the Minors' Contracts Act 1987.

101 See also *Pearce v Brain* [1929] 2 KB 310 (KBD); *Trades Hall Co v Erie Tobacco Co* [1916] 29 DLR 779 (CA of Manitoba), [22] (Perdue JA), [61], [65] (Cameron JA) (concerning a contract of sale which was *ultra vires* the buyer and therefore void; property was apparently still held to have passed).

102 *Stocks v Wilson* [1913] 2 KB 235 (headnote).

In the well-known case of *Singh v Ali*,[103] a seller sold a lorry to a buyer in a transaction which was (arguably[104]) void for illegality because the haulage permit, as then required under Malayan legislation, had been obtained by fraud on the licensing authorities. The seller delivered the lorry to the buyer and later retook it without the latter's consent. The buyer sued in detinue. Lord Denning held that property in the lorry had passed to the buyer notwithstanding the fact that the contract had been illegal and (arguably) void and granted a remedy in detinue for the return of the lorry or its value:[105]

> "Although the transaction between the plaintiff and the defendant was illegal, nevertheless it was fully executed and carried out: and on that account it was effective to pass the property in the lorry to the plaintiff. [...] Despite the illegality of the contract, the property had passed to him by the sale and delivery of the lorry."[106]

If property had indeed passed *by sale* and if the contract had indeed been *void* in those cases, they would unequivocally prove that transfers by sale are abstract. However, the position is not that straightforward. It has been contended, mainly by Swadling and Häcker, that property had actually passed *by delivery*

---

103 *Singh v Ali* [1960] AC 167 (PC); see similarly *Elder v Kelly* [1919] 2 KB 179 (KBD) (sale of milk on a Sunday which was illegal and void under the relevant statute; held that property had passed); *Watts v Seymour* [1967] 2 QB 647 (Div Ct), 653–54 (Winn LJ) (sale of a firearm to a youth without certificate which was illegal and void under the relevant statute; held that property had passed); *Belvoir Finance Co Ltd v Stapleton* [1971] 1 QB 210 (CA) (sale of cars to a finance company in breach of the hire purchase and credit sale legislation; held that property had still passed); *Kingsley v Sterling Industrial Securities Ltd* [1967] 2 QB 747 (CA) (sale of a car in alleged breach of hire purchase and credit sale legislation; held that there was no breach and no illegality but (obiter) that if the contract had been illegal, property would still have passed (782–83, Winn LJ); Harman LJ dissented and held that the contract was illegal but that property had still passed (777)). The principle that legal title may pass under an illegal contract of sale was affd in *Tinsley v Milligan* [1994] 1 AC 340 (HL), 366 (Lord Jauncey), 369–70, 375–76 (Lord Browne-Wilkinson, Lord Lowry agreeing); see also *Bowmakers Ltd v Barnet Instruments Ltd* [1945] KB 65 (CA); *Patel v Mirza* [2016] UKSC 42, [110] (Lord Toulson).

104 But cf text to fn 120 and 121.

105 Until recently, it has been settled law that illegality was not a barrier to claims and remedies which need not rely on the illegal contract *itself* but rather on some other rights (particularly ownership or possession), whether pre-existing or obtained under the executed illegal transaction; see *Bowmakers v Barnet Instruments* [1945] KB 65; *Singh v Kulubya* [1964] AC 142 (PC); *Singh v Ali* [1960] AC 167; *Belvoir v Stapleton* [1971] 1 QB 210; *Tinsley v Milligan* [1994] 1 AC 340, 366 (Lord Jauncey), 369–70 (Lord Browne-Wilkinson); Coote, MLR 1972; Treitel, Contract, 11.142–43, 11.151; Goode, Commercial Law, 3.161–64; critically Hamson, CLJ 1949 (but cf Hamson, CLJ 1964); Enonchong, LQR 1995. This "reliance-rule", however, has now been replaced by a more flexible (but still not, at least not entirely, discretionary) "range of factors approach"; *Patel v Mirza* [2016] UKSC 42, esp [82]–[121] (Lord Toulson).

106 *Singh v Ali* [1960] AC 167, 176–77 (Lord Denning).

in those cases.[107] It is their argument that the mode of transfer by sale is, in fact, a causal one, that property could not therefore have passed *by sale* in those cases but that – because the transfer by delivery has not been ousted by the SGA 1979 and because that mode of transfer is *cumulatively* available – property was still transferred by the abstract mode of transfer *delivery*. This argument entails the conclusion that property can impossibly pass prior to and without delivery if the underlying contract of sale is void.

The passages from *Stocks v Wilson* and *Singh v Ali* cited above could indeed be read with such a view; they both mentioned the fact that delivery had been made. However, even though Swadling's and Häcker's delivery-argument might explain the outcomes of those two cases, and of any other case where delivery had in fact been made, it might still not prove the contrary; it merely reinstates – to that extent – the *possibility* that transfers by sale *could* be causal.

The delivery-argument suggests that property would not have passed in *Stocks v Wilson* and *Singh v Ali* had delivery not been made. In the former case, this would have meant that the infant would not have acquired property in the furniture had the furniture still remained in the seller's possession. Suppose that the infant had already paid the price and that the seller had, prior to delivery, become insolvent or that he had profitably sold the furniture. It would have been a remarkably unjust result if the infant had, in such a case, been limited to a personal unjust enrichment claim for the price paid (failure of consideration). Rather, the infant should even then have been entitled to assume proprietary rights and to claim the profits by tracing.

Apart from that, the delivery-argument is inconsistent with at least three illegality cases. The first is *Kingsley v Sterling Industrial Securities*.[108] The claimant, in view of a refinancing scheme, sold a car to Saxon Finance and the latter sold it to the defendant finance company who let it back to the claimant under a hire-purchase agreement. Neither Saxon nor the defendant had ever got into possession of the car; Saxon had merely checked it but had always left it with the claimant. The car had thus never been delivered to either of the two buyers. The claimant failed to pay the monthly rentals and the defendant took possession of the car; the former claimed to be its owner and sued in conversion. In his dissenting judgment, Harman LJ held that the transaction, including the sale contracts between the claimant and Saxon and between Saxon and the defendant, had been in breach of the relevant hire purchase and credit sale legislation and that the contracts were therefore void for illegality. However, he still held, apparently applying *Singh v Ali*, that property in the car had passed first to Saxon

---

107 See esp Swadling, LQR 2005, 126–27, 139–42, 152; Swadling, RLR 1994, 81–82; Häcker, Impaired Consent, 136–38, 191–202; Häcker, Causality and abstraction, 211–12; cf also Fox, Property Rights, 4.6–8; cf already Diamond, MLR 1960, 453.

108 *Kingsley v Sterling Industrial Securities* [1967] 2 QB 747.

and then to the defendant.[109] The majority held that the transaction had not violated the relevant legislation and that the sale contracts had therefore been valid. But Winn LJ held obiter, in very clear terms, that, had the contract been illegal, property would still have passed and that nothing would have turned on the question whether delivery had been made:

> "[I]t does not seem to me to follow, from a finding that any particular contract of sale by which the parties intended – as they clearly did in the present case on the findings of the judge – to pass property in the article sold by force of the contract itself was illegal, that the property in the article did not pass from vendor to purchaser. In the course of the argument I myself referred to the opinion of the Privy Council in *Singh v Ali* and I am bound to say that I do not think that that case was satisfactorily distinguished from the present case [...]. The Privy Council held that notwithstanding that the contract for the sale of the lorry was unlawful, yet when in pursuance of the contract the lorry was sold and delivered to the plaintiff the property in it passed to him and he was entitled to sue the defendant in detinue. *I have not, of course, overlooked the fact that in the present case there was no real delivery of the car by the plaintiff to either Saxon Finance or the defendants, but in my opinion it is clear that the parties intended property to pass without delivery, and it is clear from the Sale of Goods Act that delivery is not an essential condition of the passing of property unless the parties intend that it should be such a condition.*"[110]

These are clear words. Winn LJ thought that property would – even prior to or without delivery – still have passed by sale under the SGA 1979. Equally clear is the case of *Belvoir v Stapleton*.[111] A car dealer sold cars to Belvoir (a finance company) who let them out to Belgravia who, in breach of the hire-purchase agreement, sold them to third parties. The contract of sale between the car dealers and Belvoir, as well as the hire-purchase agreement between Belvoir and Belgravia, was "void and unenforceable"[112] for illegality due to a breach of the relevant hire purchase legislation. The car dealer had never delivered the cars to Belvoir (the latter had never obtained possession) but directly to Belgravia. Belvoir sued Belgravia's salesman personally in conversion; this depended on Belvoir's legal title in the cars. Notwithstanding the fact that the sale contract between the car dealers and Belvoir had been void and even though delivery had never been made,[113] the Court of Appeal unanimously held that property

[109] Ibid, 777 (Harman LJ).
[110] Ibid, 782–83 (Winn LJ) (emphasis added).
[111] *Belvoir v Stapleton* [1971] 1 QB 210.
[112] These were the words of Sachs LJ (218).
[113] But cf Fox, Property Rights, 4.8, arguing that the case should be explained in terms of some sort of a *constructive delivery* (on the basis that Belvoir had instructed the car dealers to deliver the goods directly to Belgravia). This is difficult to accept. Belvoir had never had *any* form of possession, neither actual nor constructive; Belgravia had never intended to possess as a bailee for Belvoir. But quite apart from that, Lord Denning MR and Sachs LJ have clearly rejected the counsel for defendant's delivery-argument; they made utterly clear that delivery, including constructive delivery, was irrelevant.

in the car had passed to Belvoir. Lord Denning MR referred to and applied his own judgment in *Singh v Ali* and explicitly rejected the counsel for defendant's argument that the case should have been distinguished on the basis that delivery had not been made:

> "[Counsel for defendant] laid great stress on the fact that here [Belvoir] had never taken delivery of the car. It had gone straight from the dealers to Belgravia. [...] So [Belvoir] had to rely on the agreement of sale to them in order to give them title or a right to possession. But the agreement was illegal and the courts would not allow them to rely on it. [...] I do not accept this distinction taken by [counsel for defendant]. *I think that the proposition stated in [Singh v Ali] applies even where the transferee has not taken possession of the property, so long as the title to it has passed.* [...] Although [Belvoir] obtained the car under a contract which was illegal, nevertheless inasmuch as the contract was executed[114] and the property passed, the car belonged to [Belvoir] and they can claim it. This was the view of Winn LJ in [*Kingsley v Sterling Industrial Securities*] and I agree with it."[115]

Sachs LJ's judgment is to the same effect:

> "It is quite clear that the title to the cars passed as soon as the agreement between [Belvoir] and the dealers was executed[116] and that the passing of this property was not affected by the illegality of that contract nor that of the hire-purchase agreement. *It is not in point that the cars were not at any stage physically in the possession of [Belvoir]*; in that behalf I respectfully agree with what was said by Winn LJ in [*Kingsley v Sterling Industrial Securities*]. Any other view would produce highly artificial distinctions."[117]

The third case is *Watts v Seymour*.[118] A firearm dealer illegally sold a gun to a youth without permission but remained in control and in possession of the firearm throughout; the seller had only promised to (and apparently did) bring the gun to the rifle club, to which they had both belonged, whenever the youth demanded so. It appears that the seller had never delivered the firearm to the youth; though he allowed him to use it at the club in his presence, he remained in control throughout. Notwithstanding this fact, Winn LJ held that property in the gun had still passed to the youth.

Those three cases establish that legal title in goods may, in illegal sale transactions, pass prior to and without delivery.[119] It follows that – contrary

114 "Executed" here arguably only refers to the fact that counter-performance had been made (i.e. payment by Belvoir to the car dealers); see further Chapter 2 section 3.2.2.2.
115 *Belvoir v Stapleton* [1971] 1 QB 210, 217–18 (Lord Denning MR) (emphasis added).
116 Cf fn 114.
117 Ibid, 220 (Sachs LJ) (emphasis added).
118 *Watts v Seymour* [1967] 2 QB 647.
119 See also Goode, Commercial Law, 3.161 (fn 549); Bridge et al, Benjamin's Sale of Goods, 3.30; van Vliet, EdinLR 2008, 284 (fn 46).

to Swadling's and Häcker's delivery-argument – the transfer of property is not (necessarily) effected by delivery but by sale and by mere intention in such cases. Unfortunately, however, these cases may still not form an unequivocal positive proof that transfers by sale are conceptually abstract, rather than causal, since there is an argument that illegal contracts are not actually "void" but merely "unenforceable".[120] If this is correct, the illegality-cases could alternatively be explained on the basis that unenforceable illegal contracts are not wholly inexistent but that they can, once executed, still provide a valid contractual obligation based on which a causal transfer by sale might operate. There may be force in the argument that illegal contracts are merely unenforceable rather than void.[121] However, without expressing a final view on this question, it is clear that this argument would, if correct, only reinstate the possibility that transfers by sale *could* still be causal; but it would not, of course, positively prove it. Apart from that, there are at least three arguments against such an unenforceability-explanation of the mentioned illegal sale cases.

First, an unenforceability-explanation could not operate in cases where a statute – such as s 1 of the old Infants Relief Act 1874 or one which uses even clearer words – explicitly and unambiguously renders a contract or obligation "absolutely void and not merely unenforceable". It would be very unlikely that a court would distinguish such a case from the *Singh v Ali*[122] and *Belvoir v Stapleton*[123] line of authority.

Second, the unenforceability-argument may not explain *Stocks v Wilson*[124] where the statute in question had in fact declared that the relevant contract of sale was "absolutely void".[125] It is true that, on the facts of the case, delivery had been made. However, it seems unlikely that the result would have been

---

120 See (e.g.) van Vliet, Transfer of movables, 113–14; van Vliet, EdinLR 2008, 184; Goode, Commercial Law, 3.153–65; Bridge et al, Benjamin's Sale of Goods, 3.27–30; Prentice, Chitty on Contracts, vol 1, 16.33, 16.218; Coote, MLR 1972, 40–41; cf also Diamond, MLR 1960, 452. According to an alternative view, property does not in fact pass in such cases but recovery of possession by the owner is prevented by the principle *"in pari delicto potior est conditio defendentis"*; Higgins, MLR 1962; but cf Häcker, Impaired Consent, 195.

121 That illegal contracts are merely unenforceable rather than absolutely void was perhaps also the majority's view in *Tinsley v Milligan* [1994] 1 AC 340, 366 (Lord Jauncey), 369–70, 375–76 (Lord Browne-Wilkinson, Lord Lowry agreeing); cf also *Patel v Mirza* [2016] UKSC 42, [248] (Lord Sumption; in dissent, though on other points).

122 *Singh v Ali* [1960] AC 167.

123 *Belvoir v Stapleton* [1971] 1 QB 210.

124 *Stocks v Wilson* [1913] 2 KB 235.

125 It would be difficult to see how such a contract could still be considered as being merely unenforceable or voidable rather than void; see *Nottingham Permanent Benefit Building Society v Thurstan* [1903] AC 6 (HL), 10 (Earl of Halsbury LC): "[I]t is hopeless, as it appears to me, to try to get rid of the express language of the statute [s 1 of the Infants Relief Act 1874], which renders [the contract and the security] absolutely and entirely void"; Treitel, LQR 1957, 200–5; but cf the reply of Atiyah, LQR 1958, 99–101 (arguing that such contracts were merely "void as against the infant"); but cf the counter-reply of Treitel, LQR 1958, 104–6.

different had the seller remained in possession throughout. It has already been pointed out that, supposing that the infant had paid the price and that the seller had become insolvent or had profitably invested the furniture, it would have been unacceptably unfair – at least if the infant had not acted fraudulently – if the infant had been limited to a personal unjust enrichment claim for the price paid. Property must still have passed by the seller's mere intention in such a case.

Third, the unenforceability-explanation would, if combined with the principle of causality, encounter serious conceptual difficulties in explaining the passage of property in illegal sale cases prior to delivery. An *executed* illegal obligation might – if indeed unenforceable rather than void – justify an enrichment transferred under it[126] and it could be argued that, once delivery (execution) has been made, the seller's unenforceable obligation to transfer property becomes fully effective and might, if one follows the principle of causality, explain the transfer of property. However, it would be very difficult to see how an *unexecuted* unenforceable obligation – i.e. the seller's obligation to transfer property *prior to delivery* – could *alone and by itself effect* the transfer of property. This would – under the regime of the old "reliance rule" as in force until recently[127] – certainly have been more than a merely indirect enforcement of the illegal obligation. If the principle of causality were to apply, the buyer would have had to rely on the illegal contract in order to establish the passage of property prior to delivery.[128] In that regard, the new and more flexible "range of factors approach", as set down in *Patel v Mirza*,[129] has not changed anything. A combination of the unenforceability-explanation and the principle of causality would still lead to the remarkable result that – if property may still pass prior to delivery in illegal transactions – the actually *unenforceable* (or even void) executory obligation would in substance *execute and enforce itself.*

By contrast, the principle of abstraction would largely dispose of those conceptual problems. If the transfer of property is independent (abstract) from the illegal contract, the buyer does not need to rely on it to establish his title.[130] He would solely need to rely on the seller's intention to transfer ownership and

---

126 See Chapter 1 section 2.1.1.1. and Chapter 1 section 2.1.3.

127 *Tinsley v Milligan* [1994] 1 AC 340, 369–70 (Lord Browne-Wilkinson), 366 (Lord Jauncey); *Bowmakers v Barnet Instruments* [1945] KB 65, 71 (du Parcq LJ).

128 See also Treitel, Contract, 11.151; Prentice, Chitty on Contracts, vol 1, 16.218, who sought to reduce the *Belvoir*-ratio to claims between the buyer and *third parties*, asserting that a buyer could not, under an illegal contract and prior to delivery, enforce property rights against the seller himself.

129 *Patel v Mirza* [2016] UKSC 42, esp [82]–[121] (Lord Toulson).

130 However, the buyer must, if prior to delivery, still in a sense rely on the illegal agreement to show that his payment counted as *consideration* (exempting from the delivery requirement); see Chapter 2 section 3.2.2.2.

his own intention to receive it, both of which are not generally – as such – tainted with illegality.

Some authority in favour of the theory of abstraction in the law of sales may be derived from an obiter dictum of Lord Upjohn in *Branwhite v Worcester Works Finance Ltd*.[131] The claimant went to a car dealer, intending to buy a car on hire-purchase terms. He signed the finance company's blank form, paid a deposit (by transferring his old car to the dealer) and immediately took the new car away. The fraudulent dealer then filled in a purchase price and instalment rates higher than agreed and submitted the form to the finance company who purported to accept it; yet, the contract between the finance company and the claimant was void for lack of consent. The latter refused to pay the instalments and the finance company retook possession of the car. The House of Lords was mainly concerned with the question whether the claimant was entitled to claim the value of the deposit paid to the dealer by a personal unjust enrichment claim against the finance company; we are not here concerned with that issue. Interestingly, however, it was assumed without more that the finance company, who had purchased the car from the dealer (for the forged price), had obtained legal ownership in it which entitled it to retake possession. Since the dealer had made a fraudulent misrepresentation that the price stated in the form was the price agreed with the claimant, the contract of sale between the dealer and the finance company was at least *voidable*. Yet, it was argued that the contract had even been *void* because it had been conditional upon the conclusion of a valid hire-purchase agreement with the claimant. Notwithstanding that argument, Lord Upjohn (Lord Guest agreeing) suggested that it was *unnecessary* to decide whether the contract had been void or merely voidable and, accordingly, assumed that the finance company would have acquired legal ownership in the car even if the contract had been void.[132] Delivery had never been made to the finance company; the claimant had immediately taken the car away (even prior to the sale between the dealer and the finance company being concluded). Accordingly, Lord Upjohn's suggestion that property would have passed even if the contract had been void seems to endorse the notion of abstraction in transfers by sale.

It is concluded that the principle of abstraction – though perhaps not being the *only* one possible explanation – *best* explains the difficult case law where property has passed notwithstanding the underlying contract's ineffectiveness. Both the delivery-argument and the unenforceability-explanation have – far from positively proving the contrary – their own shortcomings. By contrast, any of those conceptual difficulties disappear if abstraction is recognised.

---

131 *Branwhite v Worcester Works Finance Ltd* [1969] 1 AC 552 (HL).

132 Ibid, 581 (Lord Upjohn).

2.3.3. *Arguments in Favour of Abstraction Derived from the Law of Rescission*

One might easily be misled to believe that the law of rescission militates in favour of causality.[133] If a contract is voidable, for example on the basis of misrepresentation, property revests in the transferor upon rescission;[134] this might look like a causal mechanism. In fact, however, rescission provides compelling arguments in favour of abstraction. The *contract's* avoidance is *not*, as such, the actual reason why ownership revests in such cases, not even with regard to transfers by sale.[135] The proprietary effects of rescission have nothing to do with rescission of the *contract*.[136]

This becomes evident by the fact that proprietary rescission is – by way of a power in rem to revest (legal or equitable) ownership – arguably available in exactly the same way in voidable *non-contractual* transfers, for example in cases of fraudulently induced gifts or double payments,[137] or in other cases where property is voidably transferred by the *abstract* mode of transfer by delivery, for example in voidable transfers of money.[138] At least in those cases, the actual reason

---

133 See van Vliet, EdinLR 2008, 179–84; Bridge et al, Personal Property, 10.28. Similarly, one could be led to believe that certain mechanisms in the law of *termination de futuro* equally militate in favour of causality. On the one hand, a buyer's rejection of the goods as non-conforming revests legal ownership in the seller (cf *Kwei Tek Chao v British Traders & Shippers Ltd* [1954] 2 QB 459 (QBD), 487–88 (Devlin J)); this might look like being based on the principle of causality (the contract's avoidance *ex nunc* leading to a retransfer of property *ex nunc*). The better view, however, is that such a revesting is, in fact, based on an explicit or implied (resolutive) condition imposed by the parties on their real agreement that the buyer will accept the goods (cf similarly Goode, Commercial Law, 8.19–22). On the other hand, the Court of Appeal in *RV Ward Ltd v Bignall* [1967] 1 QB 534, esp 550–51 (Diplock LJ), has rationalised the unpaid seller's right to resell the goods (s 48 of the SGA 1979) on the basis that legal title first revests in him upon termination of the contract. van Vliet, EdinLR 2008, 184–87, has used this as an argument in favour of causality. In our view, however, the revesting of legal title must equally be based on an implied resolutive condition in the parties' real agreement that property shall revest in the circumstances envisaged by ss 38–48 of the SGA 1979; see convincingly Bridge, Sale of Goods, 11.51–58.

134 See (e.g.) *Car & Universal Finance Co Ltd v Caldwell* [1965] 1 QB 525 (CA); *Newtons of Wembley Ltd v Williams* [1965] 1 QB 560 (CA) (both at common law); *El Ajou v Dollar Land Holdings plc (No 1)* [1993] BCC 698 (ChD), 713 (Millett J) (revd on other grounds in [1994] BCC 143 (CA)); *Bristol and West Building Society v Mothew* [1998] Ch 1 (CA), 22–23 (Millett LJ); *Twinsectra Ltd v Yardley* [1999] Lloyd's Rep Bank 438 (CA), [96]–[100] (Potter LJ) (revd on other grounds in [2002] UKHL 12, [2002] 2 AC 164) (all in equity).

135 Contra (e.g.) Häcker, Causality and abstraction, 209–10; Häcker, Reply, 106; Häcker, Impaired Consent, 200; Fox, Property Rights, 6.18; L. Smith, Unjust Enrichment, 44; van Vliet, EdinLR 2008, 177–78; cf also Swadling, LQR 2005.

136 See now in detail Zogg, Proprietary Consequences, Chapter 4.

137 See (e.g.) *Allcard v Skinner* [1887] 36 ChD 145 (CA), 181, 184–87 (Lindley LJ); *Pesticcio v Huet* [2003] EWHC 2293 (Ch), [133]–[134] (Neuberger J) (affd in [2004] EWCA Civ 372); *Re Glubb* [1900] 1 Ch 354 (CA); Zogg, Proprietary Consequences, Chapter 4 section 3; Häcker, Impaired Consent, 142–53; Häcker, CLJ 2009.

138 See (e.g.) *Banque Belge pour l'Etranger v Hambrouck* [1921] 1 KB 321 (CA); *Moynes v Coopper* [1956] 1 QB 439 (QBD), 445 (Lord Goddard CJ); Zogg, Proprietary Consequences, Chapter 4 section 2.2.4; Fox, Property Rights, ch 6.

for the fall back of ownership can obviously not lie in the avoidance of a contract. The preferable view is that it is simply the law of property which imposes a new power in rem to revest legal or equitable ownership in such cases. This power in rem is imposed if and because the real intention of the transferor to transfer ownership is sufficiently vitiated but not wholly absent.[139] This applies in any voidable transfer of property, whether effected *by sale* or *by delivery*. Crucially, the power in rem is imposed *irrespective* of the existence of a (voidable) contract; if a voidable contract does exist, the law of contract grants an *additional* but *notionally distinct* personal power to rescind the contract. This analysis allows a broad rationalisation of the difficult law of rescission putting this branch of the law on a more coherent and principled basis. By contrast, if it were – as dictated by the principle of causality – indeed the avoidance of the contract *as such* which effects the revesting of ownership in voidable transfers by sale (at least if prior to delivery), the law of rescission would become very obscure and would basically operate on two entirely different regimes, depending on whether the transfer has been effected causally by sale (then the *contract's* rescission would, *as such*, suffice to revest property) or abstractly by delivery (then the law of property would still have to impose a *power in rem* to revest ownership).

The principle of causality in transfers by sale and the consequent operation of two entirely different mechanisms of proprietary rescission would apparently lead to very unequal and unacceptable results with regard to the question of whether proprietary rescission is one- or two-sided. If a defrauded *seller* rescinds a contract of sale, he might revest ownership in the goods which he had transferred to the buyer but it is arguable that this does not, and should not, equally lead to a revesting of ownership in the money which the fraudulent buyer has transferred to the seller. Proprietary rescission is, and should be, only *one-sided*.[140] The buyer's transfer of money by delivery is abstract and the law of property does not confer on him a proprietary power to revest ownership by reason of his own fraud. If a defrauded *buyer* rescinds a contract of sale, he might equally revest ownership in the money which he has abstractly transferred to the seller, namely by exercising a power in rem granted by the law of property. However, the buyer's collateral rescission of the contract would, if the premise of causality in the transfer by sale were correct, also and inevitably result in an automatic revesting of legal title in the goods to the fraudulent seller. Proprietary rescission would, accordingly, be *two-sided* if the transaction is rescinded by

---

139 See now in detail Zogg, Proprietary Consequences, Chapter 4.

140 Zogg, Proprietary Consequences, Chapter 4 section 2.2.3.1(c); Häcker, Causality and abstraction, 208–212; Häcker, Impaired Consent, 201; Häcker, LQR 2012, 495, 497; cf also *Independent Trustee Services Ltd v GP Noble Trustees Ltd* [2010] EWHC 3275 (Ch), [50]–[55] (Smith J), [2012] EWCA Civ 195, [2012] 3 WLR 597, [43]–[44], [52]–[57] (Patten LJ); contra: Worthington, RLR 2002, 30 (fn 17), 36–37, 48–49; Burrows, Restitution, 19 (fn 98); Goode, Commercial Law, 14.2. The guilty party's rights are arguably limited to personal counter-restitution coupled with the defence or condition of *restitutio in integrum*.

the *buyer* but only *one-sided* if it is rescinded by the *seller*. There would be no principled reason which could justify such an unequal treatment.[141] Proprietary rescission must be the same in both cases, either one- or two-sided, but it would be completely arbitrary if fraudulent sellers were better protected than fraudulent buyers.

Häcker sought to overcome that problem by what she called a "theory of double effect".[142] According to her, though title revests automatically in the fraudulent seller upon the buyer's rescission of the contract as far as the transfer of legal title *by sale* is concerned, title should be regarded as *passing over a second time* by the abstract transfer by delivery which might then back up the transfer and immunise it against a causal-automatic revesting of property upon the buyer's rescission of the contract. However, this theory would only narrow down the ambit of the problem but it would not solve it. The unequal treatment between fraudulent sellers and fraudulent buyers would then only but still continue to exist as long as delivery has not yet been made.

The injustice caused by a causal-automatic property-revesting-system becomes particularly evident in cases such as *Branwhite v Worcester Works Finance*.[143] Suppose that the contract of sale between the finance company (buyer) and the fraudulent dealer (seller) has been voidable (rather than void) due to the dealer's fraud.[144] The finance company, had it wished to rescind the obligatory contract with the dealer and to claim back the excessive price paid by a personal or a proprietary claim, would – if the principle of causality had indeed applied – inevitably have lost its real security (legal ownership) in the car which had never been delivered to it and which had always been in the customer's possession.

Another argument – perhaps the most compelling one – which may be derived from the law of rescission relates to an issue of fusion. It is quite obvious that rescission of an obligatory contract *in equity*, for example on the basis of innocent misrepresentation or undue influence, must inevitably lead to an avoidance of the contract in equity *and* at law; in so far, the law must be regarded as fused.[145] It would certainly be nonsense to suggest that a contract, which has been avoided in equity, still remains valid at law. However, it is equally

141 The difference must not be downplayed; but cf Häcker, Causality and abstraction, 210. Even though a rescinding party's trustee in bankruptcy must probably make personal *restitutio in integrum* if he claims the revested property rights, the question whether or not the guilty party might assert proprietary rights has many other serious consequences, such as claims to profits based on tracing, claims against third-party recipients or procedural advantages.

142 Häcker, Causality and abstraction, 208–12 (but cf still Häcker, Reply, 109).

143 *Branwhite v Worcester Works Finance* [1969] 1 AC 552.

144 Whether the contract was void or only voidable was left open by their Lordships; see text to fn 132.

145 This is perhaps not technically a case of veritable fusion but rather an instance of a genuine conflict between the common law and equity where equity must prevail; s 49 of the Senior Courts Act 1981; cf *Redgrave v Hurd* [1881] 20 ChD 1 (CA), 12 (Jessel MR) (emphasis in original): "As regards the rescission of a contract, there was no doubt a difference between

well settled that rescission of a transaction in equity may not revest *legal* but only *equitable* ownership.[146] This result could impossibly be explained if the transfer of legal title by sale were indeed governed by a principle of causality. If a contract of sale is rescinded in equity, it is equally avoided at law. Yet, if a contract of sale is entirely avoided (at law and in equity), the principle of causality would actually dictate that *legal* ownership in the goods automatically and inevitably revests in the seller. But this is indubitably not the case. There is no fusion on the proprietary level. If a transaction is rescinded in equity, the contract is entirely eradicated but property only revests in equity. This demonstrates that proprietary rescission is independent from the contractual position and that the transfer of legal title must, whether effected by delivery or by sale, inevitably be abstract. A seller rescinding the transaction in equity does not, thereupon, automatically reacquire legal title in the goods. Rescission of the contract of sale does not, accordingly, *by itself* and without more effect a revesting of property; rather, equity simply imposes an independent new equitable power in rem to revest equitable ownership.

Häcker's theory of double effect could explain why legal title does not revest upon an equitable rescission of the contract as far as delivery has already been made because the supervening abstract transfer by delivery would then have immunised the transfer of legal ownership against a rescission of the contract. However, this theory would still not solve the problem if delivery has not yet been made. If a buyer's innocent misrepresentation has induced a seller to conclude a contract of sale of specific goods, property in which was agreed to pass prior to delivery, the seller's equitable rescission of the contract would, if the principle of causality indeed applied, still automatically revest *legal* title in the goods. But this is not the current state of English law.[147]

Finally, a principle of causality and a view that legal title in goods transferred by sale revests automatically upon rescission of the *contract* would seem to

---

the rules of Courts of Equity and the rules of Courts of Common Law – a difference which of course has now disappeared by the operation of the *Judicature Act*, which makes the rules of equity prevail"; *Newbigging v Adam* [1886] 34 ChD 582 (CA), 592 (Bowen LJ) (affd in [1888] 13 App Cas 308 (HL)): "A contract obtained by fraud, being voidable and not void, remains until it is set aside, and when it is set aside it is treated both at law and in equity as non-existing." See also Zogg, Proprietary Consequences, Chapter 2 section 1.1 and Chapter 4 section 2.2.1.

146 See (e.g.) *El Ajou v Dollar Land Holdings (No 1)* [1993] BCC 698, 713 (Millett J) (revd on other grounds in [1994] BCC 143); *Bristol and West Building Society v Mothew* [1998] Ch 1, 22–23 (Millett LJ); *Twinsectra v Yardley* [1999] Lloyd's Rep Bank 438, [96]–[100] (Potter LJ) (revd on other grounds in [2002] UKHL 12); *Shalson v Russo* [2003] EWHC 1637 (Ch), [2005] Ch 281, [120]–[127] (Rimer J); *Independent Trustee Services v GP Noble Trustees* [2012] EWCA Civ 195, [53] (Patten LJ); *National Crime Agency v Robb* [2014] EWHC 4384 (Ch), [2015] 3 WLR 23, [40]–[51], [80], [83] (Etherton C); Zogg, Proprietary Consequences, Chapter 4 section 2.2.3.1; Häcker, Impaired Consent, 125–53; O'Sullivan et al, Rescission, 15.4–13; Cartwright, Misrepresentation, 4.11; Worthington, RLR 2002, 31–32.

147 See also Häcker, Causality and abstraction, 212.

encounter difficulties in explaining the effects of rescission in relation to third parties. On the one hand, it would at least not be self-evident how a party's (the seller's) *personal* power to rescind the contract of sale could bind third parties – such as innocent volunteers, recipients with notice or the buyer's trustee in bankruptcy – by its supposed effect of automatically revesting legal title. Contractual powers generally operate exclusively *inter partes*. By contrast, an abstractly imposed power *in rem* would have no problems to explain its effects against third parties. On the other hand, it would not be easy to see how rescission could – without recognising an abstractly imposed power *in rem* – trigger the so-called "proprietary connection exception" to establish personal unjust enrichment claims against unprotected third-party recipients.[148] Though it could be argued that property should revest retroactively for unjust enrichment purposes, but only prospectively with regard to wrong-based claims,[149] that would be an unnecessary convoluted and rather artificial analysis. It is preferable to recognise that the law of property imposes – at the inception, independently from the contractual position and whether legal title has been transferred by delivery, by sale or by deed – a power in rem to revest ownership. That power in rem is binding on third parties, can be traced *as such* and can trigger the proprietary connection exception.[150]

2.3.4. History and Coherence

It has already been pointed out that the historical development of the transfer of legal title by sale seems to militate in favour of abstraction.[151] Originally, chattels could only be transferred upon and by delivery. The transfer of legal title by sale, which developed in the 14th or 15th century, is arguably a genuine descendant from the original mode of transfer by delivery. It appears that the former organically emerged from the latter by a gradual emancipation which eventually resulted in a complete exemption from the delivery requirement. Arguably, the sale exception *only* exempted from the delivery requirement but did not, besides that, alter the underlying structure of the original mode of transfer. If this is correct, the requirement of a distinct and separate real agreement (intention to transfer and receive ownership) is still the same and the mode of transfer is still

---

148 For the "at the expense of requirement" and the "proprietary connection exception" in the law of unjust enrichment, see generally Burrows, Restatement, 44–62 (ss 8–9); Burrows, Restitution, 69–76; Birks, Unjust Enrichment, 86–98.

149 See (in the context of tracing) *Lonrho plc v Fayed (No 2)* [1992] 1 WLR 1 (ChD), 11–12 (Millett J); *Bristol and West Building Society v Mothew* [1998] Ch 1, 22–23 (Millett LJ); *London Allied Holdings Ltd v Lee* [2007] EWHC 2061 (Ch), [276] (Etherton J); cf also (with regard to wrong-based claims) *Lipkin Gorman v Karpnale Ltd* [1991] 2 AC 548 (HL), 573 (Lord Goff).

150 Zogg, Proprietary Consequences, Chapter 4 section 2.2.3.

151 See the introductory remarks of Chapter 2.

independent (abstract) from the existence of an underlying contractual or other obligation.

Apart from that, abstraction in the transfer by sale paves the way for a coherent picture of how proprietary transfers of tangible movable chattels are effected in English law. Legal ownership may pass by three modes of transfer – delivery, sale and deed[152] – all of which are governed by the principles of separation and abstraction. Though it would not be impossible to imagine that those modes of transfer are governed by different principles, this would lead to hardly justifiable results. Similar cases would be treated unequally. An obvious example would be the resulting preference of fraudulent sellers over fraudulent buyers if transfers by sale but not transfers by delivery were governed by the principle of causality.[153]

Similarly, abstraction in the transfer of legal title by sale brings the legal position in line with the position in equity. Transfers[154] of equitable ownership are evidently governed by a principle of abstraction. A beneficial legal owner may settle property on trust or declare a trust without any underlying obligation to do so. Furthermore, a resulting trust does certainly not arise in *every* case – but only in *some* cases – where property has been transferred pursuant to a void contract, even in sale transactions. Equitable ownership *may* but *need not* be retained in such cases.[155]

2.3.5. Conclusions

Though there is admittedly no unequivocal proof, it has been argued that the available case law – particularly cases in the context of incapacity and illegality where the underlying contract of sale was void but where property was still held to have passed – may best be explained by the principle of abstraction. Apart from that, there are strong arguments of principle which militate in favour of abstraction. Causality would encounter serious, if not insurmountable,

---

152 It will be argued that transfers of legal title by deed are equally abstract; see Chapter 2 section 4.5.

153 See text to fn 140–144.

154 There is a controversy about the question whether a beneficial legal owner has legal *and* equitable ownership and whether, accordingly, equitable ownership can at all be "transferred" or "retained" (see Zogg, Proprietary Consequences, Chapter 5 sections 3.5 and 3.6; Sweet, LQR 1919; Hackney, Trusts, 148–49, 153–54; Penner, Resulting Trusts, 257–66; Rickett/Grantham, Limited Doctrine, 48–59; Worthington, Commercial Transactions, viii–x, ch 7.2) or whether there is simply no equitable ownership as long as the beneficial estate is not separated from the legal one which would mean that a beneficial legal owner could neither "transfer" nor "retain" equitable ownership (cf *Westdeutsche Landesbank v Islington* [1996] AC 669, 706, 714 (Lord Browne-Wilkinson); Chambers, Resulting Trusts, 51–55, 102–4; Birks, Introduction, 59, 70–72; Birks, NZ L Rev 1997, 629, 643–45; Fox, Property Rights, 3.23–28).

155 Equitable title is arguably only retained if a real defect entirely eradicates the transferor's intention to transfer equitable ownership; see generally Zogg, Proprietary Consequences, Chapter 5 section 3.

obstacles in the law of rescission. On the one hand, it would lead to the unacceptable result that fraudulent sellers would be better protected – receiving proprietary rights as a windfall product of causality if the defrauded buyer rescinds the contract of sale – than fraudulent buyers. On the other hand, causality could not explain the fact why, as is well settled in English law, *legal* title in goods transferred by sale does not automatically revest upon an *equitable* rescission of the contract. By contrast, abstraction does not encounter any of those conceptual difficulties. The imposition of an abstract power in rem may explain why proprietary rescission operates in the same way in contractual and non-contractual transfers (and in other transfers effected by delivery), why proprietary rescission is always only one-sided and why equitable rescission only revests equitable ownership.

It is crucial to note that abstraction does of course not mean that a transfer of legal title (by sale or otherwise) is *always* effective where an underlying contract is void; that would be absurd. There may be *dual defects* which do not only render contracts void but which equally infect the parties' real agreement, particularly the transferor's (seller's) intention to transfer ownership. The principle of abstraction does not dictate the range of defects which are dual or only obligatory. Theoretically, it would even be possible to recognise a principle of abstraction in the absence of any single defect which is only obligatory but not also real; abstraction would then not be visible in practice but still doctrinally explain the transfer's operation. Yet, it appears that there *are*, in fact, defects which only render contracts void but which do not equally affect the passage of property. For example, this is the case with regard to common mistakes, which nullify a contract at law, and mutual mistakes as to the contract price or other consideration, which negative a contractual agreement.[156]

However, there is still one conceptual problem associated with the principle of abstraction in transfers by sale which relates to the *very applicability* of the transfer by sale (without delivery). Even if a transfer of legal title by sale is – theoretically – abstract, the question still arises whether that mode of transfer may at all ever be available if the underlying contract of sale is void or inexistent or whether – similarly as in gift cases – a transfer by delivery would inevitably be required. To this question we shall turn in the next section.

3. SCOPE OF THE TRANSFER BY SALE AND THE TRANSFER BY DELIVERY

The exact ambit of the strict delivery requirement and the respective scope of a transfer by sale (i.e. by mere intention) is uncertain in several respects. What is

[156] See Chapter 4 section 2.1.2. and Chapter 4 section 2.5.

apparently uncontroversial is that *corporeal money* (domestic or foreign currency) may – whether for consideration or gratuitously – only ever be transferred *by delivery*. This does not merely reflect the general rule that the transferred chattels must be strictly identified, as explicitly laid down for goods in s 16 of the SGA 1979. It rather seems that legal title in corporeal money can still only pass upon and by delivery even if the payer has (exceptionally) already identified and set aside specific coins and notes at the time of conclusion of the contract or if he later unconditionally appropriates them prior to delivery.[157]

In relation to *goods*, delivery is indubitably required to transfer property by way of gift (otherwise than by deed) and in transfers without any basis whatsoever, for example in cases of mistaken double deliveries of goods. In other words, delivery is strictly required to effect a transfer of legal title in goods for no consideration.[158] Conversely, it clearly follows from the SGA 1979 that goods may be transferred by mere intention at least if the transaction in question is a proper sale, i.e. a transfer of goods for money consideration; this must at least include valid and voidable contracts of sale. There are, however, two difficult issues in that regard: (i) May legal title in goods pass by mere intention and without delivery in (valid or voidable) exchange transactions for non-money consideration, such as barters? (ii) May legal title in goods ever pass by mere intention and without delivery in transfers carried out under void contracts of sale (or under other void exchange transactions) or is delivery – due to a possible lack of consideration – inevitably required in those cases? To those issues we shall now turn.

3.1. TRANSFER OF GOODS FOR NON-MONEY CONSIDERATION

There is no conclusive authority in England on the question whether legal title in goods may pass by mere intention if the transfer in question is made for *non-money* consideration, as for example in cases of barters, loans of goods or transfers of goods in exchange for work. In *Cochrane v Moore*, Fry LJ (Bowen LJ agreeing) merely referred to "contracts of sale" when he explained how the second

---

157 Häcker, Causality and abstraction, 203 (fn 7); Häcker, Impaired Consent, 135–36; but cf Fox, Property Rights, 3.50–52 (apparently regarding this only as an issue of identification). Arguably, delivery may only be exempted from in cases where specific coins or notes are sold as specific items of property; in those cases, money would not be excluded from the ambit of the SGA 1979 (s 61(1)); see Bridge et al, Benjamin's Sale of Goods, 1.84; Twigg-Flesner et al, Atiyah and Adams' Sale of Goods, 11–12.

158 See only *Cochrane v Moore* [1890] 25 QBD 57; *Irons v Smallpiece* [1819] 2 B&A 551; *Re Stoneham* [1919] 1 Ch 149; *Thomas v The Times Book* [1966] 2 All ER 241; *Rawlinson v Mort* [1905] 93 LT 555.

exception of the delivery requirement – apart from deeds – had historically developed;[159] yet, he had evidently not considered the position with regard to barters or similar transactions. By contrast, Lord Esher MR clearly extended (obiter) the sale of goods exception to any transfer "for good consideration", explicitly including barters and other exchange transactions:

> "[I]t always was the law of England that an owner of a chattel could transfer his ownership thereof to another person by way of exchange or barter, or by way of bargain and sale for a consideration, or by way of and as a mere gift, or by will. [...] I have no doubt that in every one of the propositions above enumerated [i.e. transfers by exchange or barter, sale or gift], unless it be in the case of a gift by will, there was a time when, as part of the evidence of the existence of the proposition in a particular case, the Courts always required that there should have been an actual delivery of the chattel in question. Though there was proof of a contract for good consideration, in a form which would now pass the property in a chattel without delivery, proof of actual delivery was required. [...] The evidence required in all cases was not complete without proof of an actual delivery. But in some of the cases the Courts undoubtedly do not now require proof of an actual delivery. They do not require that piece of evidence. They do not in the case of a transfer by deed, or in the case of a *transfer by a contract for good consideration*, shewing in its terms an intention that the ownership should pass at once before or without immediate delivery."[160]

Koppel v Koppel[161] concerned a written agreement whereby A was to transfer all goods contained in his house to B in return for work, namely the looking after A's house and children. The case inter alia concerned the question whether the transaction was void in relation to A's executor under the Bills of Sale Act 1878; we are not here concerned with that issue.[162] But Harman LJ held that – though B had apparently obtained possession of the goods – delivery was not required to pass property in them:

> "I think that the property in the goods, this being a document evidencing a *transaction for consideration*, passed under section 18 of the Sale of Goods Act, 1893. [...] The observation by the registrar that there had been no formal delivery is not in point. There is no question of a gift here. *It was money or moneysworth*."[163]

---

159 *Cochrane v Moore* [1890] 25 QBD 57, 65–71 (Fry LJ); see further the introductory remarks of Chapter 2.

160 Ibid, 74–75 (Lord Esher MR) (emphasis added); see also *Seath & Co v Moore* [1886] LR 11 App Cas 350 (HL), 370 (Lord Blackburn) (concerned with contracts to build and transfer engines and to fit them into ships): "A contract for a valuable consideration, by which it is agreed that the property in a specific ascertained article shall pass from one to another, is effectual according to the law of England to change the property."

161 *Koppel v Koppel* [1966] 1 WLR 802 (CA).

162 See only fn 4.

163 *Koppel v Koppel* [1966] 1 WLR 802, 811 (Harman LJ) (emphases added).

The opposite view was apparently adopted by Walsh J in the Irish case of *Flynn v Mackin*.[164] A had agreed to transfer "a new blue Vauxhall Viva motor car" to B against B's used car plus £250; the parties had not determined the price of either car. A was driving with the new car to B's town in order to deliver it to B when he was involved in a serious accident. The sale was one of future generic goods by description and Walsh J held that the driven and demolished car had not (yet) been unconditionally appropriated; for that reason, property could not have passed to B. Alternatively, however, he stated (obiter) that the SGA-regime of transfers of property would anyway have been inapplicable since the transfer had (partly) been a barter (rather than two sales where the prices had been set-off against each other) which would in any case have been outside the Act's ambit as defined by s 2(1). Based on this, he apparently concluded that delivery was inevitably required:

> "Therefore, the provisions of s 18 of the Act of 1893 are not applicable to the transaction under review. The particular transaction was one which, on the evidence, was an agreement to transfer the Vauxhall Viva in consideration of a particular sum of money together with another chattel which was not valued; this transaction was one of exchange or barter. In such a case the ownership of the new Vauxhall Viva would only have been transferred when it was handed over to [B] with the intention of transferring ownership. That point was never reached in the present case."[165]

It is certainly right that contracts to transfer goods for non-money consideration, i.e. in exchange for other goods, work or something else, do *not* fall within the ambit of the SGA 1979; s 1(1) in combination with s 2(1) clearly limits the Act's scope of application to contracts "by which the seller transfers or agrees to transfer the property in goods to the buyer *for a money consideration*". It follows that the regime of ss 16–19 of the SGA 1979 cannot directly apply to barters and other exchange transactions. In so far, Harman LJ's suggestion in *Koppel v Koppel* that the SGA 1893 applied *directly* to the transaction in question (a transfer of goods in exchange for work) cannot be strictly correct.[166]

In relation to such transactions, it is rather the Supply of Goods and Services Act 1982 which is applicable. However, this Act does not contain any provisions relating to the transfer of property. It follows that the transfer of property in barters and similar exchange transactions is today still governed by the common law and that the answer to the question whether property may pass by mere intention or only by delivery must, accordingly, still be found therein.

---

164 *Flynn v Mackin* [1974] IR 101 (SC of Ireland); cf also *O'Regan v White* [1919] 2 IR 346 (CA of Ireland), 362–63 (Ronan LJ).

165 *Flynn v Mackin* [1974] IR 101, 111–12 (Walsh J).

166 Perhaps unless he conceived the transaction as including, in fact, two separate contracts (a contract to sell goods and a contract to work against a price) where the prices had been set-off.

The common law originally only recognised a transfer by delivery. Two exceptions of that delivery requirement emerged in the 14th and 15th century, one relating to deeds and the other relating to (at least) contracts of sale.[167] The crucial question thus seems to be whether the second of those exceptions was (and still is) confined to actual contracts of sale or whether it extends – as the same exception or as a new one – to barters and other transfers for non-money consideration. Such an extension of the sale exception to other transfers for consideration was suggested by Lord Esher MR in *Cochrane v Moore* and seems – contrary to the view expressed by Walsh J in the Irish case of *Flynn v Mackin* – clearly preferable in terms of principle.[168] It would be difficult to understand why transfers of goods in return for money should not require delivery whereas transfers of the same goods in return for other goods or work should do so. Drawing the line between money and non-money consideration with regard to the scope of the delivery requirement would certainly be much less sensible than drawing it between transfers for (any) consideration and transfers for no consideration. Gifts differ from transfers for consideration in various respects and their protection is much weaker in general. Volunteers cannot rely on the bona fide purchase defence and donors are free to withdraw from an oral promise to give prior to perfection. By contrast, promisors in exchange transactions cannot, even if delivery has not yet been made, withdraw from the transaction; their promise is binding. It therefore appears that delivery is a natural and logical requirement to perfect a gift since – if legal title could be transferred without delivery – an unenforceable (oral) gift would, in a sense, perfect and enforce itself. But there is no apparent reason whatsoever why delivery should, in contrast to sale transactions, be inevitably required to transfer legal title in barters or other exchange transactions.

Apart from that, there is a general judicial and legislative tendency to harmonise contracts for the transfer of goods for non-money consideration with contracts of sale and the Sale of Goods Act.[169] The adoption of a uniform regime of how property may pass in such transactions would certainly be in line with those developments.

---

167 See the introductory remarks of Chapter 2.

168 See also Bell, Personal Property, 323–27; Enright, Halsbury's Laws of England, vol 80(3), para 859; Twigg-Flesner et al, Atiyah and Adams' Sale of Goods, 11–12 (fn 30); Bridge et al, Personal Property, 10.27, 10.30; Bridge, Sale of Goods, 3.2 (fn 9), 3.5; R. Smith, Property Law, 116–17; Kersley, Goodeve's Modern Law of Personal Property, 92, 144; left open by Bridge et al, Benjamin's Sale of Goods, 1.31, 1.34–38 ("a matter for speculation"); Häcker, Impaired Consent, 135; Häcker, Causality and abstraction, 203; cf also Canton, MLR 1976, 591–92.

169 See Bridge et al, Benjamin's Sale of Goods, 1.31; Twigg-Flesner et al, Atiyah and Adams' Sale of Goods, 9; cf also *Young & Marten Ltd v McManus Childs Ltd* [1969] 1 AC 454 where the House of Lords de-emphasised the relevance of classification of contracts (but cf the remark of Lord Upjohn, 473, that the passage of property was amongst the issues where a distinction might be relevant).

3.2. TRANSFER OF GOODS FOR NO CONSIDERATION

3.2.1. *General Remarks*

It transpires that the crucial distinguishing feature to delimit the scope of the delivery requirement and, respectively, of the transfer by mere intention – i.e. of the transfer by sale under the SGA 1979 and the "transfer by exchange" under the common law – is whether or not the transfer in question has been made for (any sort of) consideration. Transfers of goods (other than corporeal money) for consideration do not require delivery. Transfers of goods for no consideration do require delivery (or a deed).

That delivery is required is plainly established in relation to *gifts*[170] but this must equally apply with regard to transfers of goods made *without any basis whatsoever*,[171] such as mistaken double deliveries of goods or deliveries of goods or deliveries of goods to the wrong person. Such transfers are clearly made *without consideration* and can therefore – just as intentional gifts – not be perfected without delivery. Even if the transferor believes (as he generally does) that there is a contractual or other obligation to carry out the transfer in question and even if he has set aside the goods to be transferred – perhaps even informing the transferee that he has appropriated certain goods, promising to deliver them – such a promise may not (even less than an oral promise to give) be self-enforced by an immediate passage of legal title prior to delivery. Upon and by delivery, however, legal title may pass even if there is no obligation of the transferor whatsoever to effect the transfer in question. Delivery is abstract and property passes unless the transferor's real intention to transfer ownership is fundamentally infected.

This leaves one very difficult issue: May legal title in goods ever pass by mere intention and without delivery in transfers carried out under *void contracts* of sale (or other void exchange transactions) or is delivery inevitably required in such cases? The possibility of a transfer prior to delivery would essentially require two things: First, that the mode of transfer by sale under the SGA (or the transfer by exchange under the common law) is *abstract*. It has been argued that this is in fact the case.[172] Second, that the mode of transfer by mere intention – by sale under the SGA or by exchange under the common law – is *applicable* at all in such cases; and this again requires that the transfer in question is made *for consideration*. But may transfers under void contracts ever be regarded as made for consideration or does a contract's voidness inevitably destroy any "nexus of

[170] See only *Cochrane v Moore* [1890] 25 QBD 57; *Irons v Smallpiece* [1819] 2 B&A 551; *Re Stoneham* [1919] 1 Ch 149; *Thomas v The Times Book* [1966] 2 All ER 241; *Rawlinson v Mort* [1905] 93 LT 555.

[171] See Chapter 1 section 2.2.2.

[172] Chapter 2 section 2.3.

reciprocity" between the two promises or performances? To this question we shall now turn.

3.2.2. *Transfers Carried Out Under Void Contracts: Delivery Required?*

3.2.2.1. Sale of Goods Act 1979 May Apply to Void Contracts of Sale

A first argument or an indication that delivery might not, at least not always, be required regarding transfers of goods carried out under void contracts of sale might be derived from the SGA 1979 itself. Section 1(1), in combination with s 2(1), states that the Act applies to "contracts of sale of goods". It is uncontroversial that this at least includes *valid* and *voidable* contracts of sale. Property may pass prior to delivery in voidable sales because such transactions are initially valid (pending rescission).[173] By contrast, it could be argued that the SGA does not apply in relation to *void* contracts of sale because void contracts are no "contracts" at all[174] and because void "contracts" are, accordingly, a priori excluded from the very scope of the SGA 1979.[175] The consequence of such an argument would be that the (abstract) transfer of property regime of ss 16–19 of the SGA 1979 would not apply to void contracts of sale altogether (but this would still not answer the question whether the common law, which applies outside the ambit of the SGA 1979, could still allow a transfer by mere intention).

It appears, however, that the very applicability of the SGA does not, as such, depend on the validity of the contract of sale. On the one hand, the mere existence of s 6 indicates that it cannot logically have been the intention of the draftsmen to exclude void contracts from the Act's ambit *altogether*.[176] Though this provision merely codifies an old common law rule (as most provisions of the SGA do),[177] its inclusion into the Act would have been completely futile if the SGA did a priori not apply to void contracts at all. Section 6 would otherwise first render an envisaged contract void, the very fact of which would then again deprive the Act and that section of their very applicability which would again mean that the contract could still be valid and that the SGA and s 6 could still

---

173 See (e.g.) *Branwhite v Worcester Works Finance* [1969] 1 AC 552.

174 Cf *Fawcett v Star Car Sales* [1960] NZLR 406, 412 (Gresson P); *Shogun Finance v Hudson* [2003] UKHL 62, [2] (Lord Nicholls); Whittaker, Chitty on Contracts, vol 1, 1.115.

175 It is possible that Swadling, LQR 2005, 126, had such an argument in mind when he said: "[W]here the contract is void, [...] the legislation [i.e. the SGA 1979] has nothing to say"; see also Twigg-Flesner, Halsbury's Laws of England, vol 91(1), para 153.

176 A similar argument (though perhaps less obvious) could be made in relation to s 62(2) which preserves, inter alia, the common law rules relating to the effect of various vitiating factors some of which render contracts void. If the SGA did a priori not apply to void contracts, s 62(2) would not have to say anything with regard to such defects which render contracts void.

177 See *Bell v Lever Bros Ltd* [1932] AC 161 (HL), 217–18 (Lord Atkin); Bridge et al, Benjamin's Sale of Goods, 3.19.

again apply (unless the old common law rule jumped in at some point). On the other hand, the case law which has been cited in support of the view that property might still pass prior to delivery in void sale transactions suggests that the SGA 1979 is, at least in principle, applicable even with regard to void contracts of sale.[178]

This seems to reveal that void contracts of sale are not per se *completely* devoid of *any* legal effects; they might at least trigger the scope of application of the SGA 1979 (at least to some extent). Transfers carried out under void contracts may, at least in so far, be distinguished from transfers which have no basis whatsoever, such as mistaken double deliveries of goods, though the latter may perhaps be made in pursuance of a *putative* contract of sale.

However, the mere fact that the SGA 1979 is, in principle, applicable to void contracts of sale cannot conclusively decide the question of whether and in how far a transfer by mere intention (without delivery) is possible in relation to transfers carried out under void contracts. On the one hand, it might be imagined that, though the SGA 1979 applies in principle, not all of its provisions – particularly ss 16–19 – apply to void contracts of sale or that those provisions only apply to void transactions in certain cases. On the other hand, the decisive criterion – whether within the regime of the SGA or at common law – rather seems to be whether the transfer in question can be regarded as being *for consideration* or whether it is in fact *gratuitous*.

3.2.2.2. Consideration in Transfers Made Under Void Contracts?

Consideration is an elusive concept which has different meanings in different contexts. In the context of restitution, failure of consideration refers to a condition imposed by the transferor, on a joint understanding shared by the transferee, which has initially or subsequently failed.[179] We are not here concerned with the restitutionary meaning of consideration. In the contractual

---

178 See Chapter 2 section 2.3.2. The clearest statement – provided that illegal contracts are indeed void (see text to fn 120–121) – may be found in *Kingsley v Sterling Industrial Securities* [1967] 2 QB 747, 782–83 (Winn LJ) (emphasis added): "[I]t does not seem to me to follow, from a finding that any particular contract of sale by which the parties intended [...] to pass property in the article sold by force of the contract itself was illegal, that the property in the article did not pass from vendor to purchaser. [...] I have not, of course, overlooked the fact that in the present case there was no real delivery [...] but in my opinion it is clear that the parties intended property to pass without delivery, *and it is clear from the Sale of Goods Act that delivery is not an essential condition of the passing of property unless the parties intend that it should be such a condition*"; see also *Belvoir v Stapleton* [1971] 1 QB 210.

179 *Fibrosa Spolka Akcyjna v Fairbairn Lawson Combe Barbour Ltd* [1943] AC 32 (HL), 48 (Viscount Simon LC); *Guinness Mahon & Co Ltd v Kensington and Chelsea Royal LBC* [1999] QB 215 (CA), 236 (Walker LJ); Goff/Jones, Unjust Enrichment, 12.1; Burrows, Restitution, 319–22; Virgo, Restitution, 308–11.

context, consideration refers to the requirement that a promise may only be binding and enforceable as a contract if it is supported by some counter-promise or some counter-performance as *quid pro quo* which need not, however, be adequate. Finally, consideration might perhaps again have a slightly different meaning in the context of the defence of bona fide purchase for value (i.e. for valuable consideration).[180]

It would certainly not be impossible to introduce a fourth meaning of "consideration" in the context of the scope of the delivery requirement. But this is not apparently necessary. The notion of consideration required to exempt from the delivery requirement on the *proprietary* level appears to operate on similar lines as the *contractual* concept of consideration. This is *not*, however, because it is the contract which *itself* effects the transfer of property by mere intention (the transfer is rather effected by the abstract real agreement[181]) but apparently because allowing a mere real agreement to take immediate effect without delivery would, in the absence of contractual consideration, indirectly enforce a non-binding gratuitous promise. English law has chosen to not enforce gratuitous executory promises (unless made by deed) and the abstract mode of transfer by mere intention may not indirectly circumvent this rule. This is why delivery is required.

Now the question arises whether and in how far a transfer of goods made under a void contract may be regarded as made for consideration. Suppose that seller A and buyer B conclude a contract of sale which is void (or unenforceable[182]) so that neither party is under an (enforceable) obligation to execute the promised performances.[183] May B's void (or unenforceable) *executory counter-promise* to pay be sufficient consideration to potentially allow a transfer of legal title in the goods prior to delivery (if A's intention to transfer ownership is not, as such, fundamentally infected by the defect)? If not, may at least B's *actual performance* of the void (or unenforceable) counter-promise provide sufficient consideration? These are very delicate questions which have not yet received

180 See esp Fox, Property Rights, 8.29–49. Though there does not seem to be much of a difference regarding the bona fide purchase defence at law, it is possible (though not preferable) that equity only accepts *executed* consideration to defeat equitable interests by bona fide purchase.

181 See Chapter 2 sections 2.2. and 2.3.

182 The distinction between "void" and "unenforceable" contracts is difficult and elusive; it seems even possible that there are not just two categories of black and white (void and unenforceable) but that there are different shades of grey in between. However that may be, it will be argued that to ask whether a *contract* is "void" or "unenforceable" is – on the *proprietary* level – to ask the wrong question. The relevant question rather is whether the particular defect in question wholly destroyed the nexus between the two promises/performances and whether performance of one may still be consideration for the other.

183 Contracts may for example be void by reason of a lack of consent or authority, a contractually fundamental mistake, illegality or by way of a statute, such as s 1 of the Infants Relief Act 1874 or s 18 of the Gaming Act 1845 (both repealed today).

sufficient attention.[184] They shall be briefly considered here but further work certainly needs to be done in this area.

A first relevant case is *Clayton v Jennings*[185] where A and B betted at a horse race. A promised to pay 10 guineas and B promised to pay 5 in the event of losing respectively. A won and claimed the 5 guineas. A statute then in force rendered bets exceeding an amount of £10 void but left unaffected bets below that amount. It appears that 10 guineas were above that limit but 5 were not. The court held that, though B's promise to pay 5 guineas (upon which A's claim was founded) was not, as such, affected by the statute, A's void promise was no consideration for it since B could not have enforced it. Therefore, it dismissed A's claim for the 5 guineas for lack of consideration.

In some contrast with this stands *Laythoarp v Bryant*,[186] which concerned s 4 of the Statute of Frauds 1677 (as then in force) which required – inter alia for contracts for the sale of land – the signature on a written document by "the party to be charged" for the respective promise to be valid. The defendant buyer purchased certain leasehold premises at an auction under a contract which he but not the seller had signed; the buyer refused to pay. In an action for damages by the seller, based on the buyer's duly signed promise, the buyer argued that there was a lack of consideration since the contract was unenforceable by him against the seller (the latter's promise being unenforceable for lack of signature) and that, therefore, the executory contract was not binding on him. The court, however, rejected this argument and held that the buyer's signed promise was still enforceable; apparently, it decided so on the basis of the statute's language which at least implicitly provided that the signing party's promise should remain enforceable even if the other party's was not. Arguably, this meant that the statute provided, at least implicitly, that the unenforceable promise (here: the seller's) was still sufficient consideration for the enforceable one (here: the buyer's).[187]

Fishmongers' Co v Robertson[188] concerned a contract which was not – as required by the common law (prior to the Corporate Bodies' Contracts Act 1960[189]) – under the corporation's seal and therefore not binding on the corporation. The court left open the question whether the unenforceable *executory* promise of the corporation could *itself* have constituted sufficient consideration and whether the corporation could have sued on the contract prior to its own actual performance but it held that at least the *actual performance* of its own

184 See only Treitel, LQR 1961; Treitel, Chitty on Contracts, vol 1, 4.186–90; Treitel, Contract, 3.153–57; cf also Unger, MLR 1956; Fox, Property Rights, 8.29–30.

185 *Clayton v Jennings* [1770] 2 WBl 706, 96 ER 416.

186 *Laythoarp v Bryant* [1836] 2 BingNC 735, 132 ER 283.

187 See Treitel, LQR 1961, 91–92.

188 *Fishmongers' Co v Robertson* [1843] 5 M&G 131, 134 ER 510, 534–35 (Tindal CJ).

189 See now ss 43–47 of the Companies Act 2006.

unenforceable promise *was* sufficient consideration. In the case of *Kidderminster Co v Hardwick*,[190] which was likewise concerned with a contract not under the seal of the claiming corporation, it was held that the unenforceable executory promise was not itself, prior to actual performance, consideration and that the corporation could not, accordingly, have sued on the contract prior to that.

Similarly, in *R v A-G of England and Wales*,[191] the Crown sued a member of a military regiment on a contract by which the latter had promised to not publish certain information and by which the Crown had promised to not move him to another regiment; yet, the Crown's promise was void since it purported to fetter the Crown's unrestrictable public law discretion. Lord Hoffmann held that the Crown's void executory promise alone would not have been consideration but that actual performance of it, i.e. the actual forbearance from moving the defendant to another regiment, *was*. The Crown was accordingly entitled to sue on the contract (only but still) after actual performance of its own void promise.

The cases cited so far were all concerned with a rule of law which rendered only *one* of the two promises void or unenforceable but which left unaffected the other one; in each of those cases, the claimant sued on the valid promise and the question arose whether that promise was still unenforceable for lack of consideration. With regard to such types of cases, it may be concluded, first, that the void or unenforceable *executory counter-promise* is not by itself consideration unless the invalidating statute or rule of law provides otherwise.[192] Second, however, it appears that *actual performance* of the void or unenforceable counter-promise generally *is* consideration.[193]

If this is correct, it appears that in a case where a seller's obligation to transfer ownership is valid but where a buyer's obligation to pay is void or unenforceable, there is – unless the relevant statute or rule of law provides otherwise – no consideration for the seller's transfer, unless and until the buyer has actually performed his void or unenforceable counter-promise, i.e. unless and until he has actually paid. Accordingly, the seller's valid promise is no more than a promise to give, unsupported by consideration, until payment has been made but it becomes thereafter a promise for good consideration. It follows that delivery is, in such cases, required as long as the buyer has not paid yet but not anymore thereafter.

---

190 *Kidderminster Co v Hardwick* [1873] LR 9 Ex 13 (Ct of Exchequer).

191 *R v A-G of England and Wales* [2003] UKPC 22, [2003] EMLR 24, [31]–[32].

192 An example of a statute (implicitly) providing that the unenforceable executory counter-promise *is* consideration arguably was s 4 of the Statute of Frauds 1677; see *Laythoarp v Bryant* [1836] 2 BingNC 735. Another example is s 34 of the Matrimonial Causes Act 1973 which, in contrast to the common law, provides that a wife's void promise to not apply to the court for a maintenance order is sufficient consideration to sue on a husband's promise to pay an allowance; see esp Treitel, LQR 1961, 91–97 (with further examples); Treitel, Chitty on Contracts, vol 1, 4.189; Treitel, Contract, 3.156.

193 Treitel, LQR 1961; Treitel, Chitty on Contracts, vol 1, 4.188–89; Treitel, Contract, 3.155–56; cf also Unger, MLR 1956, 99–100.

Now what is the position if *both* promises are void or unenforceable? Certainly, if we have concluded that a mere *executory* void or unenforceable counter-promise cannot be consideration until it has been actually performed in cases where the relevant statute or rule of law only invalidates *one* of the two promises, such an *executory* void or unenforceable counter-promise cannot – *a fortiori* – be consideration in cases where *both* promises are invalidated. But may at least *actual performance* of the void or unenforceable counter-promise count as consideration? If, in a sale transaction, not only the buyer's promise to pay but also the seller's promise to transfer goods is void or unenforceable, might the buyer's actual payment still be consideration for the seller's void or unenforceable promise?

This is at least the case as far as *illegality* is concerned. It has already been pointed out that there are at least three illegal sale cases where property in the goods was held to have passed even though delivery had never been made.[194] This must logically mean that the courts have supposed that there had been sufficient consideration for the seller's illegal promise in those cases; had this been otherwise, delivery would inevitably have been required. Though it appears that the buyer's *executory* illegal (void or unenforceable) promise to pay did not count as consideration, *actual performance* of it did. In fact, in all of the mentioned illegality cases, where delivery had not yet been made but where property was still held to have passed, the buyer had already made payment. In *Kingsley v Sterling Industrial Securities*,[195] Saxon Finance (the first buyer) had paid over the agreed "purchase price" (which was functionally a loan and from which it had deducted a contractually agreed upfront payment relating to the hire-purchase transaction) to the claimant seller by cheque; the finance company (the second buyer) had equally sent a cheque to Saxon. In *Belvoir v Stapleton*[196] and in *Watts v Seymour*,[197] the buyers had equally paid their sellers and thereby provided consideration by actually performing their illegal counter-promises.

If this analysis is correct, it follows that property would not have passed in those cases – prior to and without delivery – had the buyer not actually paid the price, because the illegal *executory* counter-promise would not by itself have constituted consideration. Hence, it appears that property may pass in illegal transactions either upon and by *delivery* or – if by mere intention – upon *payment*.

With this consideration-analysis in mind, some of the judicial statements in the leading illegality cases appear – perhaps somewhat surprisingly – in an

194 *Kingsley v Sterling Industrial Securities* [1967] 2 QB 747; *Belvoir v Stapleton* [1971] 1 QB 210; *Watts v Seymour* [1967] 2 QB 647; see Chapter 2 section 2.3.2.

195 *Kingsley v Sterling Industrial Securities* [1967] 2 QB 747; see text to fn 108–110.

196 *Belvoir v Stapleton* [1971] 1 QB 210.

197 *Watts v Seymour* [1967] 2 QB 647.

entirely new light:[198] When Lord Denning in *Singh v Ali* said that the illegal transaction was effective to pass property because it was "fully executed and carried out" and that property passes "so soon as the contract is executed",[199] his Lordship might not – or not only – have had in mind that *delivery* of the goods (the lorry) had in fact been made but also – if not only – that the buyer had already *paid the price*. In any event, he has apparently made such an amendment himself in *Belvoir v Stapleton* when he rejected the counsel for defendant's argument that the case should have been distinguished from *Singh v Ali* on the basis that the goods had never been delivered:

> "I do not accept this distinction taken by [counsel for defendant]. I think that the proposition stated in [*Singh v Ali*] applies even where the transferee has not taken possession of the property, so long as the title to it has passed. [...] Although [Belvoir] obtained the car under a contract which was illegal, nevertheless *inasmuch as the contract was executed* and the property passed, the car belonged to [Belvoir] and they can claim it."[200]

With the term "executed" Lord Denning MR and Sachs LJ could not have meant "delivery of the cars to Belvoir" since that had never happened. Though they might perhaps also have had in mind that the car dealers had already delivered possession of the cars to Belgravia, it is submitted that "execution" should be read as referring to "execution of the void counter-promise", i.e. payment. Had Belvoir not paid the price yet, property in the cars could not, in the absence of delivery to Belvoir, have passed to it since the dealers' (sellers') promise would then have been a mere promise to give. But if and as soon as Belvoir had effected payment, the sellers' promise was supported by consideration and property could have passed by mere intention (even if the dealers had still been in possession of the cars).

In some contrast with the illegality cases stands the case of *Lipkin Gorman v Karpnale Ltd.*[201] Apart from fundamental issues in the context of tracing and unjust enrichment, this landmark decision also concerned the question

---

198 See also *Scarfe v Morgan* [1838] 4 M&W 270, 150 ER 1430, 1435, which concerned a lien created on a Sunday; though Parke B rejected illegality under the relevant statute, he said obiter (emphases added): "[But even if this had been an illegal contract], this is not the case of an executory contract; both parties were in pari delicto – *it is one which has been executed, and the consideration given*; and although in the former case [i.e. in the case of an executory contract] the law would not assist one to recover against the other, *yet if the contract is executed*, and a property either special or general has passed thereby, the property must remain."

199 *Singh v Ali* [1960] AC 167, 176 (Lord Denning).

200 *Belvoir v Stapleton* [1971] 1 QB 210, 217–18 (Lord Denning MR) (emphasis added), see equally 220 (Sachs LJ) (emphasis added): "It is quite clear that the title to the cars passed *as soon as the agreement between [Belvoir] and the dealers was executed.*"

201 *Lipkin Gorman v Karpnale Ltd* [1991] 2 AC 548 (HL).

of consideration. Though this issue arose in the context of the bona fide purchase defence (at law), this case is equally relevant in the present context since the notion of consideration has arguably a broadly similar meaning in the contractual context as with regard to the bona fide purchase defence (at least at law).[202] The gaming contracts between the casino and Cass, under which the latter had transferred corporeal money to the former, had been "null and void" by reason of s 18 of the Gaming Act 1845.[203] Having rejected the argument that the handing over of the gambling chips and/or the power of the possessor of such chips to buy refreshments was sufficient consideration to invoke the bona fide purchase defence with regard to the money received,[204] the House of Lords not only rejected the view that the casino's void *executory counter-promise* to pay over a certain amount of money in the event of winning was consideration for the receipt of the money but also held that *actual performance* of this void promise was neither sufficient consideration:

> "[T]he casino cannot, in my opinion, say that it has given valuable consideration for the money, whether or not the gambler's bet is successful. It has given no consideration if the bet is unsuccessful, because its promise to pay on a successful bet is void; nor has it done so if the gambler's bet is successful and the casino has paid him his winnings, because that payment is in law a gift to the gambler by the casino."[205]

Hence, their Lordships adopted the view that the actual payments of Cass to the casino (to buy gambling chips) and the actual payments of the casino to Cass (payouts of winnings) were, in fact, two entirely unrelated performances which were not consideration for each other, and which were *both gratuitous*. Where, however, is the difference between the *Lipkin*-type of case, where the two performed void promises were not regarded as mutual consideration, and the illegality cases, where the courts did allow such an attribution of the invalid promise's performance to the respectively other promise? It appears that the distinction lies in the respective type of defect as laid down by the respective statute or rule of law. In the illegality cases, the courts apparently conceived the respective statutes or rules of law involved as – though rendering the contracts void (or unenforceable) – not entirely destroying the parties' bargain in every single respect and as at least leaving behind some kind of a *nexus of reciprocity*

---

202 See fn 180 and esp Fox, Property Rights, 8.29–49; but cf *Lipkin Gorman v Karpnale* [1991] 2 AC 548, 576–77 (Lord Goff), suggesting obiter – without citing authority – that an executory consideration would not be enough to invoke the bona fide purchase defence, even at law.

203 Now repealed by the Gambling Act 2005.

204 *Lipkin Gorman v Karpnale* [1991] 2 AC 548, 566–67 (Lord Templeman), 575–77 (Lord Goff); this was contrary to the majority's view in the Court of Appeal ([1989] 1 WLR 1340); see critically on this point Treitel, Chitty on Contracts, vol 1, 4.16–17.

205 *Lipkin Gorman v Karpnale* [1991] 2 AC 548, 575–77 (Lord Goff), see also 562, 566–67 (Lord Templeman).

between the two promises.[206] The preserved nexus of reciprocity, as originating from the parties' otherwise invalidated bargain, still allowed a (retrospective) attribution of a certain performance as consideration for another promise;[207] in so far, illegality still allows a retrospective healing of the initial lack of consideration by executing one or both of the promises. By contrast, the House of Lords in *Lipkin* apparently regarded s 18 of the Gaming Act 1845 as effectively destroying the contract in every single respect, not leaving behind anything whatsoever, not even a nexus of reciprocity; s 18 thereby somehow broke apart the agreed interrelation between the two performances and rendered them both gratuitous.

It is extremely difficult, if not impossible, to state in abstract terms in which cases such a nexus of reciprocity is preserved and in which it is not. This probably simply depends on the individual statute or rule of law in question. By contrast, it could be argued that the answer, in fact, rather lies in the distinction between contracts which are actually *void* and such which are only *unenforceable*, the nexus of reciprocity being destroyed in the former but not in the latter case. However, the categories of "void" and "unenforceable" contracts are inherently vague; they have rarely, if ever, been clearly distinguished by the courts and it is thus rarely, if ever, exactly known whether and in how far a contract is indeed void or merely unenforceable. Statutes often use ambiguous language and it may often be alleged that statutes or courts did not actually mean what they appeared to say. Furthermore, it is even conceivable that there are not just two black and white categories of contracts which are either void or unenforceable (once voidable is out of question) but that there are in fact various different degrees of voidness or unenforceability in between.[208]

A good example is s 1 of the old Infants Relief Act 1874 which rendered certain contracts concluded by infants "absolutely void". In light of the statute's clear language, combined with other features,[209] it is very difficult to argue that such contracts were not actually void but merely unenforceable, voidable

206 The notion of a nexus of reciprocity may perhaps be compared with the distinction drawn by Treitel, LQR 1961, between "mutuality of undertaking", which denotes the requirement that both parties must have made some promise *at all* failing which consideration is clearly lacking, and "mutuality of obligation", which means that in principle both promises must be valid and enforceable but that even *defective promises* (illegal, void, voidable or unenforceable) may, in certain cases, constitute consideration.

207 Evidently, the nexus of reciprocity defines *what kind* of performance may be regarded as consideration; in *Belvoir v Stapleton* [1971] 1 QB 210, for example, anything else than payment by Belvoir to the car dealers (as agreed in the illegal contract) would not have amounted to consideration.

208 Cf also Atiyah, LQR 1958, 101: "[T]he consequences of voidness in the law of contract are by no means universally the same. Contracts may be void for a variety of reasons [...], but it does not at all follow that the results in all these cases are the same."

209 See esp Treitel, LQR 1957, 200–5.

or something else.[210] Reference has already been made to the case of *Stocks v Wilson* where an infant had purchased furniture under a contract which was void under that statute but where property in the furniture was still held to have passed to the infant.[211] On the facts of the case, the furniture had already been delivered to the infant. But what would have been the position had delivery not yet been made? Could property still have passed to the infant by mere intention? This depends on the question whether the infant had given sufficient consideration. The infant's void executory promise to pay could certainly not have counted as consideration. But what if the infant had already paid the agreed price and the seller had still not delivered the goods? The preferable view is that property would then still have passed to the infant; the latter's actual payment should be regarded as sufficient consideration even though it was made in pursuance of a void contract. The statute cannot be taken to have destroyed any nexus of reciprocity between the parties' promises. Suppose that the seller had been a trustee of the goods for a third-party beneficiary (selling them in breach of trust) or that he had stolen them from a third party (selling them to the infant in a market overt as required by the market overt exception as then in force). In such a case, the infant's actual payment would certainly have been regarded as good consideration to allow invocation of the bona fide purchase defence.

This example apparently demonstrates that asking whether a contract is indeed void or merely unenforceable is – at least as far as the transfer of property is concerned – simply to ask the wrong question. Transfer of legal title – whether by delivery or by mere intention – is *abstract* and may, in principle, be effective whether or not there is a contract and whether a contract is void or merely unenforceable. The actually relevant question rather is whether the transferee has in fact provided sufficient *consideration* for the receipt of property in the goods since the abstract transfer by mere intention is only *applicable* if that has been the case. Otherwise, i.e. if the promised transfer of property must (still) be regarded as gratuitous, delivery is required.

The ultimately relevant question accordingly is whether the concrete invalidity in question – voidness or unenforceability or something in between – has swept away what would otherwise have been a good consideration. It has been argued in this section that a void or unenforceable *executory counter-promise* may not generally – unless the relevant statute or rule of law provides otherwise[212] – by itself count as consideration; however, *actual performance* of that promise *may* constitute consideration in *some* cases. This is most usually the case if only *one* of the two promises is defective but it may also be the case if *both* promises are void or unenforceable. In that regard, the relevant question is whether the particular

---

210 See fn 125.

211 *Stocks v Wilson* [1913] 2 KB 235; see Chapter 2 section 2.3.2.

212 Cf fn 192.

defect in question – as provided by the relevant statute or rule of law – is so severe as to destroy any nexus of reciprocity between the two "agreed" promises/performances or not. This question is *not* strictly tied to the question whether the promises are void or merely unenforceable. It is possible that the relevant nexus is preserved even though the contract is "absolutely void", as for example in the case of s 1 of the old Infants Relief Act 1874. Such a nexus is furthermore generally preserved in cases of illegality but it was destroyed under s 18 of the old Gaming Act 1845. Whether a nexus of reciprocity is preserved or destroyed in other cases must be examined individually with regard to every specific statute or rule of law. It is impossible to provide a comprehensive overview within the confines of this book; yet, two further examples shall be briefly mentioned.

First, with regard to *contractually fundamental mistakes*, i.e. mistakes which are serious enough to render a contract void but which may still not affect the real agreement,[213] one must probably distinguish between mutual mistakes in communication, which *negative* the parties' apparent consent, and common mistakes as to the subject-matter, which do not relate to the terms of the contract but to some exterior state of affairs and which merely (but still) *nullify* an otherwise existing agreement.[214]

An example regarding the former is the case where A and B agree that A shall transfer a specific car to B, property in which is agreed to pass immediately upon conclusion, but where A and B are at cross-purposes regarding B's counter-performance, for example if A understands that B shall pay £10,000, whereas B understands that he merely has to pay £1,000 or that he has to transfer his old car to A in exchange or that A's transfer is in fact a gift. If the objective principle – i.e. the understanding of a reasonable person in the parties' respective positions – may not provide an answer (for example if what A and B respectively said or did could objectively be understood likewise as an offer or an acceptance to pay £10,000 or £1,000), there is *no contract*. The parties' apparent consent is negatived and has never existed at all.[215] However, such a

---

213 See in detail Chapter 4; examples of contractually but not proprietarily fundamental mistakes are *common mistakes* as to the subject-matter (see Chapter 4 section 2.1.2.) and *mutual mistakes* in communication relating to the consideration, i.e. the contract price (see Chapter 4 section 2.5.).

214 See esp *Bell v Lever Bros* [1932] AC 161, 217–18 (Lord Atkin); Cartwright, Misrepresentation, ch 15.

215 See Chapter 4 section 1.1. and (e.g.) *Raffles v Wichelhaus* [1864] 2 H&C 906, 159 ER 375 (goods sold "ex Peerless from Bombay"; objective ambiguity as to whether goods "ex Peerless from Bombay, October shipment" or "ex Peerless from Bombay, December shipment" was meant); *Falck v Williams* [1900] AC 176 (PC) (mutual misunderstanding with regard to coded telegrams which could objectively have had either meaning); *South East Windscreens Ltd v Jamshidi* [2005] All ER (D) 317 (Dec) (QBD) (sale of business and mutual mistake as to the price and exact counter-performance to be made by the buyer; no unambiguous single objective meaning could be found); see generally Beale, Chitty on Contracts, vol 1, 3.13–21; Cartwright, Misrepresentation, 13.1–29.

mistake does still not affect the parties' abstract *real agreement* with regard to the transfer of property in the car. A still intended to transfer ownership in the car to B and B still intended to receive it.[216] There is no mistake in that regard. Property may at least pass upon and by delivery. But is there sufficient consideration to allow a transfer by mere intention even prior to that? B's void executory promise (whatever its content) is certainly no consideration and it appears that even actual payment of whatever amount by B to A (or a transfer of B's old car to A) would neither amount to consideration.[217] The mutuality or nexus of reciprocity between the parties' promises is entirely negatived. This is a *Lipkin*-type of case where both parties' performances are gratuitous.

By contrast, a nexus of reciprocity is not necessarily destroyed if there is an *actual consent* between the parties about A's performance and B's counter-performance but if both parties act under some fundamental mistake as to the subject-matter (common mistake). Suppose that A and B agree on the sale of a specific item, property in which shall pass immediately upon conclusion, in return for £1,000 and that they are – in a way satisfying the test of *Bell v Lever Bros*[218] – both fundamentally mistaken about that item's qualities or characteristics or about some other fundamental state of affairs exterior to the terms of the contract.[219] Such a common mistake *nullifies* the parties' otherwise existing consent and renders the contract void *ab initio*. Yet, the parties' real agreement is arguably still not affected by such a mistake, at least if the parties have physically identified the item, and property may still pass at least upon and by delivery.[220] But may it pass even prior to that? It seems that B's void executory promise to pay cannot provide consideration. However, it is arguable that

216 See Chapter 4 section 2.5.

217 It is submitted that in *Felthouse v Bindley* [1862] 11 CBNS 869, 142 ER 1037, where the parties agreed on the transfer of property in a horse but where they were in disagreement about the price, property in the horse would not have passed even if the buyer had already paid the (supposed) price; however, it will be argued that property would have passed had delivery been made; see Chapter 4 section 2.5.

218 *Bell v Lever Bros* [1932] AC 161; see also *Great Peace Shipping Ltd v Tsavliris Salvage (International) Ltd (The Great Peace)* [2002] EWCA Civ 1407, [2003] QB 679. Concrete examples are difficult to find since the hurdles of this test are extremely high; see (e.g.) *Nicholson & Venn v Smith-Marriott* [1947] 177 LT 189 (sale of a set of linen napkins and tablecloth which both parties believed to have been the authentic property of the monarch Charles I; this proved to have been wrong and Hallett J held – obiter, due to the way the case was pleaded – that this was a common mistake which would have satisfied Lord Atkin's test in *Bell v Lever Bros* and which would thus have rendered the contract void); but cf the examples given by Lord Atkin in *Bell v Lever Bros*, 224, which his Lordship assumed to be insufficient (e.g. the sale of a painting believed to be the work of an old master at a high price which turned out to be a copy).

219 Obviously, where the parties' fundamental common mistake as to the subject-matter went to the goods' very existence (cf s 6 of the SGA 1979) or to some other feature which rendered the transfer factually impossible, there is little sense to think about a transfer of property.

220 See Chapter 4 section 2.1.2.

B's actual payment of the £1,000 may be regarded as consideration and that property may thereupon pass by mere intention. There is a crucial difference in nature between mistakes which negative the parties' consent and such which merely nullify it. The latter type of mistake does arguably not completely eradicate the parties' consent so as to even destroy the nexus of reciprocity.[221]

Second, there can be little doubt that *voidable* executory or executed promises are consideration for the respective counter-promise. Hence, property may pass by mere intention and without delivery in voidable contractual transfers of property.[222] It could be argued, however, that *rescission* of the obligatory contract retroactively avoids consideration, thereby turning the transfer into a gratuitous one.[223] But the preferable view is that rescission of a voidable contract neither destroys an existing nexus of reciprocity, which means that at least actual performance of an avoided counter-promise remains sufficient consideration, nor in any other sense retroactively avoids consideration for the purposes of the delivery requirement. Arguably, this is even the case with regard to avoided executory promises. However that may be, the consideration/delivery requirement could at most be an obstacle to effect the *initial* transfer of legal title but it cannot – once title has passed – operate to *revest* property even if consideration were subsequently found to have disappeared.[224]

3.3. CONCLUSIONS

It has been argued that both transfers by delivery and transfers by sale are abstract, which means that they both operate independently from an underlying obligation's existence or validity. It has furthermore been argued that the strict delivery requirement should – transfers of corporeal money and transfers by deed apart – only (but still) apply with regard to gratuitous transfers unsupported

---

221 Cf Cartwright, Misrepresentation, 15.3: "In the case of a mistake about the subject-matter, however, there is not only an apparent agreement between the parties about their respective obligations, but (in law) an actual agreement. In making a contract void, therefore, the mistake must operate in a different way. It was said by Lord Atkin [in *Bell v Lever Bros*] not to 'negative' the parties' consent but to 'nullify' it [...]. This difference in the underlying theory about why the contract is void gives rise to a different general approach to mistakes about the subject-matter, as compared with mistakes as to terms or identity."

222 See only *Branwhite v Worcester Works Finance* [1969] 1 AC 552.

223 Cf *Independent Trustee Services Ltd v GP Noble Trustees Ltd* [2012] EWCA Civ 195, [2012] 3 WLR 597, which was, however, only concerned with consideration for the purposes of the bona fide purchase defence in equity.

224 This issue is only relevant with regard to the question whether legal title in goods transferred without delivery by the guilty party to the rescinding party automatically revests upon the latter's rescission (cf text to fn 140). With regard to assets transferred by the rescinding party, however, property will almost always revest by the concomitant exercise of the notionally distinct power in rem; cf Chapter 2 section 2.3.3.

by consideration. It follows that there is, apart from transfers by sale governed by the SGA 1979, another variant of the transfer by mere intention, namely a *transfer by exchange* which is – still today – governed by the common law but which, besides that, operates on the same lines as transfers by sale under the SGA 1979.

Gifts and transfers made without any basis whatsoever, such as mistaken double deliveries of goods, are gratuitous transfers which inevitably require delivery to be perfected. By contrast, transfers made under void contracts may either be gratuitous or – depending on the particular defect in question – for consideration. Hence, delivery is required in some cases of void contract transfers but not in others.

The distinction between void and unenforceable contracts is delicate and inherently vague. It has been argued, however, that asking whether a contract is in fact void or only unenforceable is – on the proprietary plane – to ask the wrong question. The actual relevant issue rather is whether the particular defect swept away what would otherwise have been a good consideration. As far as it does, delivery is required; as far as it does not, property may still pass abstractly by mere intention.

It has furthermore been argued that void or unenforceable executory counter-promises may not usually – unless the relevant statute or rule of law provides otherwise – by themselves constitute consideration. Actual performance of such a promise may, however, count as consideration in some cases, namely if only one of the two promises is void or unenforceable or – if both promises are invalid – if the defect in question has not entirely eradicated the parties' consent so as to even destroy a nexus of reciprocity between the two promises/performances. Again, this question is not strictly tied to the question whether the contract is void or unenforceable. It is rather possible that the relevant nexus is preserved even though the contract is "absolutely void"; an example is s 1 of the old Infants Relief Act 1874. Such a nexus is furthermore generally preserved in cases of illegality and common mistakes but not in cases of mutual mistakes in communication.

4. TRANSFER OF LEGAL TITLE BY DEED

A third method of how legal title in tangible movable property may be transferred is by deed. Deeds are of central importance in relation to land. Generally, legal estates in land can only be created or conveyed by deed;[225] transfers of registered[226]

---

225 Section 52(1) of the Law of Property Act 1925.

226 For the question whether legal estates may or must be registered, see s 3 et seq of the Land Registration Act 2002.

legal estates furthermore require registration at the Land Registry.[227] In relation to tangible personal property, however, the practical relevance of transfers by deed is (settlements on trust apart) very limited. A deed is only required to effect a gratuitous transfer prior to and without delivery of a chattel; yet, gifts are most usually effected simply by delivery. In the commercial context, where a transfer by mere intention is generally possible, deeds are almost never used to transfer personal property.

Though transfers by deed (and registration) are well known in the context of land, the doctrinal underpinnings of transfers of tangible movable property by deed are poorly understood. This correlates with a distinct shortage of case law in this regard which may apparently be explained by the mentioned practical insignificance. For that reason, it is not easy to set out a clear view as to how exactly such transfers operate and how exactly defects may affect them. Many things are left for speculation.

4.1. HISTORY

In early days, tangible movable property could only be transferred upon and by a physical delivery of the chattel itself, whether or not there was consideration and whether or not the transaction was contained in a deed or similar document.[228] In the 14th and 15th century, the sale exception emerged and it appears that this went hand in hand with the development of binding executory obligations. In those days, a sale did not impose binding obligations on the parties unless one of them has performed its part of the bargain or – in a later stage of development – if the buyer has given an "earnest money". It furthermore appears that payment or the giving of an earnest money resulted in a fiction that possession of the goods has passed to the buyer, what may be regarded as some form of a constructive delivery. This apparently helped to eventually overcome the delivery requirement entirely in sale transactions.

The deed exception similarly emerged during the 14th[229] or 15th century[230] and it is arguable that this equally correlated with the development of binding obligations created by deeds and that there was, initially, a similar fiction that execution of a deed resulted in a transfer of possession – or some sort of

227 Section 27, Sch 2 of the Land Registration Act 2002; see also the Land Registration Rules 2003.

228 See the introductory remarks of Chapter 2 and *Cochrane v Moore* [1890] 25 QBD 57, esp 64–73 (Fry LJ).

229 Baker, English Legal History, 383–84, citing *Pynchoun v Geldeford* [1385] YB Hil 8 Ric II.

230 *Cochrane v Moore* [1890] 25 QBD 57, 67–70 (Fry LJ); Holdsworth, History of English Law, vol 3, 357–58.

constructive delivery of the goods – which entitled the transferee to sue in detinue.[231] Delivery (execution) of the deed might initially have been equated with delivery of the goods themselves.

If this is correct, it is arguable that the mode of transfer by deed is – similarly as transfers by sale – a genuine descendant from the original mode of transfer by delivery and that it has organically emerged from the latter by a gradual emancipation which eventually resulted in a complete exemption from the delivery requirement. That latter requirement was replaced by a requirement to deliver (execute) the deed. Besides that, however, transfers by deed are arguably not fundamentally different from transfers by delivery. A transfer by deed apparently still requires – just as transfers by delivery and transfers by sale do – a real intention of the transferor to transfer ownership and, at some point, a real intention of the transferee to receive ownership (real agreement). This also implies that the underlying structure of transfers by deed is still broadly the same as that of transfers by delivery and that they are, accordingly, also governed by a principle of separation and abstraction.

4.2. SCOPE OF TRANSFERS BY DEED

Theoretically, the scope of transfers by deed is all-embracing. Practically, however, it is minimal. Deeds may be used to transfer any chattels (goods or corporeal money) for consideration (money or non-money) or gratuitously.[232] Though this will almost never happen in practice, there seems to be nothing in theory which would preclude a transfer of corporeal money by deed and without delivery if the money has been sufficiently identified and separated, for example in an envelope.[233] Transfers by deed are available in any type of transaction – gifts, sales, barters and other exchange transactions – but a deed is never strictly required to transfer movable property. If there is consideration, the transfer may also be effected by mere intention, unless corporeal money is concerned, or by delivery. If there is no consideration, legal title may also pass by delivery, which is usually less cumbersome.

The practical relevance of transfers by deed in the context of personal property is even further curtailed by the fact that the other two modes of transfer – sale and delivery – are always *cumulatively* available.[234] If a transfer by

231 Holdsworth, History of English Law, vol 3, 357–58, citing *Dockeray's Case* [1536] YB 27 Hy VIII Trin; Holdsworth, History of English Law, vol 7, 507–8.

232 *Cochrane v Moore* [1890] 25 QBD 57.

233 See Fox, Property Rights, 3.45–47.

234 Cf (though only with regard to transfers by delivery and transfers by sale) Swadling, LQR 2005, 126–27, 141–42, 152; Häcker, Impaired Consent, 136–37, 194–96; Häcker, Causality and abstraction, 210–12.

deed is ineffective due to some formal defect, for example because the document has not been signed, property might still pass by mere intention (if goods are transferred for consideration) or by delivery (if and as soon as delivery has been made). Hence, a transfer by deed only ever becomes actually relevant if neither a transfer of goods for consideration is concerned, in which case property can pass by mere intention, nor delivery has been made.

4.3. REQUIREMENTS TO EFFECT A TRANSFER BY DEED

4.3.1. Drawing Up and Delivery of a Deed

In transfers by deed, the counterpart of the delivery requirement is the requirement that a deed must be drawn up and delivered in a formally correct way. Originally, the common law required that the deed was written on parchment or paper and that the person bound by it has sealed – individuals also had to sign it or place their marks on it – and delivered it.[235] The Law of Property (Miscellaneous Provisions) Act 1989[236] modified those requirements and particularly abolished any rules, which (i) limited the substances on which a deed may be written, which (ii) required a seal for deeds executed by individuals and which (iii) required authority to execute a deed on behalf of another to be given by deed (s 1(1)). It is now required that the document makes clear on its face that it is intended to be a deed (s 1(2)(a)) and that it is executed by the person bound by it or by his authorised agent (s 1(2)(b)). Execution of a deed by an individual[237] requires that it is signed by that person in the presence of a witness who attests the signature (or that it is signed at that person's direction and in his and two witnesses' presence who must both attest the signature) and that it is delivered by that person (s 1(3)).

The common law requirement of "delivery" to execute a deed still applies under the Law of Property (Miscellaneous Provisions) Act 1989. Delivery of a deed does not, however, require a physical handing over of possession of the deed – or of the transferred chattels – to the transferee. Rather, any act is sufficient by which the person bound by the deed (or his agent) evinces an intention that this shall be his deed and that he shall be bound by it. No special form is required. Delivery can be made by words, conduct or a physical handing

---

235 See generally Thompson, Halsbury's Laws of England, vol 32(2), paras 201, 227–31.

236 As amended by the Regulatory Reform (Execution of Deeds and Documents) Order 2005 (SI 2005/1906).

237 For an execution by companies and other persons, see Whittaker, Chitty on Contracts, vol 1, 1.126–27, 1.135–36.

over of the deed; but mere signature is insufficient.[238] Furthermore, delivery can be made conditionally (delivery as an escrow) in which case execution is only effected upon satisfaction of those conditions.[239] As opposed to transfers by delivery, where the transferee must at least have formed an intention to exercise *possession* over the chattel in question,[240] execution (delivery) of a deed does not, as such, require any knowledge of the transferee.[241]

4.3.2. Conveyance: Real Agreement

In contrast to registered land, a transfer of tangible movable property by deed does not, in principle, require registration. Execution of the deed is by itself effective as a conveyance. However, transfers by deed will generally come within the ambit of the Bills of Sale Act 1878 – except in the cases excluded by s 4 – and must, to be fully effective prior to delivery, comply with the formal requirements of the Act and be registered as a bill of sale (ss 8 and 10). Otherwise, the transfer will be void in the case of insolvency, i.e. ineffective against a trustee in bankruptcy, an assignee for the benefit of creditors or executing persons.

A transfer of property by deed requires – just as transfers by delivery and transfers by mere intention do – that the transferor has intended to pass legal ownership to the transferee; in addition, it is required that this intention is contained within the deed itself. The deed must state, explicitly or implicitly, that property in certain goods shall pass by the deed itself. A deed which merely expresses the desire to make a transfer or which merely imposes an obligation to convey a chattel will not by itself pass ownership.[242] In other words, the deed must contain a *conveyance*, whether or not coupled with an *obligation* to execute that transfer.

Furthermore, a transfer of property by deed also requires – at some point – an intention of the transferee to receive ownership. No one can be forced to accept property against his will. But the transferee's acceptance of ownership is

---

238 See *Xenos v Wickham* [1867] LR 2 HL 296 (HL); *Macedo v Stroud* [1922] 2 AC 330 (PC), 337 (Viscount Haldane); *Vincent v Premo Enterprises (Voucher Sales) Ltd* [1969] 2 QB 609 (CA), 619 (Lord Denning MR); *Silver Queen Maritime Ltd v Persia Petroleum Services plc* [2010] EWHC 2867 (QB), [107]–[114] (Lindblom J); *Bibby Financial Services Ltd v Magson* [2011] EWHC 2495 (QB), [335] (Seymour QC); see also Thompson, Halsbury's Laws of England, vol 32(2), para 231 (with further references).

239 Ibid; see also Thompson, Halsbury's Laws of England, vol 32(2), paras 237–39; Whittaker, Chitty on Contracts, vol 1, 1.140–41.

240 See fn 24 and text to it.

241 However, the transferee has an option to retrospectively repudiate the transfer of legal title; see Chapter 2 sections 1.3. and 4.3.2.

242 *IRC v G Angus & Co* [1889] 23 QBD 579 (CA); Newman, Halsbury's Laws of England, vol 52(2), para 232; cf also Häcker, Impaired Consent, 48 (fn 155).

not – just as with regard to transfers by delivery[243] – a constitutive requirement to *initially* effect the passage of property. Whereas a transfer by delivery at least requires that the transferee intends to exercise *possession* over the chattel in question,[244] there is no such requirement in transfers by deed to become effective. Property may pass by deed, in a first step, without any knowledge of the transferee thereof.[245] However, just as with regard to transfers by delivery,[246] the transferee is – upon becoming aware of it – entitled to *reject* the transfer of ownership with retrospective effects.[247] Rejection retroactively revests ownership in the transferor and relieves the transferee from any burdens and liabilities in connection with the chattel.

It follows that even transfers by deed are essentially bilateral acts. Similarly, as with regard to transfers by delivery and transfers by mere intention, the transferor's intention to transfer ownership, which must be contained within the deed itself, coupled with the requirement that the transferee must at some point, at least tacitly, accept the receipt of ownership, which need not be contained within a deed, may conveniently be called a *real agreement*.

4.4. PRINCIPLE OF SEPARATION: DEED MAY CONTAIN AN OBLIGATION AND/OR A CONVEYANCE

The principle of separation refers to the fact that a sharp distinction must be drawn between the underlying personal obligation to effect a transfer and the conveyance itself. According to the view adopted in this book, the principle of separation ought to apply not only with regard to transfers by delivery and transfers by mere intention but also with regard to transfers by deed.

A deed may basically contain three different things, namely (i) the creation or transfer (conveyance) of some proprietary interest, (ii) the creation of binding obligations and/or (iii) the confirmation of some act whereby some proprietary interest has passed.[248] Leaving aside the last item, the content of a deed may,

---

243 See Chapter 2 section 1.3.

244 See fn 24 and text to it.

245 See esp *Standing v Bowring* [1885] 31 ChD 282, 286 (Lord Halsbury LC), 288 (Cotton LJ), 289–90 (Lindley LJ); Hill, LQR 2001, 133–34; see also references in fn 247.

246 See Chapter 2 section 1.3.

247 *Butler and Baker's Case* [1591] 3 Co Rep 25; *Townson v Tickell* [1819] 3 B&A 31; *Standing v Bowring* [1885] 31 ChD 282, 286 (Lord Halsbury LC), 288 (Cotton LJ), 289–90 (Lindley LJ); *Re Birchall* [1889] 40 ChD 436 (CA); *Cochrane v Moore* [1890] 25 QBD 57, 75–76 (Lord Esher MR); *Re Paradise Motor* [1968] 1 WLR 1125; *R v Hinks* [2001] 2 AC 241, 266–67 (Lord Hobhouse); see also Thompson, Halsbury's Laws of England, vol 32(2), para 263, 274–75; Newman, Halsbury's Laws of England, vol 52(2), paras 249–50; Crago, UWALR 1999; Hill, LQR 2001; Bell, Personal Property, 221.

248 See (e.g.) *R v Morton* [1873] LR 2 CCR 22 (Crown Cases Reserved), 27 (Bovill CJ); *IRC v Angus* [1889] 23 QBD 579; Whittaker, Chitty on Contracts, vol 1, 1.120; Thompson, Halsbury's Laws of England, vol 32(2), para 201.

firstly, be limited to a personal *obligation* to effect a transfer of property without any conveyance already contained therein.[249] It may particularly contain a contract for consideration, in which case the deed must be executed by both parties, or a gratuitous obligation to make a gift. The latter is arguably not a contract strictly speaking but still an enforceable obligation.[250] Secondly, a deed may (and often does) contain *both*, a personal obligation to execute a transfer and a conveyance effecting that transfer. This requires that the deed states, explicitly or implicitly, that the transfer of the property right shall take effect by the deed itself.[251] Thirdly, it is possible that a deed only and exclusively contains a *conveyance* without any corresponding obligation to make such a transfer. This might for instance be the case if a mere obligation to carry out a transfer – without a conveyance – has already been created by a previous deed or if such an obligation has otherwise pre-existed (contractual, statutory or other obligation) and if the transferor decides to execute that transfer by deed.[252] It follows that the personal obligation to make a transfer and the conveyance itself are – even if contained within one and the same deed – two notionally distinct and separate elements.[253]

4.5. ABSTRACTION OR CAUSALITY?

The observation that an underlying obligation and the respective conveyance are two notionally distinct elements (principle of separation) paves the way for a principle of abstraction, i.e. that the conveyance's effectiveness is independent from an underlying obligation's existence or validity, but it does not dictate such a conclusion. In theory, causality would equally be possible. The preferable view, however, is that transfers of personal property by deed are abstract, just like transfers by delivery and transfers by mere intention.[254] Though there is apparently no unequivocal proof in the case law, there are still good reasons of principle militating in favour of such a view.

---

249 See *IRC v Angus* [1889] 23 QBD 579.

250 Thompson, Halsbury's Laws of England, vol 32(2), para 259 (fn 1 and 3); Bridge et al, Personal Property, 8.23; Treitel, Contract, 3.170; contra: Whittaker, Chitty on Contracts, vol 1, 1.143.

251 Cf *IRC v Angus* [1889] 23 QBD 579; Newman, Halsbury's Laws of England, vol 52(2), para 232; cf also Häcker, Impaired Consent, 48 (fn 155).

252 This is routinely the case in relation to transfers of legal estates or interests in land. In practice, the parties first draw up and conclude a written contract of sale; s 2 of the Law of Property (Miscellaneous Provisions) Act 1989. In relation to unregistered conveyancing, i.e. transfers of unregistered interests, conveyance is then effected (only) by deed; s 52(1) of the Law of Property Act 1925. In relation to registered conveyancing, it is additionally required that the conveyance by deed is registered at the Land Registry; s 25(1) and s 27, Sch 2 of the Land Registration Act 2002.

253 Holdsworth, History of English Law, vol 3, 357–58; *IRC v Angus* [1889] 23 QBD 579.

254 See also van Vliet, Transfer of movables, 118–19, 130.

First, the fact that a deed may contain only a conveyance but no corresponding personal obligation seems to be a compelling argument in favour of abstraction. The transferor might thereby for example give effect to a previously made (unenforceable) oral promise to give. Certainly, a deed *may* also contain an enforceable gratuitous obligation to make a gift (a so-called specialty) but that *need not* be so. A conveyance contained in a deed is effective even if there is no personal obligation – neither within nor outside the deed – to carry out the transfer in question. Similarly, there is nothing in theory which would preclude a transferor from effecting a payment or a transfer of goods by a deed, which only contains a conveyance, that turns out to have been a mistaken double or overpayment or a transfer to the wrong person. Such a conveyance would be effective to transfer legal title even though there is no underlying obligation whatsoever, provided that the respective chattels have been sufficiently identified and that the transferor has not laboured under a proprietarily fundamental mistake. Such a deed, that only contains a conveyance, would not create a personal obligation. Hence, the transferor may claim personal restitution in unjust enrichment if he acted under a causative mistake or, if the mistake was induced, revest ownership by rescission. That must also apply if the transfer by deed has been effected in pursuance of a void contract. Suppose that A and B conclude a contract, written or oral, under which A has to transfer money or goods to B for a consideration, and that the contract is void for some reason. If A then conveys such an amount of money or goods to B by deed, property still passes unless there is a real defect which (also) infects the conveyance by deed in the execution stage. The position is just the same as in the case where A delivers the chattel to B after having concluded a void contract.

Second, the law of rescission provides the same compelling arguments in favour of abstraction in transfers by deed as it does in the context of transfers by sale.[255] As O'Sullivan, Elliott and Zakrzewski have pointed out, an obligation contained in a deed – whether a contract or an enforceable gratuitous promise – can be rescinded for the same reasons and in the same way as in the context of oral or written contracts. This applies even with regard to rescission at common law[256]

---

255 See Chapter 2 section 2.3.3.

256 With regard to rescission *in equity*, O'SULLIVAN et al, Rescission, 11.56–108, advocate the view that equitable rescission – whether of an oral or a written contract or of an obligation contained within a deed – can only ever be effected by a constitutive court order. The orthodox and preferable view, however, is that equitable rescission may generally be effected extra-judicially; see (e.g.) *Abram Steamship Co Ltd v Westville Shipping Co Ltd* [1923] AC 773 (HL), 781 (Lord Atkinson); *Reese River Silver Mining Co Ltd v Smith* [1869] LR 4 HL 64 (HL), 73–75 (Lord Hatherley LC); *TSB Bank plc v Camfield* [1995] 1 WLR 430 (CA), 438–39 (Roch LJ); *Brotherton v Aseguradora Colseguros SA (No 2)* [2003] EWCA Civ 705, [2003] 2 CLC 629, [27], [45]-[48] (Bayley J); *Bristol and West Building Society v Mothew* [1998] Ch 1 (CA), 22–23 (Millett LJ); ZOGG, Proprietary Consequences, Chapter 4 section 2.1.2;

for fraud or duress.[257] If a deed only contains an obligation or a contract, the victim only obtains a personal power to rescind that obligation or contract. If the deed contains both, an obligation or contract *and* a conveyance, the victim *additionally* obtains a power in rem to revest ownership, i.e. to undo the conveyance contained within the deed, at law and/or in equity. These two powers are notionally distinct and independent of each other; the victim may exercise only one or both of them.[258] If the deed only contains a conveyance, the victim only obtains a power in rem to revest ownership. In so far, there is no structural difference between voidable transfers by deed and voidable transfers by mere intention or delivery.

If this is correct, the true reason for the revesting of ownership upon rescission cannot lie in the fact that an underlying contract or obligation has been avoided. The revesting of property upon rescission is not a "causal mechanism" triggered by the underlying contract's avoidance. This applies whether the deed only contains a conveyance or also an obligation or a contract. Apart from that, causality in the transfer by deed might lead to unequal and unjustifiable results if, for example, a sale transaction has exceptionally been effected by deed. Rescission of the deed by a defrauded seller would not confer any proprietary rights on the fraudulent buyer (since a transfer of money by delivery is abstract), whereas rescission by a defrauded buyer would, *ex hypothesi*, revest legal title in the goods to the fraudulent seller (at least if delivery has not yet been made).[259] This seems wrong in principle. Moreover, causality in transfers by deed could impossibly explain why – as it is indubitably the position in English law – rescission in equity only revests equitable but not also legal ownership. Equitable rescission of an obligation contained in a deed has the effect of avoiding the obligation altogether, even at law (fusion on the obligatory level); and this would – if the transfer were indeed causal – again mean that legal title would equally revest upon equitable rescission. But this is not the case.[260] A principle of causality and a view that legal title in goods transferred by deed revests automatically upon and by rescission of the contract or obligation *as such* (as contained in the deed) would also encounter difficulties in explaining the effects of rescission in relation to third parties. It would not be self-evident why third-party recipients

---

Bridge et al, Personal Property, 15.78; Beale, Chitty on Contracts, vol 1, 7.120; Treitel, Contract, 9.94–95; Worthington, RLR 2002, 31–32; Bant, OJLS 2012, 475–80; Burrows, Restitution, 17; contra: J. O'Sullivan, CLJ 2000; Elliott, Snell's Equity, 15.12; Virgo, Equity, 639–40; Virgo, Restitution, 23.

257 O'Sullivan et al, Rescission, 29.63–86; see also Thompson, Halsbury's Laws of England, vol 32(2), paras 267–68.

258 Cf Chapter 2 section 2.3.3.

259 Cf text to fn 140–144.

260 Cf text to fn 145–147.

would be bound by the transferor's *personal* power to rescind the deed (contract or obligation).[261]

Third, the historical development of the deed exception, as previously explained,[262] militates in favour of abstraction. Originally, chattels could only be conveyed upon and by delivery. The transfer of legal title by deed, which apparently developed in the 14th or 15th century, is arguably a genuine descendant from the original mode of transfer by delivery. Delivery of the deed might initially have been equated with delivery of the goods – as some form of a constructive delivery – and it appears that execution of a deed initially resulted in a fiction of possession of the transferee, by way of some form of a constructive bailment.[263] In so far, it is arguable that the actual delivery requirement was gradually exempted from in transfers by deed but that the other requirements and the nature of the transfer as such were left unaffected, namely the requirement of a real agreement and the fact that the conveyance is effective without a corresponding obligation.

Fourth, abstraction in transfers by deed leads to a coherent overall picture of transfers of movable chattels in general. A transfer of legal ownership by delivery is certainly abstract and it has been argued that transfers by sale are equally abstract. Also, equity broadly operates on an abstract basis.[264]

However, it is crucial to note that abstraction does not, of course, mean that transfers of legal title by deed are always effective if an underlying obligation is void or inexistent; that would be absurd. There may be *dual defects* which do not only affect an obligation or a contract, contained within a deed, but which equally infect the conveyance, as purportedly effected by the deed. This is plainly the case with regard to formal defects which affect the validity of the deed as such, for example lack of form, lack of execution, forgery or non est factum. Furthermore, a real defect may – even if the deed is formally valid as such – still substantively affect the parties' real agreement, particularly the transferor's intention to transfer ownership. The main examples are proprietarily fundamental mistakes. In such a case, the formally valid deed does still not operate to transfer legal ownership, even if it is not formally cancelled. Transfers by deed are dependent on an effective real intention of the transferor to carry out the transfer in question; they are *abstract* but *not* "*super-abstract*".[265]

---

261 Cf text to fn 148–149.

262 See the introductory remarks of Chapter 2 and Chapter 2 section 4.1.

263 Cf Holdsworth, History of English Law, vol 3, 357–58.

264 See text to fn 154.

265 The term of "super-abstraction" will be used to denote the fact that a certain mode of transfer is not only independent (abstract) from an underlying personal obligation but even independent ("super-abstract") from a real intention of the transferor to execute the very transfer in question.

5. TRANSFER OF LEGAL TITLE BY REGISTRATION (A BRIEF OVERVIEW)

5.1. TRANSFER OF REGISTERED LEGAL ESTATES IN LAND: "SUPER-ABSTRACT" TRANSFER

Statutes may deviate from the rules of transfer of property as set out above. They might in particular provide that legal ownership may only pass by registration in relation to certain kinds of assets. The most prominent example is the transfer of registered[266] legal estates or interests in land. Though transfers of real property are beyond the scope of this book, this is an example of a statute providing for different and new rules governing the transfer of a certain kind of property. It furthermore illustrates that transfers effected by registration may not only be *abstract*, i.e. independent from an underlying personal obligation, but even what may conveniently be called "*super-abstract*", i.e. independent from an effective or apparent real intention of the transferor to execute the transfer in question.[267]

According to s 27 of the Land Registration Act 2002, registered estates can only be transferred by registration. The transfer is not operative unless and until the required registration has been made.[268] On the other hand, registration as proprietor of a legal estate is – once made[269] – absolutely conclusive. According to s 58 of the Land Registration Act 2002, if a person is registered as proprietor of a legal estate which would not otherwise, but for registration, have vested in that person, the estate shall still be *deemed* to have vested in that person as a result of registration. In other words, registration is *by itself* effective to vest legal estate in the registered person even if it was, for example, made without an underlying obligation or according to a transaction which was a nullity or if it was made wholly by mistake of the registrar or even if it was obtained by forged documents and by fraud on the registrar. Registration is effective even if it is

266 The possibility or requirement of first registration is governed by ss 3 et seq of the Land Registration Act 2002 (formerly by the Land Registration Act 1925); today, most legal estates or interests are registered.

267 Closely connected with this, transfers of registered legal estates are an example where common law rescission may not operate to automatically revest *legal* ownership; rather, equity must intervene by its auxiliary jurisdiction to revest equitable ownership; see Zogg, Proprietary Consequences, Chapter 4 section 2.2.3.1. Similarly, retention of equitable ownership due to a complete lack of intention to execute the transfer in question may – since legal title passes regardless of intention – without more lead to an immediate resulting trust; ibid, Chapter 3 section 2.1. and generally Chapter 3 section 1.

268 See also s 25(1) and Sch 2 of the Land Registration Act 2002 and generally the Land Registration Rules 2003.

269 Certainly, a registrar will not make registration unless being convinced that the transferee, who must make the respective application in the correct form and who must submit the instrument of transfer and any other relevant documents, is indeed entitled to the registration. However, once made, registration is – until rectified – super-abstractly effective.

made without any intention – even if wholly without knowledge – of the legal owner.[270] Transfers by registration are, accordingly, not only abstract but even *super-abstract*.

A good example is the case of *Collings v Lee*[271] which concerned a transfer of a legal estate under a proprietarily fundamental mistake which would – but for the "statutory magic"[272] of registration – have prevented legal ownership from passing. A couple tried to sell their house and employed an agent (Lee) for that purpose. Lee soon after told them that he had found a buyer, called Styles, who would be ready to buy for £250,000. In fact, however, that buyer was actually Lee himself and the name Styles was merely an alias. "Styles" was registered as the proprietor at the Land Registry and the Court of Appeal apparently assumed that registration of "Styles" as proprietor was just the same as if "Lee" had been registered (this being his alias).[273] Legal estate passed to Lee by way of super-abstract registration. However, Nourse LJ held that *equitable* ownership had been retained by the couple since their fundamental mistake as to the transferee's identity had completely negatived their intention to dispose of their equitable interest which meant that Lee had received legal estate on an immediate resulting trust for the couple.[274] Apart from that, the former legal owner, whose legal estate has been transferred away without his intention to do so, might in

---

270 See (e.g.) *Collings v Lee* [2001] 2 All ER 332 (CA); *Malory Enterprises Ltd v Cheshire Homes (UK) Ltd* [2002] EWCA Civ 151, [2002] Ch 216, [64]–[65] (Arden LJ); *Fitzwilliam v Richall Holdings Services Ltd* [2013] EWHC 86 (Ch), [2013] 1 P&CR 19; *Farakh Rashid v Teyub Nasrullah* [2018] EWCA Civ 2685, [56]–[57] (Lewison LJ); Harpum, Registered Land; Hill-Smith, CPL 2009; Burn/Cartwright, Cheshire and Burn's Modern Law of Real Property, 1079–80; Harpum et al, Megarry & Wade, The Law of Real Property, 7.115–17.

271 *Collings v Lee* [2001] 2 All ER 332.

272 *Argyle Building Society v Hammond* [1985] 49 P&CR 148 (CA), 153 (Slade LJ).

273 *Collings v Lee* [2001] 2 All ER 332, [10]–[13] (Nourse LJ).

274 See also *Malory Enterprises v Cheshire Homes* [2002] EWCA Civ 151, [64]-[65] (Arden LJ) (applied in *Fitzwilliam v Richall Holdings Services* [2013] EWHC 86 (Ch) with regard to the Land Registration Act 2002), where a fraudster managed to obtain registration of a transfer of a registered legal estate to a good faith purchaser without the former owner's knowledge; it was similarly held that legal estate had passed but that the former owner had retained equitable ownership (that decision is, however, questionable on another point, namely that the forged transfer had not been regarded as a disposition allowing a priority protection under what is now s 29 of the Land Registration Act 2002; in so far, the author fully agrees with the remarks of Hill-Smith, CPL 2009). The view that equitable ownership had been retained in this case was criticised (for example by Harpum, Registered Land, 195–202; Harpum et al, Megarry & Wade, The Law of Real Property, 7.115–17), mainly on the basis that what is today s 58 confers both, legal and equitable title, on the registered transferee. The better view, however, is – as Hill-Smith, CPL 2009, 133–35, has rightly observed – that s 58 only provides for a super-abstract transfer of legal but not also of equitable title (in contrast to s 11 regarding first registration) and that extinction of equitable title can only be obtained by way of s 29. If there is no statutory provision which provides that equitable title is equally transferred super-abstractly, it is – as a result of the absence of a sufficient intention of the transferor to dispose of it – retained under an immediate resulting trust; see Zogg, Proprietary Consequences, Chapter 5 section 5.1.3; cf also *Farakh Rashid v Teyub Nasrullah* [2018] EWCA Civ 2685, [56]–[58] (Lewison LJ).

some cases also be entitled to alter or rectify – with prospective effects[275] – the register in accordance with s 65 and Sch 4 of the Land Registration Act 2002.[276]

5.2. REGISTRATION REQUIREMENTS IN TRANSFERS OF PERSONAL PROPERTY: SHARES AND BRITISH SHIPS

The super-abstract transfer of a registered legal estate by registration has two main features: (i) Legal title may not pass unless and until registration has been made (s 27 of the Land Registration Act 2002); and (ii) legal title is – in any case and however defective the transfer may have been – deemed to have passed if and because registration has been made (s 58 of the Land Registration Act 2002). In relation to personal property, there are two particular kinds of chattels where a general registration requirement exists, namely shares and British ships. Transfers of those kinds of property *may* but *need not* share either of the two mentioned features of transfers of registered legal estates. They may also share none or only one of them.

Regarding shares,[277] certificated or uncertificated, it is apparently uncontroversial that legal title may generally only pass by a constitutive registration of the transferee as owner in the company's register of members.[278] However, it appears that a transfer of shares by registration is not, at least not in its fullest sense, "super-abstract". The entry in the register of members is – though being a constitutive requirement to acquire the shares – merely prima facie evidence (s 127 of the Companies Act 2006) but not absolutely conclusive.[279]

---

275 Paragraph 8 of Sch 4 of the Land Registration Act 2002.

276 Rectification may be made by the court or the registrar inter alia to correct a mistake (paras 2(1)(a) and 5(a) of Sch 4); however, if the transferee is already in possession, this is only possible if he consents, if he has fraudulently or negligently caused or contributed to the mistake or if it would otherwise be unjust if rectification were not made (paras 3(2) and 6(2) of Sch 4); see Hill-Smith, CPL 2009, 129, 133–40; Burn/Cartwright, Cheshire and Burn's Modern Law of Real Property, 1080–2; Harpum et al, Megarry & Wade, The Law of Real Property, 7.131–39; R. Smith, Property Law, 279–88; cf also *NRAM Ltd v Evans* [2017] EWCA Civ 1013.

277 There is a special provision for bearer shares (s 122(3) of the Companies Act 2006) according to which legal title may be deemed to have passed off the register if the company's articles so provide.

278 See (e.g.) *Société Générale de Paris v Walker* [1885] 11 App Cas 20 (HL); *Enviroco Ltd v Farstad Supply A/S* [2011] UKSC 16, [2011] 1 WLR 921, [37]–[39] (Lord Collins): "[It is] a fundamental principle of United Kingdom company law [that], except where express provision is made to the contrary, the person on the register of the members is the member to the exclusion of any other person, unless and until the register is rectified. [...] [M]embership [is] determined by entry on the register of members. [...] [T]he legislation makes it clear that the member is the person on the register, and where it is necessary to apply the legislation to persons who are not on the register, special provision is made"; Davies/Worthington, Gower's Principles of Modern Company Law, ch 27, esp 27.5.

279 *Reese River Silver Mining v Smith* [1869] LR 4 HL 64, 80 (Lord Cairns).

It appears that, for example in a forged but registered transfer, the former owner retains legal title throughout and that he is entitled to a merely declaratory rectification of the register.[280]

Regarding registered British ships,[281] the position is less clear. A transfer of such a ship must, unless it results in the ship ceasing to have a British connection, be effected by a bill of sale[282] and registered at her port of registry.[283] Yet, the exact effects of such registration are not quite clear. On the one hand, there is ambiguous authority[284] with regard to the question whether the buyer might obtain legal title by way of the bill of sale even prior to registration being made, thus whether or not registration is a formal and constitutive requirement to obtain title (as in the case of shares and legal estates).[285] On the other hand, it appears that – notwithstanding the wording of para 1(1) of Sch 1 of the Merchant Shipping Act 1995[286] – the register is, once registration has been made, only prima facie evidence but not absolutely conclusive as to the passage of legal title.[287] Hence, it seems that this kind of transfer is not super-abstract and that any rectification of the register is only declaratory in nature. Apart from that, there is no doubt that equitable interests in British ships may arise or pass off the register.[288]

We need not pursue these matters further. It suffices to note that registration is, at least in principle, required to transfer legal title in British ships and that it is at least possible that registration is a constitutive requirement in that regard but that it is rather unlikely that registration, once made, super-abstractly transfers legal title to the registered person.

---

280 See Davies/Worthington, Gower's Principles of Modern Company Law, ch 27, esp 27.5.

281 In the sense of s 1 of the Merchant Shipping Act 1995.

282 In the form as prescribed by reg 44 of the Merchant Shipping (Registration of Ships) Regulations 1993, SI 1993/3138.

283 Section 16(1), Sch 1, para 2 of the Merchant Shipping Act 1995.

284 Very instructive is the Australian authority of *Tisand Pty Ltd v The Owners of the Ship MV Cape Moreton (Ex Freya)* [2005] FCAFC 68 (FC of Australia), [152]–[159] (concerned with the similar Australian statutory counterpart); for English authorities, see esp *Stapleton v Haymen* [1864] 2 H&C 918, 159 ER 380 (cf the conflicting views of Pollock CB and Martin B); cf also *The Spirit of the Ocean* [1865] B&C 336, 167 ER 388; *The Two Ellens* [1871] LR 3 A&E 345 (HC of Admiralty), 354–55 (Sir Phillimore); *Hughes v Sutherland* [1881] 7 QBD 160 (QBD); *The Evpo Agnic* [1988] 1 WLR 1090 (CA), 1096 (Lord Donaldson MR); *The Tjaskemolen (now named Visvliet) (No 1)* [1997] CLC 521 (QBD); *Dornoch Ltd v Westminster International BV* [2009] EWHC 889 (Admlty), [98], [103] (Tomlinson J).

285 The wording of Sch 1, para 2 of the Merchant Shipping Act 1995 rather militates in favour of a transfer of legal title by the bill of sale and off the register; but cf Sch 1, para 1(1) and 1(2) (the latter *e contrario*).

286 "Subject to any rights and powers appearing from the register to be vested in any other person, the *registered owner* of a ship or of a share in a ship *shall have power absolutely to dispose of it* provided the disposal is made in accordance with this Schedule and registration regulations" (emphases added).

287 *Parrott v Parkin (The Up Yaws)* [2007] EWHC 210 (Admlty), [18] (Aikens J).

288 Schedule 1, para 1(2) of the Merchants Shipping Act 1995; cf also the references in fn 284 and 287.

CHAPTER 3

DEFECTS WHICH PREVENT THE PASSAGE OF LEGAL OWNERSHIP

In the previous chapter, we have examined the mechanics of how legal title may be transferred from one person to another. There are basically three different modes of transfer, namely delivery, sale and deed. What is common to all of them – "super-abstract" transfers by registration apart – is that, on the one hand, a sufficient intention of the transferor to transfer legal ownership is necessary and that, on the other hand, the transferee's acceptance of ownership is at some point required. This *real agreement* is the minimum requirement to convey legal title in tangible chattels, though conveyance may have further requirements, such as delivery or the execution of a deed. The mentioned modes of transfer have equally in common that conveyance is distinct and independent from an underlying contract or obligation (principle of separation and abstraction).

In this and in the next chapter, we shall now analyse certain types of defects – particularly mistakes – with regard to the question whether they are serious enough to prevent the passage of legal ownership. As a result of the mentioned similarities between transfers by sale, transfers by delivery and transfers by deed, this inquiry can broadly be made without reference to any particular mode of transfer. The principles elaborated in the following chapters accordingly apply to all of them.

Real defects, i.e. defects which prevent the passage of property, may basically operate in two different ways. They may either negative a *transferor's* intention to transfer property or they may negative a *transferee's* intention to accept the receipt of ownership.[1] Since the latter, however, only very rarely occurs in practice,[2] our focus shall lie on cases where defects infected the transferor's intention to pass property. Real defects may already occur in the *formation stage*, affecting the parties' initial real agreement (often expressed *uno actu* with the

1 If property has only passed provisionally (subject to the transferee's rejection; see Chapter 2 section 1.3.) and if the transferee's subsequent acceptance or rejection has been ineffective by reason of a fundamental defect in his intention, legal title apparently still remains vested in him but he may still reject the transfer (which he must do as soon as the defect has disappeared; see Crago, UWALR 1999, 76–78).

2 An example might be the case of *Hardman v Booth* [1863] All ER Rep Ext 1847, 158 ER 1107; see Chapter 2 fn 78.

conclusion of a corresponding obligatory contract), or – also or only – in the *execution stage*, affecting a party's real intention to carry out a conveyancing act, such as delivery.[3]

It will be recalled that the range of real defects, which prevent the passage of property, is *narrower* than the range of obligatory defects, which affect the validity of a contract.[4] A defect which is not serious enough to render a contract void may not prevent the passage of legal ownership. A defect which may not entirely negative the parties' contractual agreement may neither entirely negative their real agreement. Two things seem to follow: First, a defect allegedly rendering the real agreement/conveyance void at law must – if it has already existed in the formation stage – at least be able to render the contract equally void. Second, if no (apparent) contract has been concluded at all or if the defect has only occurred in the execution stage, but not yet existed at the time of the contract's (purported) conclusion, the defect must at least be of such nature that it would *hypothetically* have rendered a contract void (had one been concluded or had the defect already existed at the time of its conclusion).

Real defect cases, i.e. cases where legal ownership is retained *ab initio*, may accordingly only occur in one of the three following scenarios, namely (i) in transfers carried out under void contracts or void gifts, (ii) in transfers carried out without any basis whatsoever, such as double or overpayments or deliveries to the wrong person, and (iii) in transfers where the relevant real defect has only occurred in the execution stage (whether there being a valid, voidable, unenforceable or a void contract).

We shall not consider all possible kinds of defects which might potentially prevent the passage of property. Our focus will lie on the most difficult one, namely mistake. Apart from that, three rather straightforward categories shall be briefly considered, namely complete absence of intention (theft, loss and misappropriation), lack of authority and fundamental duress. It must be noted that those categories are not conclusive and that there may be other defects – for example illegality[5] or incapacity[6] – which could potentially prevent the passage of property *ab initio*.

---

3 See Chapter 1 section 3.

4 See Chapter 1 section 2.1.1.2.

5 Yet, it emerges from the cases cited in Chapter 2 section 2.3.2. that illegality does not generally prevent the passage of property. An exception seems to apply if the transfer of property (conveyance) is illegal *as such*, namely if a statute not only attacks the contract but also or only the transfer of property to or its receipt by the transferee; see (e.g.) *Singh v Kulubya* [1964] AC 142 (PC) (Buganda and Uganda statutes prohibiting non-Africans to obtain land without permission); *Joe v Young* [1964] NZLR 24 (CA of New Zealand) (NZ statute providing that not only the contract but also the conveyance shall be of no effect; cf now generally s 6 of the Illegal Contracts Act (NZ)); see also Enonchong, LQR 1995, esp 144–46; Prentice, Chitty on Contracts, vol 1, 16.218; Bridge et al, Benjamin's Sale of Goods, 3.30.

6 Under the present state of the law, incapacity only rarely renders contracts void. As far as this is not the case, it may neither prevent the passage of property. Regarding natural persons,

By contrast, defects which only render contracts *voidable* cannot completely negative the parties' real agreement. It follows that for example fraudulently or innocently induced non-fundamental mistakes (misrepresentation), non-fundamental duress or undue influence may not prevent the passage of property to the guilty party *ab initio* (subject to rescission). Those kinds of defects only entitle the aggrieved party to revest ownership (legal or equitable) by exercising a newly imposed power in rem.[7] Even less may defects which merely render contracts *terminable de futuro* prevent property from passing.

1. COMPLETE ABSENCE OF INTENTION: THEFT, LOSS AND MISAPPROPRIATION

It may be all too obvious to mention the fact that property in tangible movable chattels does not pass if the legal owner A has never, not even apparently, intended to transfer legal ownership to B, particularly if he is wholly unaware of the "transfer". There is simply no real agreement in such a case. The most evident example is theft (in the narrow sense of taking without the owner's knowledge rather than in the broader criminal law sense[8]). If a thief (B) takes possession

contracts are only void if concluded by very young children (*Johnson v Clark* [1908] 1 303 (ChD), 311–12 (Parker J); *R v Oldham MBC Ex p Garlick* [1992] 24 HLR 726 (CA), 741–42 (Scott LJ) (affd on this point in [1993] AC 509 (HL)); Fox, Property Rights, 4.52; Whittaker, Chitty on Contracts, vol 1, 9.6) or if made in the absence of mental capacity and subject to the Court of Protection's jurisdiction under the Mental Capacity Act 2005 (*Masterman-Lister v Jewell* [2002] EWCA Civ 1889, [2003] 1 WLR 1511, [57] (Chadwick LJ); Fox, Property Rights, 4.42–50; but cf Treitel, Contract, 12.52–63). Regarding corporations, the common law *ultra vires* doctrine, which rendered contracts void, is today only very narrowly applicable (see s 39(1) of the Companies Act 2006); it only applies to charities (s 42), public authorities (but cf now the Local Government (Contracts) Act 1997) and corporations incorporated by special statutes. But even as far as it does apply, it seems that it only prevents the passage of property if the transaction has been *ultra vires* the *transferor* (*Auckland Harbour Board v The King* [1924] AC 318 (PC), 326–27 (Viscount Haldane); *Woolwich Equitable Building Society v IRC* [1993] AC 70 (HL), 177 (Lord Goff); *Tauranga Borough v Tauranga Electric Power Board* [1944] NZLR 155 (CA of New Zealand), 228–29 (Myers CJ)) but not if it has been *ultra vires* the *transferee* (*Ayers v The South Australian Banking Co* [1871] LR 3 PC 548 (PC), 559 (Mellish LJ); *Westdeutsche Landesbank Girozentrale v Islington LBC* [1996] AC 669 (HL), esp 689–90 (Lord Goff); *Exchange Bank of Canada v Fletcher* [1891] 19 SCR 278 (SC of Canada), [21] (Patterson J); *Trades Hall Co v Erie Tobacco Co* [1916] 29 DLR 779 (CA of Manitoba), [22] (Perdue JA), [61], [65] (Cameron JA), but cf [1]–[8] (Howell CJM, Richards JA agreeing)). See also Millett, LQR 1998, 410–11; Fox, Property Rights, 4.31–36.

7 See generally on the effects of rescission Zogg, Proprietary Consequences, Chapter 4 section 2.2; O'Sullivan et al, Rescission, esp chs 13–18; Cartwright, Misrepresentation, ch 4.

8 Theft has a much broader meaning in modern criminal law (s 1(1) of the Theft Act 1968); the offence of theft is today possible even if property has passed to the defendant; see s 5(4); *R v Gomez* [1993] AC 442 (HL); Fox, Property Rights, 4.74, 4.90.

of A's property without the latter's consent, B will only obtain a possessory legal title[9] but legal ownership will remain vested in A.[10] If B later transfers the chattel to a third party, the *nemo dat* rule applies, subject to exceptions, particularly in relation to money.

Very similar is the case where A has lost possession of the chattel in question. Loss of possession does not result in a loss of ownership. If a finder takes possession of the chattel, he merely obtains a possessory legal title but legal ownership remains vested in A.[11]

But even if A intentionally transfers *possession* to B under a bailment, for example on terms of hire, loan, deposit or a pledge, B only obtains a possessory legal title,[12] even if he appropriates the chattel and decides to forthwith possess as owner. Legal *ownership* still remains vested in A since he has never had an intention to transfer it to B.[13]

2. LACK OF AUTHORITY

Closely connected with the category of complete absence of intention is the category of lack of authority. A thief, whether selling in his own name or in the name of the true owner, has no authority to bind the latter and to transfer the latter's property. The same applies with regard to agents purporting to sell and transfer their principals' property to third parties if acting without or beyond their respective authority.[14]

An agent who disposes of the principal's property, whether disclosed or not, and transfers it to a third party is able to bind the principal and to effect a transfer of legal ownership if he acts within his *actual authority* (express or implied).[15] The same applies if the principal has *ratified* the disposition or if

---

9 *Costello v Chief Constable of Derbyshire Constabulary* [2001] EWCA Civ 381, [2001] 1 WLR 1437.

10 *Miller v Race* [1758] 1 Burr 452, 97 ER 398; *Neate v Harding* [1851] 6 Ex 349, 155 ER 577; *Shalson v Russo* [2003] EWHC 1637 (Ch), [2005] Ch 281, [110] (Rimer J); *Ilich v R* [1987] 162 CLR 110 (HC of Australia), 128 (Wilson, Dawson JJ); Fox, Property Rights, 4.82–91; Virgo, Restitution, 571–73.

11 *Armory v Delamirie* [1722] 1 Str 505, 93 ER 664; *Holiday v Sigil* [1826] 2 Car & P 176, 172 ER 81; *Moffatt v Kazana* [1969] 2 QB 152 (Assizes (Nottingham)); *Parker v British Airways Board* [1982] 1 QB 1004 (CA); see generally Hickey, Finders.

12 Goode, Commercial Law, 2.40–47.

13 Maitland, Equity, 46–47; *MCC Proceeds Inc v Lehman Bros International (Europe)* [1998] 4 All ER 675 (CA); *Re Bond Worth Ltd* [1980] Ch 228 (ChD), 247 (Slade J); *Morris v CW Martin & Sons Ltd* [1966] 1 QB 716 (CA), 738 (Salmon LJ).

14 The same also applies where an agent without authority purports to *accept* the receipt of property on behalf of a principal; cf *Hardman v Booth* [1863] All ER Rep Ext 1847; see Chapter 2 fn 78.

15 Bowstead/Reynolds, Agency, 8.126–27 and ch 3 (generally on express and implied authority).

the agent has acted with *apparent authority* – whether on the basis of usual authority, as normally granted to agents in the respective position, or by way of some representation made by the principal to the third party – provided that the third party has acted without notice of the agent's lack of actual authority.[16] In other words, an agent's disposition of the principal's property is, in principle, ineffective to transfer legal ownership if the disposition in question has been completely unauthorised or beyond the agent's actual authority, unless the principal has ratified it or unless the agent has acted with apparent authority and the transferee without notice. If the disposition is ineffective in that sense, the principal retains legal ownership unless some other *nemo dat* exception applies.[17] This general principle is repeated in s 21(1) of the SGA 1979.[18]

The exact requirements and the scope of the doctrines of actual and apparent authority or ratification need not be set out here; they may be found elsewhere.[19] It suffices to note that *if* property of another is disposed of by a purported agent without sufficient authority (actual or apparent or by ratification), legal ownership is retained by the former owner unless some other *nemo dat* exception applies.

Two further remarks may be added: First, if an agent has actual authority to carry out a certain act but if he acts otherwise than for the principal's benefit, particularly if in furtherance of his own interests, or if he has obtained the authority by fraud on the principal, his acts are – in general – still *outside* the actual authority provided by the principal.[20] It follows that a third party

16 See (e.g.) *Pickering v Busk* [1812] 15 East 38, 104 ER 758 (unauthorised sale by a broker of hemp which lay at a wharf and for which he was named as owner in the books of the wharfinger; held that the broker had apparent authority); *Quinn v CC Automotive Group Ltd* [2010] EWCA Civ 1412 (unauthorised sale of a car by a fraudulent employee; held that the employee had apparent authority by being allowed to act within the owner's showrooms); Bowstead/Reynolds, Agency, 8.126–38 and 3.4–5, 8.10–64 (on apparent authority in general), 2.47–98 (on ratification in general).

17 There are various *nemo dat* exceptions in the context of lack of authority: Estoppel (s 21(1) of the SGA 1979), dispositions by mercantile agents (s 2 of the Factors Act 1889), dispositions by sellers in possession (s 24 of the SGA 1979, s 8 of the Factors Act 1889), dispositions by buyers in possession (s 25 of the SGA 1979, s 9 of the Factors Act 1889); see generally Bridge et al, Benjamin's Sale of Goods, ch 7; Bowstead/Reynolds, Agency, 8.126–58.

18 "Subject to this Act, where goods are sold by a person who is not their owner, and who does not sell them under the authority or with the consent of the owner, the buyer acquires no better title to the goods than the seller had [...]."

19 See esp Bowstead/Reynolds, Agency.

20 *Hopkins v TL Dallas Group Ltd* [2004] EWHC 1379 (Ch), [87]–[89] (Lightman J); *Criterion Properties plc v Stratford UK Properties LLC* [2004] UKHL 28, [2004] 1 WLR 1846, [31] (Lord Scott); *Architects of Wine Ltd v Barclays Bank plc* [2006] EWHC 1648 (QB), [14]–[19] (Steele J) (revd on other grounds in [2007] EWCA Civ 239); *Parti v Al Sabah* [2007] EWHC 1869 (Ch), [44]–[50] (Smith J); *Lysaght Bros & Co Ltd v Falk* [1905] 2 CLR 421 (HC of Australia), 429–32 (Griffith CJ), 439 (O'Connor J); cf also *Pilgram v Rice-Smith* [1977] 1 WLR 671 (Div Ct), 675 (Lord Widgery CJ); *Rolled Steel Products (Holdings) Ltd v British Steel Co* [1986] Ch 246 (CA), 306–7 (Browne-Wilkinson LJ); see esp Bowstead/Reynolds, Agency, 3.8–10; contra: *Macmillan Inc v Bishopsgate Investment Trust plc (No 3)* [1995]

transferee may, in such a case, only obtain legal title if the agent has acted with apparent authority,[21] if the principal has ratified the act or if the third party may rely on a *nemo dat* exception other than s 23 of the SGA 1979 which is inapplicable in such a case.[22]

Second, the position is quite similar with regard to companies.[23] The *ultra vires* doctrine, which rendered acts outside the companies' objects void for lack of capacity, has been abolished for most companies by s 39 of the Companies Act 2006. But it is still possible that a director or other person acting on behalf of the company – which is itself taken to have unrestricted *capacity* – has *no authority* to do so. As a general rule, the orthodox agency principles apply. A director or other person may have actual authority to bind the company, which is conferred on him by the companies' constitution or by some internal rules or decisions. If he has no such actual authority and if the act is not ratified, he might still have apparent authority based on the usual authority of a person in his position or based on some representations attributable to the company;[24] but this requires that the third-party acts without notice of the lack of actual authority. In addition to those common law principles, there is a statutory protection (s 40) conferred on third parties, other than company directors or persons associated with them (s 41), who deal with directors in good faith and without notice of their lack of authority. If s 40 applies, a director's – but not another person's – restriction of actual authority is ignored as far as contained in the company's constitution (articles, resolutions or agreements; s 40(3)).[25]

Accordingly, if a director transfers property of the company either with actual authority or, if not ratified, with apparent authority or under s 40 to a good faith transferee, legal ownership will pass. Otherwise the company will

---

1 WLR 978 (ChD), 984 (Millett J) (affd without considering this issue in [1996] 1 WLR 387 (CA)); cf also *Whitehorn Bros v Davison* [1911] 1 KB 463 (CA), 479–80 (Buckley LJ). If this is correct, there is a serious difference between the case where B defrauds A to transfer property to him which he then sells to C (in which case s 23 of the SGA 1979 applies) and the case where B defrauds A to equip him with authority to transfer title directly to C (in which case there is no actual authority of B, s 23 of the SGA being inapplicable). In the latter case, C might only obtain legal ownership if B has acted with apparent authority, if A is otherwise estopped from denying C's acquisition of title or if some other *nemo dat* exception applies. This is much narrower than C's protection under s 23 of the SGA.

21 The agent's fraud does not prevent the application of the doctrine of apparent authority; see (e.g.) *Lexi Holdings v Pannone & Partners* [2009] EWHC 2590 (Ch); *Quinn v Automotive Group* [2010] EWCA Civ 1412; Bowstead/Reynolds, Agency, 8.62–64.

22 The requirement of s 2 of the Factors Act 1889 that the mercantile agent must have been in possession "with the consent of the owner" may, however, plainly be met even if that consent was obtained by fraud; see *Folkes v King* [1923] 1 KB 282 (CA); *Pearson v Rose & Young Ltd* [1951] 1 KB 275 (CA); *Du Jardin v Beadman Bros* [1952] 2 QB 712.

23 See generally Davies/Worthington, Gower's Principles of Modern Company Law, 7.4–29; Bowstead/Reynolds, Agency, 8.30–40.

24 See esp *Freeman & Lockyer v Buckhurst Park Properties (Mangal) Ltd* [1964] 2 QB 480 (CA).

25 See generally Davies/Worthington, Gower's Principles of Modern Company Law, 7.9–17.

retain legal ownership by reason of lack of authority.[26] The company may then sue the transferee in conversion or unjust enrichment and trace its property at common law. This is perhaps less well known than the companies' alternative option of claiming its thereby – equally by reason of lack of authority – retained *equitable* ownership under a resulting trust and of claiming equitable proprietary remedies, tracing in equity and suing third parties for knowing receipt or dishonest assistance.[27]

3. FUNDAMENTAL DURESS

What is the position if a legal owner (A) is coerced to conclude a contract to transfer a chattel and/or to deliver or otherwise convey that chattel to the coercing party? In contrast to cases of theft, finding, misappropriation or lack of authority, where the owner has never agreed to the transfer at all, the owner in a sense still does express his consent in coercion cases, though this consent is not entirely based on his free will.

It has already been observed that legal ownership may only be retained if the defect in question (coercion) is serious enough to equally render an underlying contract void, rather than merely voidable.[28] Certainly, coercion does not generally render a contract void, but merely voidable, and it does neither, accordingly, in general prevent the passage of property but merely renders the proprietary transfer voidable (imposing a power in rem). If pressure amounts to duress, the contract and the proprietary transfer are voidable at law. If it merely amounts to undue influence, the transaction is only voidable in equity.[29] This is uncontroversial in principle. However, though coercion is routinely said to merely render a transaction voidable, without expressing a reservation for

26 See (e.g.) *Clark v Cutland* [2003] EWCA Civ 810, [2004] 1 WLR 783, [23], [27] (Arden LJ) (concerned with a misappropriation of company assets by a director): "[I]n this case, there was no organ of the company which was duly authorised to form any intention about making the payments. [The director] made the payments as an agent lacking the authority. Accordingly this is not a situation where the full legal and beneficial ownership in the [misappropriated assets or proceeds] passed [...]. [W]here an agent carries out a transaction without authority, the consequence is [...] that the transaction is without legal effect. This consequence is more serious in law than that which attaches to a transaction which is voidable since the right to rescind a voidable transaction can be lost."

27 See Zogg, Proprietary Consequences, Chapter 5 section 5.1.4.

28 See Chapter 1 section 2.1.1.2.

29 Regarding duress (at law): *North Ocean Shipping Co Ltd v Hyundai Construction Co Ltd* [1979] QB 705 (QBD), 719–21 (Mocatta J); *Pao On v Lau Yiu Long* [1980] AC 614 (PC), 634–36 (Lord Scarman); *Universe Tankships Inc of Monrovia v ITWF (The Universe Sentinel)* [1983] 1 AC 366 (HL), 383–84 (Lord Diplock), 400 (Lord Scarman); *Dimskal Shipping Co SA v ITWF (The Evia Luck) (No 2)* [1992] 2 AC 152 (HL), 165–66 (Lord Goff). Regarding undue influence (in equity): *Barclays Bank plc v O'Brien* [1994] 1 AC 180 (HL); *Royal Bank of Scotland plc v Etridge (No 2)* [2001] UKHL 44, [2002] 2 AC 773.

extreme cases,[30] it seems quite obvious that a certain degree of voluntariness must inevitably be required for a person's "consent" to have any legal effects. Certainly, an offer or acceptance to conclude a contract, which is expressed under the most extreme forms of duress, cannot be taken to have any legally relevant effects whatsoever. If B for example knocks at A's door, holds a gun at his head and forces him to "accept" an offer to sell and buy a certain chattel for a certain price, A's acceptance must certainly be regarded as legally wholly inexistent. A consent given under the impression of serious and direct violence against the person or under the threat of such violence is no consent at all. Evidently, there can be no difference between a case where a robber first uses serious violence or threats of such violence to force A to conclude a contract and to deliver a chattel to him and a case where he simply takes away the chattel without "asking", merely using violence or the threat of violence to force A to not fight back.[31] Such "contracts" – concluded under the impression of direct and serious violence against the person or under the threat of such violence – must be completely void, not merely voidable.[32]

The case law concerned with duress is certainly not inconsistent with this proposition. Though contracts were regarded as merely voidable in most cases,[33] these were all concerned with rather mild forms of duress, particularly economic duress. There is only one exception, namely *DPP for Northern Ireland v Lynch*,[34] which concerned an extreme form of duress against the person and where it was still suggested (obiter) that such a contract was merely voidable. However, this was a criminal case which was concerned with the question whether the defence

---

30 Beale, Chitty on Contracts, vol 1, 8.4–8.7, 8.54; Treitel, Contract, 10.2, 10.12; McKendrick, English Private Law, 8.203; Burrows, Restitution, 260 (text to fn 46), 263 (fn 62); cf also Furmston, Cheshire, Fifoot & Furmston's Law of Contract, 394–96; contra (arguing for voidness): Lanham, MLR 1966.

31 Apparently contra Beale, Chitty on Contracts, vol 1, 8.7. With great respect, such a distinction is not only – as explicitly admitted – "artificial" but simply untenable in any civilised system of law. To give an even more extreme example than the threat of murder by a gunman: If B uses instruments of veritable torture and the victim – initially resisting to accept the offer but at some point being unable to physically withstand the torture which is getting more and more painful – "accepts" it, how could it seriously be supposed that the victim has given any actual – though voidable – consent? Consent under torture is no consent; it is a complete nullity. There is no contract. Legal ownership is retained; it does not pass voidably.

32 To the same effect Lanham, MLR 1966; Fox, Property Rights, 4.89, 6.13; Fox, RLR 1996, 68–69; Watts, RLR 1995, 53; Virgo, Restitution, 577; Friedmann, LQR 2003, 82; Häcker, Impaired Consent, 197.

33 All concerned with economic duress: *North Ocean Shipping v Hyundai Construction* [1979] QB 705, 719–21 (Mocatta J); *Pao On v Lau Yiu Long* [1980] AC 614, 634–36 (Lord Scarman); *The Universe Sentinel* [1983] 1 AC 366, 383–84 (Lord Diplock), 400 (Lord Scarman); *The Evia Luck (No 2)* [1992] 2 AC 152, 165–66 (Lord Goff); *Capital Structures plc v Time & Tide Construction Ltd* [2006] EWHC 591 (TCC), [18] (Wilcox J); concerned with a threat of requiring an act contrary to the affected party's religious belief: *Halpern v Halpern (Nos 1 & 2)* [2007] EWCA Civ 291, [2008] QB 195.

34 *DPP for Northern Ireland v Lynch* [1975] AC 653 (HL).

of duress (threats against the accused's life) was available at all in a charge of aiding and abetting murder. In his dissenting judgment, Lord Simon compared this issue with the English law of contract and stated obiter and in general terms, not specifically directed to extreme duress, that contracts procured by duress are voidable, not void.[35] But this cannot be seen as authority for the proposition that even contracts concluded under the most extreme forms of duress are merely voidable. Rather, there is authority to the contrary suggesting that such contracts are not only voidable but indeed completely void.[36]

Self-evidently, such forms of extreme duress do not only render any purportedly concluded contract void but they must equally negative any consent of the legal owner to transfer property. Fundamental duress destroys any real agreement and negatives any apparent consent to execute a conveyancing act, for example delivery. It follows that fundamental duress is a real or dual defect which prevents the passage of legal ownership.[37] This is borne out by the case of *Duke de Cadaval v Collins*[38] where the defendant obtained an arrest on a foreigner, who had just arrived in England, for an alleged debt of £10,000 which the defendant had known to not exist. The foreigner thereupon signed an agreement to pay and did pay £500 to be discharged from the arrest. In an action for money had and received, Lord Denman CJ said this:

> "[I]s it still the plaintiff's money? How is it shewn not to be so? [...] [T]he arrest was fraudulent; and the money was parted with under the arrest, to get rid of the pressure. [...] The property in the money, therefore, never passed from the plaintiff, who parted with it only to relieve himself from the hardship and inconvenience of a fraudulent arrest."[39]

To the same effect is the example given (obiter) by Lord Lowry in *R v Gomez* (comparing the old common law felony of robbery with the modern position under s 8 of the Theft Act 1968):

> "When, in response to the highwayman's threat, 'Your money or your life,' the victim delivered up his money, he did so *against his will* and there was no question of consent. The highwayman was guilty of an aggravated form of stealing and did not obtain even a

35 Ibid, 695 (Lord Simon), cf also 680 (Lord Wilberforce).

36 *Barton v Armstrong* [1976] AC 104 (PC), 120 (Lord Cross).

37 Fox, Property Rights, 4.89, 6.13; Fox, RLR 1996, 68–69; Watts, RLR 1995, 53; Virgo, Restitution, 577; Lanham, MLR 1966, 618–19; Häcker, Impaired Consent, 197.

38 *Duke de Cadaval v Collins* [1836] 4 A&E 858, 111 ER 1006; see equally *R v McGrath* [1869] LR 1 CCR 205 (Crown Cases Reserved) (payment of money at an auction for a chattel for which the victim had bidden under a threat to not otherwise allow the victim to leave the room; held that property in the money had not passed; conviction of larceny); *R v Lovell* [1881] 8 QBD 185 (Crown Cases Reserved) (payment of more money than due for services under threats of physical violence; held that property had not passed; conviction of larceny).

39 *Duke de Cadaval v Collins* [1836] 4 A&E 858, 864–65 (Lord Denman CJ).

> voidable title. The same holds good today and it would be idle to suggest that the victim of a robbery consents in any way to hand over his property, much less to transfer its ownership, to the robber."[40]

By contrast, it is equally clear that in cases of less extreme coercion,[41] for example in cases of economic duress, duress against goods or mere undue influence, a contract is not void but merely *voidable* and that legal ownership does pass *voidably* to the coercing transferee, subject to a power in rem to revest legal or equitable ownership by rescission.[42] The transferor's intention to transfer property is not, in such cases, completely *negatived* by coercion; it is merely *vitiated*.

---

40 *R v Gomez* [1993] AC 442, 480–81 (Lord Lowry) (emphasis in original).

41 The exact demarcation line between "extreme" and "non-extreme" duress need not be further drawn here; guidelines may be found in the cases of *Barton v Armstrong* [1976] AC 104 (threats against the victim's life; consent wholly negatived); *Duke de Cadaval v Collins* [1836] 4 A&E 858 (threat of an ongoing arrest; consent wholly negatived) and *Halpern v Halpern (Nos 1 & 2)* [2007] EWCA Civ 291 (threat of requiring an act from the affected party which would have been contrary to that party's religious beliefs; consent not wholly negatived but merely vitiated).

42 See further Zogg, Proprietary Consequences, Chapter 4 section 2.

CHAPTER 4
FUNDAMENTAL MISTAKE IN PARTICULAR

We shall finally turn to the most difficult type of defect, namely mistake. A profound analysis of the effects of mistakes necessitates a strict distinction between three different levels where it might respectively operate: Property, contract and unjust enrichment.[1] In particular, a mistake's effects need not be the same on the contractual level as on the proprietary plane. A mistake might render a contract void but leave unaffected the proprietary transfer (conveyance), which is abstract. Yet, the converse is arguably impossible, unless the defect has only occurred in the execution but not in the formation stage. The range of real defects is narrower than the range of obligatory defects.[2] A mistake which is unable to render a contract void may not at the same time still prevent the passage of property. But not every mistake which is serious enough to render a contract void is also sufficient to prevent property from passing.

It has already been pointed out that the standard terminology in the context of mistakes is rather confused and that it is – unless unambiguous from the context – convenient to refer to *proprietarily fundamental mistakes*, i.e. mistakes that prevent the passage of property, as opposed to *contractually fundamental mistakes*, i.e. mistakes that render contracts void.[3]

We shall start our analysis with a brief overview of mistakes which may render contracts void (contractually fundamental mistakes) before turning to the difficult question as to which of them might equally prevent the passage of property (proprietarily fundamental mistakes). Courts and commentators have so far developed three very narrow categories of mistakes which may prevent legal ownership from passing, namely (i) mistakes as to the transferee's identity, (ii) mistakes as to the transferred property's identity and (iii) mistakes as to the transferred property's quantity.[4] It accordingly appears that mistakes are only

---

1 See Chapter 1 section 1.

2 See Chapter 1 sections 2.1.1.2. and 3.

3 See Chapter 1 section 1.2.

4 *Ilich v R* [1987] 162 CLR 110, 126–27 (Wilson, Dawson JJ); Williams, Crim LR 1958, 222–23; Williams, CLJ 1977; Williams, Criminal Law, 32.133–34; J. Smith, Crim LR 1972, 586–88; Virgo, Restitution, 574–76; Fox, Property Rights, 3.99–102, 4.116–46; Fox, RLR 1996, 64–67; Pollock/Wright, Possession, 100–14, 205–12; Grantham/Rickett, RLR 1997, 88–89; Häcker, Impaired Consent, 119–20, 138; Häcker, ZEuP 2011, 346–48; Orchard, NZLJ 1973, 111–12; Sheehan, Personal Property, 154–55; cf also *R v Milne* [1990] ABCA 323

proprietarily fundamental in quite extreme cases where the transferor's intention to carry out the transfer in question is virtually absent. Crucially, the mistake must relate to the *transfer of property as such* rather than merely to the *motivation why* – but not *that* – a certain transfer shall be made. Only the former but not the latter type of mistake may be proprietarily fundamental. At the end of this chapter, it will furthermore be argued that there is, in addition to the mentioned three categories, a fourth category of proprietarily fundamental mistakes, namely mistakes as to the type of legal interest (ownership or possession) to be transferred.[5]

1. MISTAKES WHICH RENDER CONTRACTS VOID

As Lord Atkin has famously explained in *Bell v Lever Bros Ltd*,[6] there are two different ways of how a mistake might render a contract void at law,[7] namely by operating "so as to negative or in some cases to nullify consent".

1.1. MISTAKES WHICH NEGATIVE CONSENT

A mistake *negatives* consent if it relates to the essential terms of the contract and if it puts the parties so much at cross-purposes as to prevent them from reaching an agreement at all. This kind of mistake is sometimes referred to as a "unilateral mistake" although it is often impossible to say which of the parties has actually been mistaken.[8] In fact, it is better analysed as simply being part of the rules of offer and acceptance.[9]

According to a basic rule of contract law, an offer and a respective acceptance must be interpreted in accordance with the *objective principle*, unless the parties

(CanLII) (CA of Alberta), [19]–[24], [26] (Coté J) (revd on other grounds in [1992] 1 SCR 696 (SC of Canada)); critically: Swadling, Unjust Delivery (but cf still Swadling, RLR 1994, 82; Swadling, LQR 2005, 152).

5 Chapter 4 section 2.5.

6 *Bell v Lever Bros Ltd* [1932] AC 161 (HL), 217 (Lord Atkin).

7 Since the case of *Great Peace Shipping Ltd v Tsavliris Salvage (International) Ltd (The Great Peace)* [2002] EWCA Civ 1407, [2003] QB 679 (cited with apparent approval in *Pitt v Holt* [2011] EWCA Civ 197, [2012] Ch 132, [166] (Lloyd LJ), [2013] UKSC 26, [2013] 2 AC 108, [115] (Lord Walker)), it is authoritatively settled that equity has no longer any jurisdiction to render a contract, which is binding at law, void or voidable on the basis of a non-induced (shared or unilateral) mistake; in so far, *Bell v Lever Bros* [1932] AC 161 is conclusive; see also *Statoil ASA v Louis Dreyfus Energy Services LP (The Harriette N)* [2008] EWHC 2257 (Comm), [105] (Aikens J); Zogg, Proprietary Consequences, Chapter 5 section 7.1.1.

8 Treitel, Contract, 8.1.

9 See *Whittaker v Campbell* [1984] QB 318 (Div Ct), 326–27 (Goff LJ); Slade, LQR 1954; Beale, Chitty on Contracts, vol 1, 3.12–13; Cartwright, Misrepresentation, 13.1–29; Atiyah, Ottawa LR 1968, 253–60.

were *subjectively ad idem* or unless one of the parties has *known* the other party's (divergent) actual subjective intention.[10] It follows that such mutual mistakes may generally only be operative[11] to negative an apparent agreement if (i) the parties were not subjectively *ad idem*,[12] if (ii) neither[13] of the parties had knowledge of the other party's actual subjective intention[14] *and* if (iii) an unambiguous objective interpretation of the offer and acceptance is unavailable.[15]

---

10 The objective principle provides that a party is generally bound by the natural and objective meaning of his words and conduct which the other party might reasonably attach to them; see (e.g.) *Smith v Hughes* [1871] LR 6 QB 597 (QBD), 607 (Blackburn J): "If, whatever a man's real intention may be, he so conducts himself that a reasonable man would believe that he was assenting to the terms proposed by the other party, and that other party upon that belief enters into the contract with him, the man thus conducting himself would be equally bound as if he had intended to agree to the other party's terms"; *Cornish v Abington* [1859] 4 H&N 549, 157 ER 956; *Paal Wilson & Co A/S v Partenreederei Hannah Blumenthal (The Hannah Blumenthal)* [1983] 1 AC 854 (HL), 914 (Lord Brandon), 915–17 (Lord Diplock), 924 (Lord Brightman); *First Energy (UK) Ltd v Hungarian International Bank Ltd* [1993] BCC 533 (CA); *Maple Leaf Macro Volatility Master Fund v Rouvroy* [2009] EWCA Civ 1334, [10], [17] (Longmore LJ); Cartwright, Misrepresentation, 13.1–29; Friedmann, LQR 2003; Beale, Chitty on Contracts, vol 1, 3.13–48; Treitel, Contract, 1.2, 2.2, 8.47; Beatson et al, Anson's Law of Contract, 34–35, 272–78.

11 Cf Treitel, Contract, 8.47–53.

12 If the parties actually do intend the same thing but if their respective words and conducts must objectively be taken to mean something else, the parties' actual subjective consent must prevail; see Williams, MLR 1954, 154–55; Cartwright, Misrepresentation, 13.7, 13.10, 13.19; Beale, Chitty on Contracts, vol 1, 3.14; Friedmann, LQR 2003, 68–69.

13 It appears that a contract is void if *both* parties knew that the respectively other party's actual intention was divergent.

14 If A's subjective intention differs from the objective meaning of his words and conduct and if B has knowledge of this at the time of conclusion, the objective principle does not apply and the terms as objectively understood are not part of the contract. Though this issue is not finally settled in England, it seems that a contract is not inevitably void for lack of consent in such a case but that a contract comes into being on the terms as subjectively intended by A, at least if A could have reasonably believed that B intended to accept the offer as understood by him. This question needed not be answered in the seminal cases of *Smith v Hughes* [1871] LR 6 QB 597 and *Hartog v Colin & Shields* [1939] 3 All ER 566 (KBD). The approach of a valid contract on the subjectively intended terms was favoured in *Ulster Bank Ltd v Lambe* [2012] NIQB 31 (HC of Northern Ireland), [21]–[28] (Weatherup J) (offer intended to be for £155,000 mistakenly stated for €155,000 of which the offeree was aware; held that the offer was in fact for £155,000 and that the contract was binding and enforceable for that amount); see convincingly Beale, Chitty on Contracts, vol 1, 3.25, 3.29–31; see also Beatson et al, Anson's Law of Contract, 276–78; Treitel, Contract, 8.51, 8.53; Friedmann, LQR 2003, 72–73; Goodhart, LQR 1941, 231; Häcker, Impaired Consent, 178–83; contra: *Statoil ASA v Louis Dreyfus Energy Services LP (The Harriette N)* [2008] EWHC 2257 (Comm), [87], where Aikens J stated (obiter) that there is "never a contract at all" in such a case. However, an exception must apply with regard to *mistakes as to the other party's identity*: If A subjectively intends to contract with C but if his offer is objectively to be understood as being addressed to B and if B, having knowledge of this, purports to accept it, there is neither a contract with B (for lack of consent) nor a contract with C since B's acceptance cannot bind C (for lack of authority).

15 The objective principle cannot provide an answer if the parties' words and conduct are too ambiguous, particularly if a reasonable bystander might equally well understand either of the two parties' different subjective meanings; see (e.g.) *Raffles v Wichelhaus* [1864] 2 H&C 906,

Such mistakes which put the parties at cross-purposes – in the sense of an incongruence between offer and acceptance as interpreted in accordance with the mentioned amalgam of the objective and the subjective principle – may particularly relate to the other party's identity (if this was of the essence for the mistaken party[16]), the nature or the quantity of the subject-matter dealt with or the interest to be transferred. It will be seen that those kinds of mistakes are equally capable of preventing the passage of property. But mutual mistakes may also negative an agreement if they relate to other essential terms of the contract, particularly the kind or amount of consideration to be provided, for example the price to be paid.[17] Yet, it will be argued that such mistakes – though they may negative a *contractual* agreement – have no effects on the *proprietary* plane.[18]

1.2. MISTAKES WHICH NULLIFY CONSENT (COMMON MISTAKES)

A contractual agreement, which is actually existent according to the mentioned amalgam of the objective and the subjective principle, may still be *nullified* under the common law doctrine of *common mistakes*. These are mistakes which do not relate to the contractual terms but to some exterior facts or state of affairs outside the contract. Such mistakes are always motivational in nature and relate to the *why* a party has agreed to the contract in question (as it would otherwise exist). At common law,[19] such mistakes only render contracts void[20] within very narrow confines, namely only if (i) the same mistake is shared by both parties (common mistake), (ii) if neither of the parties has expressly or impliedly warranted the existence of the supposed state of affairs or otherwise taken the risk of the mistake in question, (iii) if the non-existence of the supposed state of

159 ER 375 (goods sold "ex Peerless from Bombay"; objective ambiguity as to whether goods "ex Peerless from Bombay, October shipment" or "ex Peerless from Bombay, December shipment" was meant); *Falck v Williams* [1900] AC 176 (PC) (mutual misunderstanding with regard to coded telegrams which could objectively have had either meaning); *South East Windscreens Ltd v Jamshidi* [2005] All ER (D) 317 (Dec) (QBD) (sale of business and mutual mistake as to the price and exact counter-performance to be made by the buyer; no unambiguous single objective meaning could be found).

16 See fn 82, 92 and 106.

17 See *Felthouse v Bindley* [1862] 11 CBNS 869, 142 ER 1037; *Hartog v Colin & Shields* [1939] 3 All ER 566; *South East Windscreens v Jamshidi* [2005] All ER (D) 317 (Dec); Treitel, Contract, 8.44; cf also *Woodhouse AC Israel Cocoa SA v Nigerian Produce Marketing Co Ltd* [1972] AC 741 (HL), 767–68 (Lord Cross).

18 Chapter 4 section 2.5.

19 Equity has no jurisdiction to render a contract, which is binding at law, void or voidable on the basis of a non-induced (shared or unilateral) mistake; see fn 7.

20 If a contract is not void by reason of a common mistake, it might still be *voidable* if the (unilateral or common) mistake has been *induced* by a fraudulent, negligent or wholly innocent misrepresentation; cf Cartwright, Misrepresentation, 15.8, 15.13.

affairs is not attributable to the fault of either party *and* (iv) if the mistake is so (contractually) fundamental that it renders the contractual adventure impossible or the performance essentially different from what the parties have envisaged.[21]

If those requirements are met, the contract is void at common law. This does not, however, mean that the proprietary transfer must equally be void. Though the practical relevance of this observation might be limited, it will be argued that common mistakes may never prevent the passage of legal ownership, since they are always only *motivational* in nature.[22]

2. MISTAKES WHICH PREVENT THE PASSAGE OF LEGAL OWNERSHIP

In this section, we shall examine whether and in how far mistakes may prevent the passage of property (proprietarily fundamental mistakes). It will be argued that purely motivational mistakes, which only relate to the *why* a certain transfer shall be carried out, are – however grave! – invariably insufficient to prevent ownership from passing.[23] By contrast, mistakes which directly relate to the transfer of property itself, i.e. mistakes *that* the very transfer shall be made, are sufficient to prevent the passage of title. The relevant intention *that* a certain transfer shall be made – and, conversely, the potential for a relevant mistake – not only includes (i) an intention that legal ownership shall be transferred *at all*[24] but also an intention (ii) that the *very chattel(s)*[25] in question shall be transferred (iii) in the relevant *quantity*[26] (iv) to the *transferee* in question.[27]

Basically, the argument will be made that an analogy should be drawn between the four mentioned categories of proprietarily fundamental mistakes and the respective jurisprudence on the contractual level: The general amalgam of the objective and the subjective principle relating to the interpretation of contractual offers and acceptances should be analogously applied in relation to transfers of property (real agreement). Hence, the "face-to-face principle", as established in *Shogun Finance Ltd v Hudson*,[28] should be extended to the proprietary level. Furthermore, it will be argued that the face-to-face principle, as

[21] *Bell v Lever Bros* [1932] AC 161, 217–22 (Lord Atkin); *Great Peace Shipping v Tsavliris Salvage* [2002] EWCA Civ 1407, esp [73]–[94] (Lord Phillips MR); Cartwright, Misrepresentation, 15.14–34; Treitel, Contract, 8.2–8.7; Beale, Chitty on Contracts, vol 1, ch 6; Beatson et al, Anson's Law of Contract, 300–16.

[22] See Chapter 4 section 2.1.2.

[23] Chapter 4 section 2.1.

[24] Chapter 4 section 2.5.

[25] Chapter 4 section 2.3.

[26] Chapter 4 section 2.4.

[27] Chapter 4 section 2.2.

[28] *Shogun Finance Ltd v Hudson* [2003] UKHL 62, [2004] 1 AC 919.

applied in relation to mistakes as to the other party's identity, should be extended by analogy to some "face-to-property principle" as far as the identification of the contract goods is concerned.

It will emerge from the following discussion that there are – identity mistakes apart – only a few authorities on the subject considered in this chapter and that most of them stem from the realm of criminal law. Prior to the enactment of the Theft Act 1968 and the Fraud Act 2006, the English property offences basically distinguished between larceny, including larceny by a trick and larceny by a bailee, and the obtaining of goods by false pretences.[29] Larceny required a taking and carrying away or conversion to one's own use of the chattel in question without the owner's consent coupled with a fraudulent intent to permanently deprive the owner thereof at the time of the taking.[30] Crucially, larceny was impossible if the defendant had obtained not only possession but also legal ownership in the chattel.[31] In this case, only the offence of obtaining by false pretences was available.[32] It follows that the question whether the defendant obtained legal ownership or not and whether, if the victim had apparently agreed to the transfer, a mistake was proprietarily fundamental to prevent the passage of property, was relevant to decide for which of those offences the defendant was liable. In so far, the old English criminal law directly drew on the private law position with regard to the transfer of property.

The law of theft was revised and much extended by the Theft Act 1968. Larceny was abolished and theft was made applicable even to cases where legal ownership has indefeasibly passed to the defendant, as long as the latter is under a (personal!) obligation to make restitution based on a mere restitution yielding mistake.[33] It follows that the distinction between proprietarily fundamental mistakes and merely restitution yielding (or contractually fundamental) mistakes has become largely[34] obsolete under the Theft Act 1968. Hence, English criminal law will not generally produce any more relevant authorities in this regard.[35] But the English

---

29 Sections 1 and 32 of the Larceny Act 1916; similar principles already applied under the older Larceny Acts and the common law; see generally Turner, Kenny's Outlines of Criminal Law, chs 13, 17; Turner, Russell on Crime, vol 2, chs 51, 70.

30 Section 1 of the Larceny Act 1916; see (e.g.) *R v Ashwell* [1885] 16 QBD 190 (Crown Case Reserved); *Folkes v King* [1923] 1 KB 282 (CA).

31 See (e.g.) *Folkes v King* [1923] 1 KB 282, 307 (Scrutton LJ): "[I]t is clear that if the legal property passes, dealing with it is not larceny"; Pollock/Wright, Possession, 219–21; Swadling, Unjust Delivery, 291; Fox, Property Rights, 4.72.

32 Section 32 of the Larceny Act 1916; this was the case if the owner intended to (and did) transfer possession and property to the defendant but if the latter had obtained this consent by fraud (the defendant thus obtaining a voidable title in the goods).

33 Section 5(4) of the Theft Act 1968; see *Lawrence v MPC* [1972] AC 626 (HL); *R v Gomez* [1993] AC 442; *R v Hinks* [2001] 2 AC 241 (HL); Williams, CLJ 1977, 68–71; Fox, Property Rights, 4.74; Ormerod/Williams, Smith's Law of Theft, ch 2.

34 But cf fn 57.

35 However, passage of property might, at least in theory, be considered regarding the practically unimportant question of whether a defendant is liable under s 1(1) or s 5(4) of the Theft

pre-1968 authorities – and the case law of Commonwealth jurisdictions where a similar distinction was or still is known[36] – still remain relevant with regard to the here examined private law issue of passing of property.[37]

2.1. MOTIVATIONAL MISTAKES (PARTICULARLY LIABILITY MISTAKES)

2.1.1. Property Not Prevented from Passing

Though a clear distinction may sometimes be difficult to draw,[38] it is a well-established principle that mistakes which only bear on the *why* but not on the *that* a certain transfer of ownership shall be made – including the three parameters of *what, how much* and *to whom* – may not prevent the passage of property.[39] This applies irrespective of the gravity of such a motivational mistake. Crucially, the requirement that a mistake must be proprietarily fundamental does not refer to the importance or severity of a mistake but only to the question whether or not a transferor has an actual natural intention – though perhaps vitiated – to execute the very transfer of property in question. It is sufficient for property to pass, at least voidably, that the transferor knows what he is doing, namely that he transfers legal ownership in certain chattels in a certain quantity to a certain person.

The most common form of motivational mistakes are *liability mistakes* where a transferor mistakenly believes that he is liable to make a certain transfer. This is frequently the case in transfers carried out without any basis whatsoever, such as double or overpayments, or in transfers made under void contracts.[40] But the

Act 1968; cf WILLIAMS, CLJ 1977, 68–71; WILLIAMS, Criminal Law, 32.123–37; ORMEROD/WILLIAMS, Smith's Law of Theft, 2.250–52.

36 See esp *Ilich v R* [1987] 162 CLR 110 where the Australian High Court was concerned with stealing under s 371 of the Criminal Code of Western Australia which resembled s 1 of the old English Larceny Act 1916 and the common law; cf also ORCHARD, NZLJ 1973, 110–11, concerning s 220 (now s 219) of the Crimes Act 1961 (New Zealand).

37 See FOX, Property Rights, 4.76–77; SWADLING, Unjust Delivery, 290–97.

38 See the examples provided in the following sub-sections, esp in Chapter 4 section 2.4.2.3.; cf also WILLIAMS, CLJ 1977, 64–65.

39 See the cases immediately discussed in this sub-section; see also SWADLING, Unjust Delivery, 289–90; SWADLING, RLR 1994, 82; J. SMITH, Crim LR 1972, 586–88; VIRGO, Restitution, 576; FOX, Property Rights, 4.133–37, 4.141–42; FOX, RLR 1996, 64–67; WILLIAMS, Crim LR 1958, 222; WILLIAMS, Criminal Law, 32.133–34; HÄCKER, Impaired Consent, 137–38; HÄCKER, ZEuP 2011, 346–48; apparently *contra*: MCCORMACK, CPL 1996, 96; VAN VLIET, Transfer of movables, 111–14, 130–32, who regards transfers by sale as causal, even considering whether a *causa traditionis* is required for transfers by delivery, regarding gifts (*causa donandi*) and money; cf also VAN VLIET, EdinLR 2008. Apart from the arguments already given in favour of abstraction (see Chapter 2), it may be added that VAN VLIET completely ignores the entire case law discussed in this sub-section.

40 See for example *Westdeutsche Landesbank v Islington* [1996] AC 669, esp 689–90 (Lord Goff).

transferor might also be aware of the fact that he is under no liability to execute the relevant transfer – thus intending to make a gift – but still be mistaken about some other facts or state of affairs which motivate him to do so. A motivational mistake might also occur if a transferor *is* under a liability to make the transfer in question but if he would not, but for the motivational mistake, have carried it out (yet).[41] In each of those cases, property does pass – at least voidably – by reason of the fact that the transferor has actually formed a real (natural) intention to execute the very transfer in question.

We shall now turn to the relevant case law in that regard. The first case is *Chambers v Miller*[42] where the claimant, acting on behalf of his employer, presented a cheque at the defendant's bank whereupon the cashier – mistakenly overlooking the fact that the drawer's account had been overdrawn – correctly counted out the money and placed it on the counter. The claimant took the money, counted it and was counting it a second time when the clerk discovered the mistake and immediately demanded the money back. Upon the claimant's refusal, the clerk detained him and, by threatening to give him into custody on a charge of stealing, forced him to return the money. The claimant sued in trespass to the person (assault and false imprisonment) which turned on the question whether legal title in the money had remained with the bank. The court unequivocally held that property in the money had passed to the claimant and that the clerk's motivational mistake had not negatived his intention to transfer legal title.[43]

In the case of *R v Prince*,[44] Mr Allen held a deposit account in his name at the London and Westminster Bank where his wife, intending to leave him, presented a forged order for payment of the deposit, purporting to be issued by Mr Allen. The bank clerk, having general authority,[45] mistakenly believed that the order was genuine and paid out the money. Mrs Allen thereupon left her husband, gave one of the notes to her lover and kept the rest. Concerned with a criminal charge against the lover, the court held that property in the money had, notwithstanding the clerk's motivational mistake, passed to Mrs Allen. This meant that the lover could not have been convicted for handling stolen property

41 This is a mistake exclusively occurring in the execution stage; see further Chapter 1 section 3.

42 *Chambers v Miller* [1862] 13 CBR (NS) 125, 143 ER 50.

43 Apart from that, it appears that the bank could not even have claimed personal restitution in unjust enrichment since the bank's payment had been within the mandate of the customer (drawer) and because the payee (claimant or his employer) had had a valid legal basis ("good consideration") which justified the enrichment; see *Barclays Bank Ltd v WJ Simms Son & Cooke (Southern) Ltd* [1980] QB 677 (QBD), 700 (Goff J).

44 *R v Prince* [1868] LR 1 CCR 150 (Ct for Crown Cases Reserved).

45 The court limited its decision to a case where the clerk had full authority and considered obiter that property might not have passed had the clerk merely had limited authority; see further *R v Middleton* [1873] LR 2 CCR 38 (Ct for Crown Cases Reserved) and Chapter 4 section 2.2.2.3.

and that Mrs Allen could not have committed larceny (but only obtaining by false pretences). This case plainly establishes that a motivational liability mistake may not prevent the passage of property even if it was fraudulently induced by the transferee and if it was of the most serious degree. That must be correct in principle since the question whether title passes is – if the transferee accepts the transfer – exclusively a question of the transferor's real intention and actual state of mind. If legal title passes in cases where the transferor has acted under a *spontaneous* motivational mistake, as in *Chambers v Miller*,[46] it must equally pass where he has acted under the very same – but *induced* – motivational mistake, as in *R v Prince*. In that regard, the transferee's state of mind, conduct or fault is irrelevant.[47] This is, in fact, the basis of the well-known rule that legal title passes voidably in cases of fraud or duress.[48]

In *Moynes v Coopper*,[49] a wages clerk put more money than due into a pay packet and handed it over to an employee, who did not discover the mistake until he had opened the packet at home. The clerk had not been mistaken about the amount of money he was in fact putting into the pay packet (which might well have been a fundamental mistake as to quantity); the mistake rather occurred because he had overlooked the fact that the overpaid amount had already been paid to the employee in advance. This was, accordingly, a mere liability mistake.[50] In a criminal charge for larceny, Lord Goddard CJ and Hilbery J acquitted the employee for two alternative reasons:[51] First, they held that there had been no *animus furandi* at the time of the taking; second, they held that legal ownership in the money had passed to the employee despite the clerk's motivational mistake.[52]

---

46 *Chambers v Miller* [1862] 13 CBR (NS) 125.

47 Cf Swadling, Unjust Delivery, 290, who draws an illuminating parallel with the rule that liability in unjust enrichment is equally independent from the defendant's fault.

48 See (e.g.) *Load v Green* [1846] 15 M&W 216, 152 ER 828; *Car & Universal Finance Co Ltd v Caldwell* [1965] 1 QB 525 (CA); *Newtons of Wembley Ltd v Williams* [1965] 1 QB 560 (CA); Fox, Property Rights, ch 6; cf also s 23 of the SGA 1979.

49 *Moynes v Coopper* [1956] 1 QB 439 (QBD).

50 See likewise *R v Potisk* [1973] 6 SASR 389 (SC of South Australia) where Potisk produced travellers' cheques at a bank to the value of 1,480 USD to be exchanged into Australian currency; the clerk mistakenly applied the wrong conversion rate and handed over more than double the amount due; Bray CJ (Mitchell J agreeing) held that property in the money had passed to Potisk (Wells J dissenting).

51 Stable J dissented from both (447–51).

52 Applying *R v Prince* they said (445): "Where a transfer of property is obtained by fraud, there is no doubt but that the property does pass, subject, however, to the right of the defrauded party on discovering the fraud to disaffirm the transaction and resume his property. In the present case the action would be for money had and received to the company's use as paid under a mistake of fact. For these reasons [i.e. the absence of an *animus furandi* and the passage of property], while the defendant was guilty of grave dishonesty, in our opinion he was not guilty of larceny, and in the present state of the law he was not guilty of any criminal offence." This perceived gap of criminal liability was the reason why s 5(4) of the Theft Act 1968 was later introduced; cf Ormerod/Williams; Smith's Law of Theft, 2.253–54.

The same result was reached in *Lacis v Cashmarts*.[53] The defendant selected various goods in a supermarket, put them on the counter and the manager, having full authority, asked for £85 8s. instead of £185 8s. since the till had turned back to zero when it had reached £100. Lord Parker CJ held that there was only a contract for the last couple of goods recorded after the till had turned back to zero but not for the previous ones[54,55] and concluded, applying *R v Prince*, that the manager had had a plain intention to transfer ownership in all of the goods to the defendant. The manager's motivational liability mistake did not prevent the passage of property in the additional goods. Hence, the defendant could not have been convicted for larceny. The transferor had only a personal claim in unjust enrichment.

In some contrast with this stands the difficult case of *R v Gilks*.[56] The defendant placed bets on different horses and won a total amount of £10.62. The bookmaker, however, paid out £117.25 mistakenly believing that the defendant had backed a successful horse which he had not. The defendant was aware of the mistake but still accepted and kept the money. The bookmaker exactly knew how much money he was in fact handing over; he was only mistaken as to how much had in fact been due. This was, accordingly, a mere mistake as to motive. In a charge of theft under s 1 of the Theft Act 1968,[57] the Court of Appeal,

53 *Lacis v Cashmarts* [1969] 2 QB 400 (Div Ct).

54 Whether this analysis is correct is at least doubtful. In fact, it could be argued that, because the defendant must have known that the manager's objective offer to sell the goods for £85 8s. has not corresponded with his subjective intention, there has been a binding contract of sale in relation to *all* of the goods for the price of £185 8s. (see fn 14) and that the defendant was, accordingly, still contractually obliged to pay the balance; cf also J. Smith, CLJ 1972B, 207–8.

55 His Lordship furthermore held that, to the extent that there had been a contract of sale, property had only passed – as intended by the parties – *upon payment*, but that property had passed *immediately* to the extent that there had been no contract, i.e. in relation to the first couple of goods; cf also Williams, CLJ 1977, 76–78. The preferable view, however, is that even if and as far as there has been no contract (which is doubtful as such), the parties' real agreement still had to be objectively understood as deferring the transfer of property until payment has been made, since this is very generally the nature of supermarket transactions. Property then passed upon payment and by delivery; see Chapter 2 section 1.2.

56 *R v Gilks* [1972] 1 WLR 1341 (CA); cf also the obiter dicta of Lord Wright in *Norwich Union Fire Insurance Society Ltd v WMH Price Ltd* [1934] AC 455 (PC), 461–62 (emphasis added): "The facts which were misconceived were those which were essential to liability [...]. The mistake, being of the character that it was, prevented there being that intention which the common law regards as essential to the making of an agreement or *the transfer of money or property*" and of Greene MR in *Morgan v Ashcroft* [1938] 1 KB 49 (CA), 66: "[A mistake where] [t]he payer thinks that he is discharging a legal obligation whereas in truth and in fact he is making a purely voluntary payment [...] is to my mind unquestionably fundamental or basic and may be compared, at least by way of analogy, with the class of case in which mistake as to the nature of the transaction negatives intention in the case of contract". However, those two cases were exclusively concerned with personal restitution and did not at all decide the question of passage of property.

57 Section 5(4) of the Theft Act 1968 was held to be applicable only with regard to *legal* obligations to make restoration but *not* with regard to *moral* obligations and it was

however, surprisingly held that property in the money had still not passed to the defendant.

With great respect, the reasoning of Cairns LJ, giving the judgment of the court, is unconvincing and flawed in several respects. Firstly, the judge did not offer any principled reason why property should not have passed in this case but simply agreed with the deputy chairman below and just boldly asserted that it did not. Secondly, he only cited *R v Middleton*[58] as an authority for this proposition. This case, however, is an extremely disputable one, the authority of which is markedly uncertain.[59] The decision in that case has been powerfully criticised; some commentators sought to save its result on the basis that it had actually concerned an identity mistake.[60] Cairns LJ, however, interpreted the case as establishing the proposition that property does not pass, very generally, "where a person was paid by mistake [...] a sum in excess of that properly payable".[61] This would effectively mean that *every* mistake, including *all* motivational liability mistakes, would prevent the passage of property. With respect, it is impossible to accept such an inconsiderate broad proposition based on such an uncritical adoption of *R v Middleton*. Thirdly, the ratio of *R v Gilks* is inconsistent with the well-settled rule of the English law of rescission that even fraudulently induced non-fundamental motivational mistakes may not prevent the passage of legal ownership in a first step but that legal title may be revested by rescission in a second step.[62] Fourthly, Cairns LJ's broad proposition that every or almost every causative mistake prevents the passage of property would radically disrupt the general relationship between property and unjust enrichment since almost every personal unjust enrichment claim based on mistake would then effectively be accompanied by a retained legal property right (if the transferred asset or its proceeds are still traceably identifiable). This would, inter alia, effectively result in an unwarranted preference of mistaken unjust enrichment claimants over other unsecured creditors. Fifthly, *R v Gilks* is inconsistent with the case law

held – apparently because the overpayment resulted from gambling activities (see *Morgan v Ashcroft* [1938] 1 KB 49, 60–62 (Greene MR), 67–69 (Scott LJ)) – that the defendant's restitutionary liability had only been a moral one. Theft was accordingly only possible under s 1 which presupposed that property had not passed. Hence, this was a rare case where the distinction between fundamental and non-fundamental mistakes continued to be practically relevant under the Theft Act 1968.

58 *R v Middleton* [1873] LR 2 CCR 38.

59 See Chapter 4 section 2.2.2.3.; cf also Orchard, NZLJ 1973, 111–13.

60 See the references in fn 148; it will, however, be argued that the "identity mistake" in that case should not actually have been sufficient to prevent the passage of property and that the case was, even on that basis, wrongly decided.

61 *R v Gilks* [1972] 1 WLR 1341, 1344 (Cairns LJ).

62 See (e.g.) *Load v Green* [1846] 15 M&W 216; *Car & Universal Finance v Caldwell* [1965] 1 QB 525; *Newtons of Wembley v Williams* [1965] 1 QB 560; O'Sullivan et al, Rescission, esp 14.3–6; Fox, Property Rights, ch 6; cf also s 23 of the SGA 1979.

set out above of which only *Moynes v Coopper* was cited. But even regarding that case, Cairns LJ merely considered one of the two decisive reasons, namely that there had been no *animus furandi*, but he overlooked the other, namely that property had not passed. In so far, *R v Gilks* must be regarded as wrongly decided (*per incuriam*) and should not be binding in England. Finally, it may be noted that *R v Gilks* has received powerful academic criticism[63] and that it was regarded as wrongly decided in *Ilich v R*.[64] Furthermore, there are various cases which have since been decided and which have rightly assumed that liability and other motivational mistakes may not prevent the passage of property.[65]

2.1.2. Transfers of Property Under Contracts which are Void for Common Mistakes

The principle that motivational mistakes may not – however grave – prevent the passage of property must equally apply in cases where a chattel is transferred under a contract which is void by reason of the doctrine of common mistake.[66] Certainly, the practical relevance of this observation is – owing to the very narrow confines of that doctrine – quite limited. For example, if a common mistake relates to the contract goods' existence or to the fact that the transferee is not already their true owner,[67] it is of course idle to talk about a passage of property. But it is apparently still conceivable that there may be a few cases of operative common mistakes where the question of a transfer of property might still arise. For example, where, unbeknown to both of the parties, the contractual adventure is illegal[68] or where the chattel transferred is of a substantially different nature than supposed.

---

63 J. Smith, Crim LR 1972, 586–89; Orchard, NZLJ 1973, 111–14; Williams, CLJ 1977, 72–73; Williams, Crim LR 1977, 205–7; Ormerod/Williams, Smith's Law of Theft, 2.266.

64 *Ilich v R* [1987] 162 CLR 110, 127 (Wilson, Dawson JJ).

65 *Barclays Bank v Simms* [1980] QB 677, 688–89 (Goff J); *Re Goldcorp Exchange Ltd* [1995] 1 AC 74 (PC), 102–3 (Lord Mustill); *Westdeutsche Landesbank v Islington* [1996] AC 669, esp 689–90 (Lord Goff); *R v Potisk* [1973] 6 SASR 389; *Ilich v R* [1987] 162 CLR 110, 127 (Wilson, Dawson JJ); *R v Milne* [1990] ABCA 323 (CanLII), esp [5]–[7], [11]–[18] (Coté J) (revd on pure criminal law grounds in [1992] 1 SCR 696); cf also *R v Shadrokh-Cigari* [1988] Crim LR 465 (CA) and *R v Webster* [2006] EWCA Crim 2894, [32]–[33] (Richards LJ), where legal ownership in a mistakenly transferred chattel was (impliedly) assumed to have passed but where equitable proprietary restitution was granted; the latter is questioned in Zogg, Proprietary Consequences, esp Chapter 5 sections 3 and 4.

66 Cf Chapter 4 section 1.2.

67 See *Bell v Lever Bros* [1932] AC 161, 217–18 (Lord Atkin); see also s 6 of the SGA 1979.

68 Cf Treitel, Contract, 8.13. An illegal contract might, but for the common mistake, only be unenforceable rather than void (see Chapter 2 fn 120); however, property might in any case – whether the contract being void or merely unenforceable by reason of the illegality – pass notwithstanding the contract's ineffectiveness (see Chapter 2 section 2.3.2.) and notwithstanding the common mistake.

A good example is *Nicholson & Venn v Smith-Marriott*.[69] This case concerned the sale of a specifically identified set of linen napkins and tablecloth which both parties believed to have been the authentic property of the monarch Charles I; this turned out to have been wrong (the items stemmed from the Georgian era). The buyer inter alia claimed in unjust enrichment (failure of consideration) on the basis that the contract has been void for common mistake. This was endorsed by Hallett J who held – obiter, due to the way the case had been pleaded – that "a Georgian relic [...] is an 'essentially different' thing from a Carolean relic" and, accordingly, that this was an operative common mistake, satisfying Lord Atkin's test in *Bell v Lever Bros*.[70] The buyer was thus entitled to a personal unjust enrichment claim for the value of the price paid, based on mistake and failure of consideration. Conversely, it could have been asked whether the seller had retained, as a result of his mistake, property in the transferred table linen or whether he would equally have been limited to a personal restitutionary claim. The court was not concerned with this question but the answer seems clear: The seller – just as the buyer – acted under a mere (self-induced) motivational mistake and was plainly aware that he was transferring legal ownership in the very table linen before him to the buyer. This motivational mistake could not have prevented the passage of property.[71]

Apart from the grounds set out in the previous sub-section, there is an additional compelling reason why property must pass in such cases of common motivational mistakes: Suppose that the buyer but not the seller had been aware of the goods' true nature (and that the goods' true nature had been more valuable than assumed by the seller). In such a case, the contract would not have been void for common mistake. If the buyer had fraudulently induced the

---

69 *Nicholson & Venn v Smith-Marriott* [1947] 177 LT 189 (KBD); see also *Sherwood v Walker* [1887] 66 Mich 568 (SC of Michigan) (sale of a specifically and physically identified cow which was believed to be sterile by both parties but which was in fact in calf; held that this was a mistake as to the substance of the thing and that the doctrine of common mistake applied); *Smith v Zimbalist* [1934] 2 Cal App 2d 324 (Dist CA, California) (sale of specifically identified violins which were mistakenly believed to be genuine Stradivarius and Guarnerius violins by both parties; held that this was a mistake as to the substance and that the doctrine of common mistake applied); for further examples, see Treitel, Contract, 8.18–20; Beatson et al, Anson's Law of Contract, 300–16. It must be re-emphasised, however, that the relevant test is very restrictive (at least in England); see esp the examples given by Lord Atkin in *Bell v Lever Bros* [1932] AC 161, 218–24; cf also *Leaf v International Galleries* [1950] 2 KB 86 (CA) (sale of a specifically identified painting which was mistakenly believed to be a Constable by both parties; stated obiter that the shared mistake was not serious enough); but cf the criticism of Treitel, Contract, 8.20.

70 *Bell v Lever Bros* [1932] AC 161.

71 It will furthermore be seen that, since the table linen had been specifically and physically identified, the mistake had not been one which prevented the passage of property under the head of a mistake as to the property's identity; see Chapter 4 section 2.3.

seller's mistake, the contract would have been voidable; legal title in the goods would then still have passed to the buyer, though subject to a power in rem of the seller to revest it. If the buyer had not induced the seller's unilateral mistake, the contract would have been perfectly valid in which case property would equally have passed (non-voidably). If this were otherwise, one would be confronted with the surprising result that property had not passed notwithstanding the seller's existing contractual obligation to make the very transfer in question. That could not be right. Rather, the valid contract's indirect curing effects[72] must inevitably lead to the conclusion that the proprietary transfer would neither – just as little as the contract – have been affected by the seller's unilateral motivational mistake. Defects which are not serious enough to render contracts void cannot prevent the passage of property. Now if this is correct, the seller's motivational mistake as to the goods' substance can neither become proprietarily relevant if it is shared by the buyer. The seller's intention and state of mind is exactly the same whether or not the buyer shares the mistake. In other words, the law of property does not, as opposed to the law of contract, distinguish between *unilateral* and *common* mistakes. The transferor's and the transferee's intentions to transfer and receive ownership must always be assessed separately.

2.2. MISTAKES AS TO THE TRANSFEREE'S IDENTITY

Having concluded that liability and other motivational mistakes, where the transferor is merely mistaken about the *why* he is carrying out a certain transfer, are not proprietarily fundamental, we shall now turn to cases where the transferor is actually mistaken about the fact *that* he is executing a certain transfer. The first and practically most important group of cases are those where the transferor is mistaken about the transferee's true identity. The cases commonly cited in this regard are, on the one hand, the criminal case of *R v Middleton*[73] and, on the other hand, various contract cases which have mainly concerned the question whether an identity mistake renders a contract void or voidable. It will be seen that *R v Middleton* is of very doubtful authority and that it did arguably not even concern a genuine identity mistake at all.[74] The argument will be made that a parallel should be drawn between the contractual position and the proprietary transfer, even though these are still notionally distinct and strictly independent from each other. It is convenient to first set out the applicable principles of contract law before turning to the proprietary position.

---

72 See Chapter 1 section 2.1.1.2.

73 *R v Middleton* [1873] LR 2 CCR 38.

74 See Chapter 4 section 2.2.2.3.

2.2.1. *Contract: Void or Voidable?*

Identity mistakes have constantly troubled the courts since at least the middle of the 19th century.[75] The facts of the respective cases have almost invariably followed the same pattern: A rogue (B) defrauds a seller (A) by misrepresenting his identity, the seller relies on the creditworthiness of the represented (impersonated) person and parts with the goods on credit. The rogue does not pay, or a cheque is dishonoured, and immediately resells the goods to a third party in good faith (C). The rogue disappears and a dispute arises between A and C in which the latter seeks to invoke the bona fide purchase defence which generally depends on the question whether A has retained legal ownership in the goods *ab initio* (B thus only ever taking a possessory title) or whether B has acquired a voidable title (i.e. legal ownership subject to a power in rem of A). If the former, the *nemo dat* rule applies and C will not generally be able to rely on a *nemo dat* exception. If the latter, C acquires unencumbered legal ownership by reason of s 23 of the SGA 1979; powers in rem are generally susceptible to bona fide purchases of third parties.[76]

In their analyses of this legal background, the courts have often imprecisely simplified the problem as solely and directly depending on the question whether the *contract* between A and B has been void or merely voidable. Though this approach – somewhat coincidentally – leads to correct results in the context of identity mistakes, it is, strictly speaking, conceptually inaccurate:[77,78]

---

75 For a historical analysis, see MacMillan, CLJ 2005.

76 See only *White v Garden* [1851] 10 CB 919, 138 ER 364; *Phillips v Phillips* [1861] 4 De G F&J 208, 218 (Lord Westbury); *Cundy v Lindsay* [1878] LR 3 App Cas 459 (HL), 464 (Lord Cairns); *Shalson v Russo* [2003] EWHC 1637 (Ch), [126] (Rimer J); Häcker, Third Party Rights.

77 An exception is *Shogun Finance Ltd v Hudson* [2003] UKHL 62, [2004] 1 AC 919, which concerned a hire-purchase transaction; the transferor had obviously not intended to transfer ownership to the rogue (yet) but s 27 of the Hire-Purchase Act 1964 still provided for a statutory *nemo dat* exception which required, inter alia, the existence of a valid or voidable (but not a void) hire-purchase agreement. Hence, the statutory *nemo dat* exception itself directly drew on the question whether the contract had been void or merely voidable.

78 In so far, the criticism of Thomas, LMCLQ 2008, 188, that a three-party conflict is in such cases effectively resolved by the law of contract rather than the law of property ("contractualism") somewhat misses the point. In fact, it *is* the law of property which – independently of the law of contract – decides whether the transferor retains ownership or merely obtains a power in rem. The fact that this depends on the dealings between A and B, which is generally beyond control or knowledge of C, is by no means objectionable. This is rather a direct consequence of the fact that property rights may be transferred by consensual dealings and the fact that the law recognises a broad *nemo dat* principle. In any case, it would certainly be wrong to suggest that the question whether ownership is retained by A, or whether B obtains a voidable title, should be answered in light of its impacts on bona fide acquisitions by third parties. If the *nemo dat* principle is conceived to be too rigid, new *nemo dat* exceptions should be created by the legislator. However, we may not manipulate one area of property law to correct the shortcomings of another.

It is true that defects which render contracts voidable, for example induced mistakes, duress or undue influence, generally also render proprietary transfers voidable, in the sense that the transferor loses ownership but obtains a power in rem to revest it, the power being susceptible to meanwhile bona fide purchases. In so far, the contractual and the proprietary levels provide for parallel rules. However, this must not conceal the fact that the *power in rem* is still notionally distinct and independent from the *personal power* to rescind the contract.[79] Strictly speaking, it is not relevant – as far as the bona fide purchase defence is concerned – whether a contract is voidable but only whether legal ownership passes voidably, subject to a power in rem. If the underlying contract is void, it would be equally inaccurate to say that it is the contract's voidness which *in and of itself* automatically prevents the passage of property. Rather, transfers of legal ownership, whether effected by delivery, by sale or by deed, are abstract and independent from the underlying transaction.[80] There are, however, certain kinds of defects which not only render contracts void (obligatory defects) but which also prevent the passage of property (real or dual defects) and it is submitted that identity mistakes, if operative, are precisely of that kind. They do not only negative the parties' contractual consent but also their real agreement.

The contractual identity mistake cases, as discussed in the following sub-sections, should accordingly be (re)interpreted as simply abbreviating the true legal reasoning and as leaving out one logical step in that regard. Instead of it being the contract's voidness or voidability *as such* which causes the retention of property or the proprietary transfer's voidability, it must rather be the identity mistake which, on the one hand, renders the contract void or voidable and which, on the other hand and independently of this, also renders the parties' real agreement void or voidable.

2.2.1.1. Cases Prior to *Shogun Finance*

With this in mind, we may now consider the contractual position with regard to identity mistakes. Prior to the landmark decision in *Shogun Finance v Hudson*,[81] the case law has been helplessly inconsistent. On the one hand, there were cases where the parties had dealt with each other exclusively in writing and at a distance. The most important of those cases is *Cundy v Lindsay*[82]

---

[79] See Zogg, Proprietary Consequences, Chapter 4 section 2.2.3.

[80] See Chapter 2 section 1.4. (delivery), Chapter 2 section 2.3. (sale) and Chapter 2 section 4.5. (deed).

[81] *Shogun Finance v Hudson* [2003] UKHL 62.

[82] *Cundy v Lindsay* [1878] LR 3 App Cas 459; see similarly *Boulton v Jones* [1857] 2 H&N 564, 157 ER 232; see also *King's Norton Metal Co v Edridge Merrett & Co* [1897] 14 TLR 98 (CA) where a rogue (Wallis) sent a letter to the seller by which he asked for an offer to buy metal. The letter was signed with "Hallam and Co", a fictitious firm which did not exist. The seller

where a rogue (Blenkarn), who had a room at 37 Wood Street, Cheapside, sent an order for goods (handkerchiefs) to the seller which he had signed with a name that appeared as "Blenkiron & Co". There was a highly respectable firm in 123 Wood Street whose name was "W Blenkiron & Son" and the seller thought – as the rogue had hoped – that it was that firm that had ordered the goods. The seller accordingly addressed all his letters to "Blenkiron & Co, 37 Wood Street" and eventually sent the goods to that address where they were received by the rogue, who subsequently sold them to an innocent purchaser. In an action for conversion against the latter, the House of Lords held that – because the parties had never been *ad idem* and because the seller's offer had been made to "Blenkiron & Co" rather than to Blenkarn – there was no contract between the seller and Blenkarn and that property in the goods had not passed to the latter. The action thus succeeded.

On the other hand, there were cases where the seller and the rogue had dealt with each other face-to-face. In *Phillips v Brooks Ltd*,[83] a rogue entered the store of a jeweller at Oxford Street, looked at some jewels and decided to buy a ring. He then pretended to be "Sir George Bullough", providing an address at St. James's Square, and the jeweller, who knew that there lived a person with such a name, let him have the ring against a cheque. The cheque was dishonoured and it turned out that the rogue had meanwhile pledged the goods with a pawnbroker acting in good faith. In an action for conversion by the jeweller against the pawnbroker, it was held that there had been a voidable contract between the jeweller and the rogue, that property had (voidably) passed to the latter and that the pawnbroker had thus acquired good title. The reason for this – and the feature distinguishing the case from *Cundy v Lindsay* – was that the rogue had been physically present in the seller's shop and that the seller had physically and face-to-face identified the person whom he intended to contract with:

> "[The seller] in fact contracted to sell and deliver [the ring] to the person who came into his shop [...]. [T]he seller intended to contract with the person present, and there was no error as to the person with whom he contracted, although the [seller] would not have made the contract if there had not been a fraudulent misrepresentation."[84]

---

sent the goods to Wallis' address and Wallis sold them to a good faith buyer. In an action for conversion against the latter, Smith LJ held that there was a voidable contract between the seller and Wallis and that property had passed (voidably) to the latter. The buyer therefore prevailed. This case may be distinguished from *Cundy v Lindsay* on the basis that the seller had not at all cared about the buyer's true identity – apparently, the seller would have contracted with anyone on credit – and that the offer had therefore been addressed to "the writer of the letters" according to the subjective principle; see fn 106 and text to fn 134–135; but cf Goodhart, LQR 1941, 239–40.

83 *Phillips v Brooks Ltd* [1919] 2 KB 243 (KBD).

84 Ibid, 246, 248–49 (Horridge J).

Phillips v Brooks was affirmed by the Court of Appeal in *Lewis v Averay (No 1)*,[85] a case which concerned almost identical facts, where Lord Denning MR spelled out the following principle:

> "When a dealing is had between a seller [...] and a person who is actually there present before him, then the presumption in law is that there is a contract, even though there is a fraudulent impersonation by the buyer representing himself as a different man than he is. There is a contract made with the very person there, who is present in person."[86]

In stark conflict with those cases stood *Ingram v Little* which equally concerned very similar (indistinguishable) facts.[87] Sellers LJ and Pearce LJ (Devlin LJ dissenting) pronounced the principle[88] that, though there is a presumption that the seller intends to deal with the person physically present, his offer must still be objectively construed. On the facts of the case, they concluded that the offer was to be understood as being addressed to the impersonated person.[89] It was accordingly held that there had been no contract between the seller and the rogue for lack of consent and that the seller had retained ownership.

---

85 *Lewis v Averay (No 1)* [1972] 1 QB 198 (CA) (face-to-face sale of a car against a cheque to a rogue who pretended to be "Richard Green", a famous film actor; the cheque was dishonoured and the car was meanwhile sold to a good faith buyer; held that there had been a voidable contract between the seller and the rogue and that the good faith purchaser prevailed); see also *Fawcett v Star Car Sales Ltd* [1960] NZLR 406 (CA of New Zealand).

86 *Lewis v Averay (No 1)* [1972] 1 QB 198, 207 (Lord Denning MR).

87 *Ingram v Little* [1961] 1 QB 31 (CA) (face-to-face sale of a car against a cheque to a rogue who pretended to be "P.G.M. Hutchinson", an existing wealthy person from Caterham; the cheque was dishonoured and the car was meanwhile sold to a good faith buyer); cf also *Lake v Simmons* [1927] AC 487 (HL), 500–2 (Viscount Haldane); but cf the interpretation of this case by Devlin LJ in *Ingram v Little*, 69–73, which was affd in *Shogun Finance v Hudson* [2003] UKHL 62, [140]–[141] (Lord Phillips).

88 They heavily drew on the article of Goodhart, LQR 1941, esp 240–42.

89 *Ingram v Little* [1961] 1 QB 31, 50–51 (Sellers LJ): "The mere presence of an individual cannot, however, be conclusive that an apparent bargain he may make is made with him. [...]. [*Phillips v Brooks*] is not an authority to establish that where an offer or acceptance is addressed to a person (although under a mistake as to his identity) who is present in person, then it must in all circumstances be treated as if actually addressed to him. I would regard the issue as a question of fact in each case depending on what was said and done and applying the elementary principles of offer and acceptance [...]"; 57 (Pearce LJ): "The offer is apparently addressed to the physical person present. Prima facie, he, by whatever name he is called, is the person to whom the offer is made. His physical presence identified by sight and hearing preponderates over vagaries of nomenclature. [...] Yet clearly, though difficult, it is not impossible to rebut the prima facie presumption that the offer can be accepted by the person to whom it is physically addressed."

2.2.1.2. The *Shogun Finance* Case

Some 125 years after *Cundy v Lindsay*, the House of Lords eventually got the chance to reconsider this branch of the law in the case of *Shogun Finance v Hudson*.[90] Their Lordships basically overruled *Ingram v Little* and – by a bare majority – authoritatively[91] settled the issue in favour of a distinction between cases where the parties have dealt with each other exclusively at a distance and by written correspondence, for example by an exchange of letters, e-mails or faxes, and cases where they have identified each other physically and face-to-face. If the identity of the other party is of the essence for the mistaken party,[92] an operative mistake renders a contract completely void in the former case but merely voidable in the latter.

The *Shogun Finance* case concerned a hire-purchase transaction. A rogue entered the showrooms of a motor dealer, introduced himself to the sales manager as "Mr Durlabh Patel", an existing person living in Leicester, and presented a driving licence of Mr Patel which he had obtained by dishonest means. The rogue said that he wished to purchase one of the displayed cars and they agreed on a price of £22,250, subject to obtaining hire-purchase finance. The rogue filled out a standard hire-purchase application form with the name and the details of Mr Patel and signed it with a forged signature of the latter. The manager then faxed the document together with a copy of the driving licence to Shogun Finance who, after having checked Mr Patel's creditworthiness, accepted the offer by signing the application form and by phoning the manager, communicating acceptance. The car was handed over to the rogue who merely paid a deposit of 10%, partly by a cheque which was dishonoured. The rogue then sold the car to a good faith buyer and disappeared. Shogun Finance sued

---

90 *Shogun Finance v Hudson* [2003] UKHL 62.

91 MacMillan, CLJ 2005, has argued that the interpretation of the old cases was historically incorrect since they had in fact (also) been concerned with restoration in the criminal law; yet, as she admits, the *Shogun* decision is nonetheless binding in England; cf also Treitel, Contract, 8.39 (in fine).

92 If the identity of the other party is irrelevant to the mistaken party, the misrepresentation (in face-to-face dealings) may not induce the conclusion of the contract; in contracts concluded at a distance, the offer or acceptance is subjectively addressed to the "writer of the letters"; see fn 106; *King's Norton Metal v Edridge Merrett* [1897] 14 TLR 98, 99 (Smith LJ) (and comment in fn 82); cf also *Citibank NA v Brown Shipley & Co Ltd* [1991] 2 All ER 690 (QBD), 699–702 (Waller J) (sub nom *Midland Bank plc v Brown Shipley Co & Ltd*); *Fawcett v Star Car Sales* [1960] NZLR 406. The identity of the other party is usually essential in credit transactions or ongoing relationships but not if the mistaken party would have dealt with anyone, as for example in mere retail sales; *Shogun Finance v Hudson* [2003] UKHL 62, [47]–[48] (Lord Hobhouse); Beale, Chitty on Contracts, vol 1, 3.37; Bridge et al, Benjamin's Sale of Goods, 3.12; MacMillan, CLJ 2005, 742.

the buyer in conversion. This action depended on the question whether the latter could bring himself within the *nemo dat* exception of s 27 of the Hire-Purchase Act 1964 which required that the good faith buyer's seller (the rogue) had been a "debtor" under a valid or at least a voidable – but not a void – hire-purchase agreement with the owner (Shogun Finance). Hence, the crucial issue was whether there had at least been a voidable contract between Shogun Finance and the rogue or whether their apparent agreement had been completely void. A bare majority in the House of Lords (Lord Hobhouse, Lord Phillips and Lord Walker) held that the contract had been void and that the buyer could thus not have invoked the exception of s 27.[93] The majority's line of reasoning might be summarised as follows.

First, all of their Lordships (including Lord Nicholls and Lord Millett) analysed the issue whether Shogun Finance and the rogue had concluded a contract or whether an identity mistake had negatived their apparent agreement as essentially being a problem of offer and acceptance (consent).

Second, again everyone appeared to agree that an offer may only be accepted by the person – or a person having authority to bind that person – to whom the offer was "made" or "addressed" on the facts of the case and according to the relevant legal rules.[94] Similarly, the acceptance of an offer addressed to the acceptor must be addressed to the offeror.

Third, as Lord Walker put it,[95] the crucial question was – and it was basically this question which divided their Lordships – *to whom* Shogun Finance's acceptance (or offer) had been "made", Mr Patel or the rogue. According to the minority's view, it should have been regarded as made to the person to whom it was – apparently as a matter of pure fact – *directed*.[96] By contrast, the majority regarded this as a mixed question of fact and law[97] and held that an offer or acceptance is "made" (addressed) to the person to whom it is *subjectively intended* or to whom it is *objectively deemed to be intended*.[98] As Lord Phillips emphasised, who arguably offered the most pertinent speech of the majority, the question to

---

93 The minority (Lord Nicholls and Lord Millett) would have overruled *Cundy v Lindsay*. They basically defended the view that the face-to-face principle should have been extended to all means of communication, including written correspondence at a distance, and that, in other words, an offer or acceptance is *addressed* to the person to whom it is – as a matter of fact – *directed* (as opposed to "intended" or "deemed to be intended"). They would thus have held that Shogun Finance and the rogue had been *ad idem* and that the contract had been merely *voidable* for misrepresentation.

94 See also *Whittaker v Campbell* [1984] QB 318, 326–27 (Goff LJ); *Ingram v Little* [1961] 1 QB 31, 64 (Devlin LJ); *Fawcett v Star Car Sales* [1960] NZLR 406, 419 (Gresson P); Goodhart, LQR 1941, 229–32.

95 *Shogun Finance v Hudson* [2003] UKHL 62, [184] (Lord Walker).

96 Ibid, [27]–[30] (Lord Nicholls), [63]–[82], [103] (Lord Millett).

97 Cf also *Ingram v Little* [1961] 1 QB 31, 64–65 (Devlin LJ).

98 *Shogun Finance v Hudson* [2003] UKHL 62, esp [123]–[125] (Lord Phillips), see also [183]–[184] (Lord Walker), [46]–[48] (Lord Hobhouse).

whom an offer or acceptance is made is determined by the same principles as those which determine whether the parties are *ad idem* regarding the essential terms of a contract and which determine their content.[99] The question to whom an offer or acceptance is addressed is accordingly determined by the *objective principle*, i.e. an objective interpretation of the words and conduct of the parties,[100] unless one of the parties has *known* the other party's *actual subjective intention*, in which case that subjective intention is relevant,[101] or unless both parties are *subjectively ad idem*, in which case the subjective consent prevails over the outward appearance.[102]

Fourth, the majority upheld a distinction between dealings inter praesentes and cases where the parties have dealt with each other exclusively at a distance. It was held that the application of the above principles does not give rise to any problems in the latter case where the parties have communicated *exclusively in writing*.[103] In such cases, the question of to whom an offer or acceptance is made is – unless the subjective principle applies – determined by an objective construction of the exchanged written documents. This is consistent with the general principles of contract law. The majority furthermore seemed to suggest that, if the agreement has been reduced to writing, extrinsic evidence is only admissible to fill gaps or to clarify unclear words but not where the addressee has been unequivocally identified by clear words of the document.[104] However, it is doubtful whether those remarks correctly state the law since it is generally accepted that the parol evidence rule does not apply in relation to the validity and formation of a contract but merely as to its contents, once it is established that it has been formed.[105] It follows that in cases where the parties have dealt with each other exclusively in writing, the addressee of the relevant offer or acceptance is, in principle, determined by an objective construction of the written contract and – even if the contract has been reduced to writing – of any available extrinsic

---

99 This was also the approach proposed by Goodhart, LQR 1941, 229–32, 235; see also Slade, LQR 1954, 392–95; Beatson et al, Anson's Law of Contract, 290–92.

100 See fn 10; see esp Goodhart, LQR 1941, 230–32; cf also *Cornish v Abington* [1859] 4 H&N 549; Treitel, Contract, 8.47.

101 *Shogun Finance v Hudson* [2003] UKHL 62, [123] (Lord Phillips), citing *Smith v Hughes* [1871] LR 6 QB 597 and *Hartog v Colin & Shields* [1939] 3 All ER 566; see also Goodhart, LQR 1941, 230–31; Slade, LQR 1954, 392–95. The problem whether the contract might be upheld on the subjectively intended terms does obviously not arise in mistaken identity cases; see fn 14.

102 See fn 12.

103 *Shogun Finance v Hudson* [2003] UKHL 62, esp [154], [167], [178] (Lord Phillips).

104 Ibid, esp [46]–[49] (Lord Hobhouse), see also [154]–[161] (Lord Phillips), [188] (Lord Walker); cf also *Hector v Lyons* [1989] 58 P&CR 156 (CA), 159 (Browne-Wilkinson V-C), 160 (Woolf LJ).

105 *Homburg Houtimport BV v Agrosin Private Ltd (The Starsin)* [2003] UKHL 12, [2004] 1 AC 715, [175] (Lord Millett); *Muneer Hamid v Francis Bradshaw Partnership* [2013] EWCA Civ 470 (CA), [46]–[58], esp [57] (Jackson LJ); McLauchlan, LQR 2005; Treitel, Contract, 6.16, 6.20, 8.39 (fn 216); McKendrick, Chitty on Contracts, vol 1, 13.119, 13.132.

evidence, such as drafts exchanged in negotiations. The objective principle does not apply where – which may equally be proved by extrinsic evidence – one of the parties has known of the other party's actual subjective intention or if the parties have in fact been subjectively *ad idem*.[106]

Fifth, the majority – in so far in accordance with the minority – held that in cases where the parties have dealt with each other face-to-face there is at least a "strong presumption", if not a rule, that the offer or acceptance is addressed to the person physically present, whoever that person is and whatever attributes that person may have.[107] In such cases, there is an agreement between the parties physically present and the contract may, if at all, only be voidable for misrepresentation.

The underlying basis of this "*face-to-face principle*" is the notion that a physical identification of a person is generally stronger than an identification by description, for example by providing a name, address, date of birth or other features. If a shopkeeper intends to contract with a person (rogue) physically present in his store, the former has, once the rogue has provided his wrong details, generally two things in mind: "I want to contract with *this person* physically present" and "I want to contract with X, living in Y". It is the effect of *Shogun Finance* that the former prevails. This means, on the one hand, that the shopkeeper's offer or acceptance must *objectively* be construed as being made "to the person physically present". On the other hand – and this is actually the crucial feature of the face-to-face principle –, the shopkeeper's *actual subjective intention* is equally taken to have been "to contract with the person physically present". Had one asked the shopkeeper whether he *actually* intended to deal with the person physically present or with X, living in Y, he could not have given a sensible answer since he had simply believed that these were one

---

106 Arguably, the parties *are* subjectively *ad idem* – even if a written document and an objective interpretation thereof might show that an offer has been addressed to someone else than the actual acceptor – if it is proved (even if only by extrinsic evidence) that the mistaken offeror has in fact subjectively intended to contract "with whomever might have been the writer of the letters", i.e. if the identity of the other party has simply been immaterial to the offeror and if the latter would subjectively have contracted with *anyone*; see *King's Norton Metal v Edridge Merrett* [1897] 14 TLR 98, 99 (Smith LJ) (and comment in fn 82 and text to fn 134–135); cf also *Citibank v Brown Shipley* [1991] 2 All ER 690, 699–702 (Waller J); *Fawcett v Star Car Sales* [1960] NZLR 406.

107 *Shogun Finance v Hudson* [2003] UKHL 62, [170] (Lord Phillips): "Where there is some form of personal contact between individuals who are conducting negotiations, this approach [i.e. the amalgam of the objective and subjective principle determining the addressee of an offer] gives rise to problems. In such a situation I would favour the application of a strong presumption that each intends to contract with the other, with whom he is dealing"; see also [185]–[187] (Lord Walker), considering a departure from the presumption or rule in cases of agency and where a person's senses are impaired, as for example if a blind is deceived; cf also [67] (Lord Millett); *Ingram v Little* [1961] 1 QB 31, 65–67 (Devlin LJ); contra: GOODHART, LQR 1941, 240–42.

and the same person.[108] Yet, in a retrospective assessment of the shopkeeper's subjective intention, as existing at the time of conclusion, we inevitably need an answer to this conundrum – in one or the other direction – and *Shogun Finance* now authoritatively provides that the physical element ought to prevail. In other words, *Shogun Finance* has effectively reduced a person's name, address, date of birth and the like to mere *attributes* and declared a person's physical body to constitute its *identity* in face-to-face cases, at least for the purposes of identifying the addressee of an offer or acceptance.[109]

Sixth, the majority held that the case before them did not, on its facts, concern face-to-face dealings but that this was rather a case where the parties (Shogun Finance and the rogue) had exclusively dealt with each other at a distance and in writing (fax sent by the dealer's manager[110]). Crucially, it was held that the dealer had not been an agent of Shogun Finance. Therefore, the fact that the rogue had been present in the dealer's showrooms and that the dealer had physically identified him was immaterial.[111] Hence, their Lordships objectively construed the words of the written documents and concluded that they had unequivocally shown that "Mr Patel" and not the rogue (or the person physically present in the dealer's showrooms) had been the objectively intended addressee of Shogun Finance's acceptance. There was accordingly no contract between Shogun Finance and the rogue (and of course neither between Shogun Finance and Mr Patel since the rogue had no authority to bind the latter).

It follows that there was in fact no divergence between Shogun Finance's subjective intention ("to deal with Mr Patel") and the objective construction of the documents ("to deal with Mr Patel"). The case was solved on the basis of the objective principle. However, it could equally well have been resolved on the basis of the subjective principle since (i) Shogun Finance had subjectively intended to deal with Mr Patel and because (ii) the rogue had knowledge of this.[112]

What, however, would have been the position had the parties dealt with each other face-to-face, for example if the dealer had been Shogun Finance's agent or

---

108 *Shogun Finance v Hudson* [2003] UKHL 62, [138], [153], [170] (Lord Phillips), calling this a "conundrum".

109 As to the almost philosophical issue of what defines the "identity" of a person and the role of a name in that regard, see *Shogun Finance v Hudson* [2003] UKHL 62, [60], [73]–[75] (Lord Millett), [120]–[122] (Lord Phillips); *Lewis v Averay (No 1)* [1972] 1 QB 198, 206 (Lord Denning MR); Fox, Property Rights, 4.121; Cartwright, Misrepresentation, 14.2–3, 14.13.

110 Apart from that, the dealer – but not the rogue – had also spoken with an agent of Shogun Finance by phone.

111 *Shogun Finance v Hudson* [2003] UKHL 62, [51] (Lord Hobhouse), [173]–[178] (Lord Phillips), [191] (Lord Walker).

112 See fn 101. The same is true for *Cundy v Lindsay* [1878] LR 3 App Cas 459; see also Slade, LQR 1954, 393–95; Treitel, Contract, 8.50; cf also *Fawcett v Star Car Sales* [1960] NZLR 406, 418 (Gresson P).

if another representative of Shogun Finance had been present in the showrooms? In this case, Shogun Finance's acceptance would, on the one hand, have been *objectively* addressed "to the person physically present" (documentary evidence being overridden by the extrinsic evidence of physical identification). Even more importantly, Shogun Finance's *subjective intention* would then neither have been "to deal with Mr Patel" but "to deal with the person physically present". There is nothing artificial with this. First, had the dealer had authority to bind Shogun Finance, it would have been *his* subjective intention which would have been relevant and which would have been attributed to Shogun Finance. This is orthodox company and agency law. Second, it is natural to suppose that an offeror's actual intention generally is "to deal with the person physically present" if he is dealing with that person face-to-face and if he has identified that person by sight. In such a case, that person's details (name, address, date or place of birth, nationality, bank details, creditworthiness or the like) are only *attributes* which do not *identify* the contracting party. Even though the mistaken party would not have formed a subjective intention to contract with the person physically present had it known of those attributes, it still *did* form such an intention.

2.2.1.3. Conclusions and Scope of the Face-to-Face Principle

The category of identity mistakes is not actually based on a mistake casually speaking – in the sense of a simple mistake of one party as to the other party's name, address or other details – but rather on the fact that one of the parties (offeree or acceptee) is not effectively identified as a party to the contract according the applicable rules of contract law on offer and acceptance. Identity mistakes are solely a problem of congruence of offer and acceptance and of identification of the parties to the contract. The relevant questions are: (1) To whom was the offer addressed? (2) To whom was the acceptance addressed? (3) Did they match?

The question of to whom an offer or acceptance is addressed is determined by the same principles as those applying in relation to any other term of the contract. Generally, the addressee is determined by the objective principle, i.e. by an objective construction of the words and conduct of the parties. But if the objective meaning of a party's words or conduct differs from that party's actual subjective intention, that subjective intention is relevant if the other party is aware of it. Similarly, the objective principle is displaced by the subjective principle if the parties are in fact subjectively *ad idem*, i.e. if both parties subjectively intend to contract with each other.[113]

If the parties have dealt with each other exclusively in writing, there is no additional problem (apart from the fact that one should recognise that

[113] The parties are arguably subjectively *ad idem* if the mistaken party does simply not care about the other party's true identity; see fn 106.

extrinsic evidence is always admissible to determine the addressee of an offer or acceptance). By contrast, if the parties have dealt with each other face-to-face, there is a rule or at least a very strong presumption that both parties have objectively and subjectively intended "to deal with the person physically present". In other words, the physical identification prevails – objectively and subjectively – over an identification by description, i.e. by words providing a name, address or other details of the parties.

But there remains one last difficult question: What is the exact scope of this face-to-face principle? Three particular issues shall be mentioned: First, it seems clear that the face-to-face principle does apply if the parties have had some physical face-to-face contact in their negotiations but if they have eventually concluded a written agreement, whether by signing it in physical presence of each other or by a subsequent exchange of letters and whether this merely evidenced the oral contract or reduced the contract to writing.[114] The parol evidence rule does not apply to the formation of a contract. It is the underlying rationale of the face-to-face principle to give preference to a physical identification over an identification by words and it would be difficult to see why a physical identification on one day should again be ignored on a later day.

Second, what is the position if a rogue enters the store of a blind shopkeeper and concludes a contract with the latter inter praesentes? This is a very delicate question which was explicitly left open by Lord Walker.[115] Does the face-to-face principle only apply if the other party has indeed been identified *by sight* or also if it has been identified *by hearing* or *by touching*, for example by shaking hands? Does such a form of physical identification still prevail over an inconsistent identification by description? It will later be argued that the face-to-face principle should apply neither in such a case nor in cases where the parties have contracted in the dark.[116] If this is correct, it follows that the face-to-face principle neither applies if the parties have, perhaps in combination with written correspondence, only dealt with each other by telephone. Just as with regard to blind persons, identification by hearing should not prevail over an identification by description. By contrast, the face-to-face principle should arguably apply

114 Cf *Shogun Finance v Hudson* [2003] UKHL 62, [170] (Lord Phillips) (emphases added): "Where there is *some* form of personal contact between individuals who are conducting negotiations [...]. Where, however, the dealings are *exclusively* conducted in writing [...]", see also [188] (Lord Walker); [24]–[25] (Lord Nicholls); but cf *Hector v Lyons* [1989] 58 P&CR 156, 159 (Browne-Wilkinson V-C).

115 *Shogun Finance v Hudson* [2003] UKHL 62, [187] (Lord Walker); his Lordship gave the biblical example of Jacob who impersonated his elder twin brother Esau in order to deceive his blind father Isaac (Genesis, ch 27).

116 See *R v Ashwell* [1885] 16 QBD 190 and Chapter 4 section 2.3.2.4.; see also Goodhart, LQR 1941, 240–41, who, however, denied the existence of a face-to-face principle and who effectively argued that an identification by description ought to prevail in any case over an identification by sight.

where the parties have negotiated via some modern form of video link (video conferences, Skype, or the like). Just as where the parties are physically present, identification by sight should prevail.[117]

Third, agency appears to be a general exception to the face-to-face principle.[118] If A communicates with B – whether face-to-face or at a distance! – and if it is established by an application of the objective and the subjective principle that A does not intend to deal with B as principal but only as an agent for a principal (X), a contract can only come into existence between A and X. This requires that B has authority, actual or apparent, to bind X. Otherwise, the apparent contract between A and X is void for lack of authority.[119] It follows that the face-to-face principle only applies – in a sense – *one-sidedly* in such a case: It does apply with regard to B's offer or acceptance, made on behalf of X, by which B objectively and subjectively intends to deal "with the person identified by sight". However, it does not apply with regard to A's offer or acceptance since A does not – neither subjectively nor objectively – intend to contract "with the person identified by sight" but only with that person's principal, who is not physically present.[120] Who this principal is, i.e. to whom the offer or acceptance is addressed (X or another person), must be determined by the objective and the subjective principle, just as in cases of written or telephonic communication.

This is the proper explanation of *Hardman v Booth*.[121] In this case, a seller (A) went to the premises of "Gandell & Co" where he found Edward Gandell who pretended to be a partner of that firm but who was in fact only a clerk without authority. Edward Gandell purported to conclude a contract for the purchase of goods on behalf of Gandell & Co and A delivered the goods to the premises of Gandell & Co where Edward Gandell received them and later pledged them to a party in good faith. Obviously, there was no contract between A and Gandell & Co because Edward had no authority to bind the firm. Yet, the question arose whether there had been a (voidable) contract between A and Edward Gandell. The court unanimously held that there had been no such contract either. This must be right. Even though A and Edward Gandell had dealt with each other face-to-face, A had neither objectively nor subjectively intended to contract with Edward Gandell as principal but only as an agent. Since A had thus not identified the principal by sight, his offer or acceptance was to be construed in accordance

117 The position regarding dealings by telephone or video link was left open by Lord Phillips ([168]) and Lord Walker ([188]). Lord Nicholls ([28]) and Lord Millett ([69]) used the uncertainty in this regard as an argument against the limitation of the face-to-face principle to cases where the parties have dealt with each other in physical presence and in favour of its extension to any kinds of dealings and to any means of communication.

118 *Shogun Finance v Hudson* [2003] UKHL 62, [89] (Lord Millett), [186]–[187] (Lord Walker).

119 Ibid, [48] (Lord Hobhouse), [170]–[172], [178] (Lord Phillips).

120 Evidently, companies as contracting parties can never be identified by sight.

121 *Hardman v Booth* [1863] All ER Rep Ext 1847; see also *Shogun Finance v Hudson* [2003] UKHL 62, [89] (Lord Millett), [186] (Lord Walker).

with the ordinary rules: On the one hand, it was objectively addressed only to Gandell & Co. On the other hand, A had subjectively intended to contract only with Gandell & Co and Edward Gandell had knowledge of this.[122] Hence, the latter could not accept A's offer in his own name.

2.2.2. *Proprietary Transfer: Void or Voidable?*

2.2.2.1. Parallel between the Contractual and the Proprietary Position: Identity Mistakes as Dual Defects

We can now turn to the actual question of our inquiry: Does a mistake as to the transferee's identity negative the transferor's intention to transfer legal ownership and, if so, in what circumstances? It has been explained that pure motivational mistakes, where a transferor is merely mistaken about the *why* he is carrying out a certain transfer, cannot prevent the passage of property.[123] But the identity of the transferee, i.e. *to whom* a transfer is to be made, is a parameter of the transfer itself and affects a transferor's intention *that* a certain transfer shall be carried out. An intention to transfer property to C is insufficient to effect a transfer to B. The question arises of when exactly a transferor is mistaken about the "identity" of a transferee. Is a mistake as to his name sufficient? Is this to be determined subjectively or objectively? Does the face-to-face principle apply? As the previous sub-sections have shown, giving an answer to those questions is by no means a straightforward task.

In the leading case on this subject, *Shogun Finance v Hudson*,[124] the question of a transfer of property did not actually arise. As usual in hire-purchase transactions, the original legal owner of the car in question, the motor dealer, had transferred property in the car to the finance company, Shogun Finance, and the apparent (void) agreement – real or obligatory – between the latter and the rogue had in any case not provided for a transfer of property to the rogue yet. In almost all other identity mistake cases, however, the transfer of property from the original owner to the rogue was actually the crucial issue. It has already been mentioned that the courts in those cases, including the House of Lords in *Shogun Finance* discussing them, somewhat imprecisely assumed that the question whether property had been retained *ab initio* or whether it had passed voidably to the rogue, subject to a power in rem of the former owner, was just the same as (or at least directly depended on) the question whether the underlying contract was void or voidable. Apparently, the courts supposed that the fact that a contract was void *necessarily* and *by itself* meant that property

[122] Crucially, this was not a case where the true identity of the other party has been immaterial to A.

[123] See Chapter 4 section 2.1.

[124] *Shogun Finance v Hudson* [2003] UKHL 62.

could not have passed. With respect, this cannot be right. Even if one does not share the view adopted in this book that even transfers by sale and transfers by deed are abstract, it can still not be doubted that at least transfers by delivery are abstract.[125] Since delivery had in fact been made in all identity mistake cases, the fact that the underlying contract was void could not in and of itself have been the true reason why property had been retained *ab initio*.

This is not to suggest that those cases have been wrongly decided. Quite to the contrary, it is argued that the results of each of them – *Ingram v Little* apart – was right; only their reasonings should be slightly amended or reinterpreted. Whether one is concerned with a transfer by sale or a transfer by delivery or even a transfer by deed, the transfer of property is distinct and independent from the underlying contract (principle of separation and abstraction). The grounds which render a contract voidable, particularly fraudulent misrepresentation, are generally *also* grounds which prompt the law of property to confer a new and distinct power in rem on the transferor to revest ownership in him. This is why there is a parallel between a contract's and a proprietary transfer's voidability.[126] Furthermore, such a parallel between the contractual and the proprietary position should also be recognised as far as voidness on the ground of an identity mistake is concerned. This kind of mistake is, if operative, a *dual defect* which does not only negative the parties' contractual consent but also their real agreement.

It is helpful to compare the transferor's intention to transfer ownership with an *offer* to transfer property and the transferee's intention to receive ownership with a corresponding *acceptance*. This allows us to draw a close parallel between the offer to transfer property and the offer to conclude a contract.[127] It follows, first, that there is an operative identity mistake on the proprietary level if the transferor's offer to transfer property is not addressed to the transferee in question and, second, that the question of *to whom* an offer to transfer property is addressed is determined by the same principles as those which determine the addressee of a contractual offer.

Certainly, a real agreement, i.e. the combination of a transferor's intention to transfer ownership and a transferee's intention to receive it, is not strictly a contract and it is governed by different rules. On the one hand, property might provisionally pass without the transferee's acceptance;[128] on the other hand, consideration is not required (if delivery has been made). However, there is still nothing to prevent an analogous application of the contract rules with regard

---

125 See Chapter 2 section 1.4.

126 See generally Zogg, Proprietary Consequences, Chapter 4.

127 See also Orchard, NZLJ 1973, 113; Williams, Crim LR 1958, 222: "The principles governing mistake of identity of party are probably analogous to those for mistake in the formation of contract."

128 See Chapter 2 section 1.3.

to the question of *to whom* an offer to transfer property is addressed. Arguably, this question must in principle also be determined by an objective interpretation of the words and conduct of the transferor. If the defendant is only objectively but not subjectively the addressee of the proprietary transfer, the subjective intention must still prevail if the defendant knows that the transferor does not subjectively intend to transfer property to him. Similarly, if the transferor's offer to transfer property is not objectively addressed to the defendant but if the transferor still subjectively intends to do so – and if the defendant eventually accepts the transfer –, the objective outward appearance is displaced by the parties' subjective consent.[129] Moreover, the face-to-face principle, which is authoritatively established on the contractual level, must arguably also apply on the proprietary plane: If the transferor has physically identified the transferee by sight, that identification should – objectively and subjectively – prevail over an identification by description, for example by providing a name, address, date of birth or the like. Such a "contract analogy" on the proprietary level is, as will emerge from the following discussion, broadly consistent with the available case law.

2.2.2.2. Dealings at a Distance: Identification by Description (or Otherwise than by Sight)

It is convenient to start with cases where the parties have not dealt with each other face-to-face, i.e. where the transferor has not identified the transferee by sight. Apart from *Shogun Finance*,[130] where the issue of a transfer of property from the owner (Shogun Finance) to the rogue has not arisen, the most important mistaken identity case concerned with dealings at a distance is *Cundy v Lindsay*.[131] It will be recalled that the transferor (A) received an order for handkerchiefs sent by the rogue Blenkarn who had a room at 37 Wood Street, Cheapside. The order was signed by the rogue with a name that appeared as "Blenkiron & Co", giving the address of "37 Wood Street, Cheapside". A thought, as the rogue had hoped, that the order came from the respectable firm "W Blenkiron & Son" which had its premises in the same street. A sent back a letter expressing his acceptance of the offer which he addressed to "Blenkiron & Co, 37 Wood Street, Cheapside" and sent the goods to that same address where the rogue received them. In an action for conversion against a good faith purchaser, the House of Lords unanimously held (i) that there had been no contract between A and the rogue and (ii) that property in the goods had not

129 Since the transferee's acceptance of ownership is not necessarily a constitutive requirement *ab initio* (see Chapter 2 section 1.3.), property may pass provisionally in accordance with the transferor's unilateral subjective intention.

130 *Shogun Finance* [2003] UKHL 62.

131 *Cundy v Lindsay* [1878] LR 3 App Cas 459.

passed to the latter. Though their Lordships apparently assumed that a transfer of property could only have been effected *by sale* and that a valid or voidable contract was inevitably required for those purposes,[132] this is not strictly correct. Delivery had been made to Blenkarn and an abstract transfer *by delivery* would in any event have been possible.[133] However, their Lordships' finding that no property had passed was still correct on the basis that A's intention to transfer ownership to Blenkarn had equally been negatived by the identity mistake, just as his intention to conclude a contract with the latter had been negatived by that mistake. Since A had never identified the transferee by sight, the face-to-face principle did not apply. Objectively, A's offer to transfer property was addressed to the firm "Blenkiron" and not to "Blenkarn". Furthermore, A had subjectively intended to transfer ownership to "Blenkiron" and the rogue had knowledge of this. For those reasons, A's intention to transfer property had not been addressed to Blenkarn who could therefore only have taken a possessory legal title.

This case may be contrasted with *King's Norton Metal v Edridge Merrett*.[134] A rogue (Wallis) sent a letter to the seller (A) by which he asked for an offer to buy metal. The letter was signed with "Hallam and Co", a fictitious firm which did not exist. A, who had apparently neither checked that firm's existence or creditworthiness nor otherwise cared about the buyer's true identity, sent an offer to Wallis' address, apparently made to "Hallam and Co". Wallis sent back an acceptance letter and A despatched the goods on credit to Wallis' address. In an action for conversion by A against a good faith buyer, Smith LJ held that there had been a (voidable) contract between A and Wallis and that property had (voidably) passed to the latter. The judge apparently distinguished the case from *Cundy v Lindsay* on the basis that "Hallam and Co" was a fictitious firm and not an existing entity. This seems to refer to the fact that the seller had not at all cared about the buyer's true identity as he had not even made inquiries about the firm's very existence. In so far, the case should be interpreted on the basis that, though A's offer to transfer property had objectively been addressed to

---

132 Ibid, 464–66 (Lord Cairns): "[I]f the property in the goods in question passed, it could only pass by way of contract; there is nothing else which could have passed the property. [...] My Lords, that being so [i.e. the contract being void], it is idle to talk of the property passing", 468 (Lord Hatherley) (emphasis added): "But no contract was made with Blenkarn [...] and *therefore* there could be no delivery of the goods with the intent to pass the property", but cf 470–71 (Lord Penzance): "I am not aware, my Lords, that there is any decided case in which a sale and delivery intended to be made to one man, has been held to be a sale and delivery so as to pass the property to another, against the intent and will of the vendor."

133 See Chapter 2 section 1.4. and Swadling, LQR 2005, 126–27, 141–42, 152; Häcker, Impaired Consent, 136–37, 194–96; Häcker, Causality and abstraction, 210–12.

134 *King's Norton Metal v Edridge Merrett* [1897] 14 TLR 98; cf also *Citibank v Brown Shipley* [1991] 2 All ER 690, 699–702 (Waller J); *Fawcett v Star Car Sales* [1960] NZLR 406, 429–32 (Cleary J, North J agreeing), 419–20 (Gresson P, who reached a different result).

"Hallam and Co", A had still subjectively intended to make the offer to "the writer of the letters"[135] since he had not in fact cared about the identity of the buyer. Though the case involved a credit transaction, the seller had still – carelessly – accepted to transfer property to whomever had written the letters. In so far, A's actual subjective intention displaced the objective outward appearance of his offer.

A case from the realm of criminal law is *R v Hudson*.[136] The Ministry of Food, intending to pay an existing debt to their creditor Lewis Hutson, who lived in Scunthorpe, mistakenly made out a cheque to "Mr Hudson". For some mistake, the letter enclosing that cheque was sent to the address of one James Hudson who lived in the same town. James Hudson realised the mistake, sent back the cheque to the Ministry and fraudulently asked to correct it by including his initial "J". The Ministry apologised and sent back the corrected cheque for "Mr J Hudson". James Hudson thereupon banked the cheque and was later convicted of larceny of the cheque. This conviction was upheld in the Court of Criminal Appeal. Though the court did not thoroughly discuss the issue of passage of ownership, the conviction for larceny must inevitably have meant that property in the cheque had been retained by the Ministry.[137] That must be right: Though there was no contract between the Ministry and James Hudson, property in the cheque could (potentially) still have passed abstractly by delivery. Unlike in *Cundy v Lindsay*, the Ministry's offer to pass ownership in the cheque could objectively only have been construed as being addressed to James Hudson since they had inserted the initial "J" and sent it to James Hudson's address. However, the Ministry had evidently subjectively intended to transfer ownership in the cheque to "Lewis Hutson", their creditor, and James Hudson had knowledge of this. For that reason, the objective principle was displaced by the transferor's actual subjective intention. Hence, property could not have passed to James Hudson.

So far, cases have been discussed where either both, an objective interpretation *and* the transferor's actual subjective intention pointed at a person other than the defendant (*Cundy v Lindsay*) or where, though the objective principle pointing at a person other than the defendant, the transferor's actual subjective intention still addressed the defendant as transferee (*King's Norton Metal v Edridge Merrett*) or where, though the objective principle pointing at the defendant, the

---

135 *King's Norton Metal v Edridge Merrett* [1897] 14 TLR 98, 99 (Smith LJ).

136 *R v Hudson* [1943] KB 458 (Ct of Criminal Appeal). The two similar cases of *R v Mucklow* [1827] 1 Mood CC 160, 168 ER 1225 (Crown Cases Reserved) and *R v Davies* [1856] Dears 640, 169 ER 878 (Crown Cases Reserved), the reports of which are very brief, are of little assistance since the accused was acquitted on the basis that there had been no *animus furandi* at the time of taking.

137 Larceny was impossible if ownership had passed to the defendant; see the introductory remarks of this chapter section 2.

transferor's subjective intention addressed a person other than the defendant of which the latter had been aware (*R v Hudson*). There remains one last scenario, namely where the transfer is objectively but not subjectively addressed to the defendant but where the defendant has no knowledge of this. There is apparently no case where it has ever been decided whether property would pass in such circumstances or not.

Suppose that A subjectively intends to make an offer to sell goods on credit to "Mr Lewis Hutson, Main Road 10, Scunthorpe" but that by some mistake he writes "Mr Hudson, Main Road 1, Scunthorpe" and that he sends the offer and the goods to that latter address where one Mr James Hudson is living. Suppose further that Hudson does not know – and ought not to know – that the offer is not in fact intended for him and that he sends back an acceptance letter whereupon A despatches the goods to his address. Would property pass to Hudson? Based on the objective principle, Hudson is supposedly entitled to rely on the natural meaning of the words used in the offer and to assume that it is addressed to him. His acceptance would bring a contract between him and A into existence and it is argued that A's offer to transfer property would equally be bindingly addressed to Hudson. It follows that property would pass to the latter in such a case.

Proprietary transfers are – similarly as contracts – subject to the objective principle, at least as far as the identification of the addressee is concerned. With regard to contractual transfers of property, this must already follow from the "indirect curing effects" of an existing contract formed on the basis of the objective principle. If a mistake is unable to negative a contractual consent, it cannot – *a fortiori* – negative the proprietary consent.[138] The same must apply in non-contractual settings, for example where A subjectively intends to make a gift or to discharge an existing debt to "Hutson" but where he objectively transfers property to "Hudson", unless the latter knows or ought to know of the mistake.[139] If the transferee is entitled to rely on the natural and objective meaning of the words and conduct of the transferor, property passes to him and the transferor has at most a personal restitutionary claim in unjust enrichment, subject to the change of position defence.[140]

2.2.2.3. Face-to-Face Dealings: Identification by Sight

The identity mistake cases provide clear authority for the proposition that property does pass – perhaps voidably – if the parties have dealt with each other

---

138 See Chapter 1 section 2.1.1.2.

139 An example might be where A owes debts to both, "Hutson" and "Hudson", and where he intends to discharge only the debt owed to Hutson but sends the money to Hudson by mistake.

140 A restitutionary claim is not available if there is a valid legal basis (contract, gift or otherwise) between A and Hudson, which cannot be set aside; see Chapter 1 sections 2.1.1.1., 2.2.1. and 3.

face-to-face, notwithstanding an apparent identity mistake of the transferor. In the typical case, a rogue enters a store, pretends to be someone else known to be creditworthy and the transferor transfers property on credit. The rogue does not pay and sells the goods to an innocent third party who is then sued in conversion. *Phillips v Brooks,*[141] *Lewis v Averay (No 1)*[142] and *Shogun Finance v Hudson,*[143] which has effectively overruled *Ingram v Little,*[144] provide a safe basis to conclude (i) that there is a (voidable) contract and (ii) that property passes (voidably) in such cases.

The reason for this is rooted in the face-to-face principle which, it is submitted, does not only apply on the contractual level (with regard to the offer or acceptance to conclude a contract) but equally on the proprietary level (with regard to the offer to transfer property). It is the underlying rationale of this principle that a physical identification by sight of a person as the other party to a contract or, respectively, as the transferee of property ought to prevail over an inconsistent identification by description, for example by providing a name, address, date of birth or other details. In such a case, a transferor is taken to have intended – objectively *and* subjectively – to transfer ownership to the person physically identified by sight. This is not an artificial fiction which conflicts with the transferor's actual subjective intention. Rather, the face-to-face principle simply provides a solution to a conundrum: A transferor has, in such cases, generally two things in mind, namely "I want to contract with and transfer property to this person physically present" and "I want to contract with and transfer property to X, living in Y". Since the transferor believes, at the time of the transaction, that these are one and the same person, one would never, in a retrospective assessment, get a proper answer by asking of what he has *really* intended; he simply intended both. Their Lordships in *Shogun Finance* have provided a convenient and simple solution to that impasse in favour of the physical identification by sight.

As a result, the defendant's name, address, date of birth and other features are reduced to mere *attributes* in face-to-face cases and his physical body is – for identification purposes – then regarded as exclusively constituting his *identity.* It follows that a transferor is not, in face-to-face cases, actually mistaken about the fact *that* he is transferring property to the person physically identified by sight but only about the *why* he is doing so, namely because he believes that that person has another name, another address, another date of birth, another nationality, other bank details or a better creditworthiness. These are pure motivational mistakes which may not prevent the passage of property.[145]

141 *Phillips v Brooks* [1919] 2 KB 243.
142 *Lewis v Averay (No 1)* [1972] 1 QB 198.
143 *Shogun Finance v Hudson* [2003] UKHL 62.
144 *Ingram v Little* [1961] 1 QB 31.
145 See Chapter 4 section 2.1.

In some contrast with this stands the difficult case of *R v Middleton.*[146] Middleton intended to withdraw 10s. from his Post Office bank account which stood 11s. in credit. In accordance with the bank's practices in those days, he applied for and received a warrant allowing him to withdraw such an amount at the specified branch and a corresponding letter of advice was duly sent to that branch. Middleton went to the branch and presented the warrant and his depositor's book to the clerk. But the clerk, instead of referring to the proper letter of advice for 10s., by some mistake looked at another letter of advice of a different customer which related to the amount of £8 16s. 10d. and put such an amount on the counter. Middleton realised the mistake but still took the money and went away. It is crucial to note that the clerk's mistake had not related to the amount he was actually handing over – he knew that he handed over £8 16s. 10d. – but only to the *why* he was doing so, namely because he had believed that the bank had been liable to do so. However, Middleton was still convicted of larceny and the conviction was upheld by a majority of eleven to four in the Court of Crown Cases Reserved. This must inevitably have embraced a finding that property in the money had not passed to Middleton.[147] Eventually, this case came to be seen as an authority for the proposition that mistakes as to the transferee's identity prevent the passage of property.[148]

However, the ratio of this case is markedly uncertain[149] and it is submitted that it should not be seen as authority for the proposition that the clerk's mistake had prevented the passage of ownership in that case. On the one hand, the four minority judges (Brett J, Bramwell B, Cleasby B and Martin B) apparently held that property had passed to Middleton and that the mistake had been insufficient to prevent that.[150] On the other hand, three of the eleven majority judges (Bovill CJ, Keating J and Kelly CB) based their findings that property had not passed on the narrow ground that the clerk had merely had a limited authority. This contains no finding that it had been the clerk's *mistake* which had prevented the

146 *R v Middleton* [1873] LR 2 CCR 38.

147 See the introductory remarks of this chapter section 2.

148 Virgo, Restitution, 574; J. Smith, Crim LR 1972, 587; Williams, CLJ 1977, 67–68 (fn 13, 15); Williams, Criminal Law, 32.133–34 (fn 350); Pollock/Wright, Possession, 111–12, 206–7; Fox, RLR 1996, 65 (fn 29); Fox; Property Rights, 4.123 (fn 159); Orchard, NZLJ 1973, 112; cf also *Ilich v R* [1987] 162 CLR 110, 124–27 (Wilson, Dawson JJ), but cf 136–38 (Brennan J); contra: Swadling, Unjust Delivery, 292–94; Turner, Kenny's Outlines of Criminal Law, 286–87; Turner, Russell on Crime, vol 2, 970–74; *R v Potisk* [1973] 6 SASR 389, 399–403 (Bray CJ).

149 Cf the comment of Lord Parker CJ in *Lacis v Cashmarts* [1969] 2 QB 400, 410: "It will be, I suppose, for all time debated, until that case is no longer cited, what is really the true effect of [*R v Middleton*]."

150 *R v Middleton* [1873] LR 2 CCR 38, 65–66 (Brett J): "[T]he clerk intended to pass to the man who stood before him [...] the possession of and the property in the whole of the money which he laid on the counter"; the judgments of Bramwell B and Cleasby B (with whom Martin B agreed) are to the same effect.

passage of property. Those judges might still have thought that, but for the lack of authority, property would have passed. Pigott B expressly dissented from the majority's reasoning but not from their result. It is extremely difficult to follow his judgment; he apparently felt that the intention and the mistake of the clerk (and perhaps even the question of whether property had passed at all) had been immaterial in that case.[151] This is, with respect, certainly inaccurate as long as one upholds the conviction, as he did. At any rate, Pigott B's judgment is not apparently based on the assumption that the clerk's mistake had prevented the passage of property. It follows that only seven of the fifteen judges (Cockburn CJ, Blackburn, Mellor, Lush, Grove, Denman and Archibald JJ) actually regarded the clerk's mistake as operative to prevent the passage of ownership in the money. It therefore appears that this case cannot be regarded as a strictly binding authority on this issue. Apart from that, the reasoning provided by those seven judges is, with respect, unconvincing.[152]

First, it was apparently assumed – very generally – that legal ownership could only ever pass in sale or gift transactions but in no other cases and that, since the present case had neither concerned a sale nor a gift, property in the money could not have passed to Middleton:

> "At common law the property in personal goods passes by a bargain and sale for consideration, or a gift of them accompanied by delivery; and it is clear, from the very nature of the thing, that an intention to pass the property is essential both to a sale and to a gift. *But it is not at all true that an intention to pass the property, even though accompanied by a delivery, is of itself equivalent to either a sale or a gift.*"[153]

With all due respect, the assumption that sales and gifts are the only two types of transactions which may effect a transfer of property is absolute nonsense. If this were correct, property could never pass in transactions such as barters, loans, payments of debts – owed for services, taxes, wrongs, unjust enrichment or something else – or in simple over- or double payments.[154] In fact, it would

151 Ibid, 51 (Pigott B): "I agree in the judgment of the majority of the Court, except that I do not adopt the reasons which are there assigned for holding that the mistaken intention of the clerk did not, under the circumstances here, prevent the case from being one of larceny on the part of the prisoner. I quite accede to that proposition, but my reason is that, in the view I take of the facts, the intention and acts of the clerk are not material in determining the nature of the prisoner's act and intent [...]." Pigott B then merely focused on the *animus furandi* of Middleton, held that such had been formed prior to taking and treated the case as one of finding; however, he did not apparently consider whether property had passed to Middleton though this would clearly have been an obstacle to larceny; see also SWADLING, Unjust Delivery, 293 (fn 123); *R v Potisk* [1973] 6 SASR 389, 399 (Bray CJ).

152 Critically also *R v Potisk* [1973] 6 SASR 389, 400–3 (Bray CJ); SWADLING, Unjust Delivery, 292.

153 *R v Middleton* [1873] LR 2 CCR 38, 43 (emphasis added).

154 See SWADLING, Unjust Delivery, 287–88, 292.

even follow that legal title in the money could not have passed to Middleton even if the clerk had referred to the correct letter of advice and even if he had handed over the correct amount of money since the bank's debt had neither been based on a sale nor on a gift.

Second, *R v Middleton* is – the limited authority point apart – indistinguishable from *Chambers v Miller*[155] and *R v Prince*.[156] In the former, the bank clerk mistakenly overlooked the fact that the drawer's account had been overdrawn when he cashed the cheque. In the latter, the bank clerk mistakenly believed – and this mistake was even fraudulently induced by the transferee – that the presented order for payment was genuine when he paid out the money to the fraudulent wife. In both cases, it was held that the clerk's mistake had only been a mistake as to motive and that such mistakes could not prevent ownership from passing. In *R v Middleton*, the bank clerk similarly believed by mistake that the bank had owed the amount of £8 16s. 10d. to the person standing in front of him. This was likewise only a motivational liability mistake which had been caused by the fact that the clerk had looked at a wrong document when he made up his mind whether or not – and how much – to pay to the customer before him. It follows that if the *R v Middleton*-type of mistake indeed prevents the passage of property, *every* causative motivational mistake would apparently do so. This is certainly not the case.[157]

Third, even if *R v Middleton* were to be regarded as an authority for the proposition that the clerk's (identity) mistake prevented the passage of property, such a ratio would have been overruled by the face-to-face identity mistake cases of *Phillips v Brooks*,[158] *Lewis v Averay (No 1)*[159] and *Shogun Finance v Hudson*.[160] Though *R v Middleton* concerned, unlike those cases, a mistake which had exclusively occurred in the execution stage – there being no (voidable) contract with regard to the excess – and though Middleton had not induced the

155 *Chambers v Miller* [1862] 13 CBR (NS) 125; for discussion see Chapter 4 section 2.1.1.

156 *R v Prince* [1868] LR 1 CCR 150; see the comment of Martin B in *R v Middleton* [1873] LR 2 CCR 38, 53: "[T]he act of the accused in [*R v Prince*] was a grosser act, and more akin to larceny than that of the prisoner in this case; yet it was held not larceny. I defy any man to explain to any one not a lawyer the difference between the two cases. The distinction seems to me worthy of an ancient casuist"; cf also Swadling, Unjust Delivery, 292; Orchard, NZLJ 1973, 114; *R v Potisk* [1973] 6 SASR 389, 400–1 (Bray CJ). The majority's point of distinction is very dubious (44): "In that case [*R v Prince*], however, the money was paid to the holder of a forged cheque payable to bearer, and therefore vested in the holder, subject to the right of the bank to divest the property. In the present case, the property still remains that of the Postmaster-General and never did vest in the prisoner at all. There was no contract to render it his which required to be rescinded; there was no gift of it to him, for there was no intention to give it to him or to any one. It was simply a handing it over by a pure mistake, and no property passed."

157 See Chapter 4 section 2.1.

158 *Phillips v Brooks* [1919] 2 KB 243.

159 *Lewis v Averay (No 1)* [1972] 1 QB 198.

160 *Shogun Finance v Hudson* [2003] UKHL 62.

transferor's mistake, the position must still be the same. On the one hand, the proprietary transfer by delivery is abstract and operates independently from a collateral contract. On the other hand, if a proprietary transfer is not even void (but only voidable) in cases of fraud, a similar transfer may *a fortiori* not be void in the absence of fraud.

The correct analysis of *R v Middleton* is the following: The transfer in question was a transfer by delivery because corporeal money was concerned. Since transfers by delivery are inevitably abstract, the crucial question was whether the clerk – supposing that he had sufficient authority to bind the owner (bank) – had a sufficient intention to transfer ownership in the money to Middleton. The clerk was neither mistaken about the actual amount of money he was handing over nor, apparently, about the transferee's name, address, date of birth or other features since he had in fact consulted and stamped the latter's depositor's book. The clerk's mistake was a mere motivational liability mistake caused by the fact that he had looked at a wrong document.[161] But even assuming that the clerk had been mistaken about Middleton's name, address, date of birth or the like, the face-to-face principle would – at least from a modern perspective – still have applied. The clerk had identified the transferee by sight and had, accordingly, objectively and subjectively intended to transfer property to the very person standing physically in front of him. The mistake would still have been merely motivational in nature, only relating to one of Middleton's attributes. In any case, property in the money should – the limited authority point apart – have passed to Middleton.[162] In so far, the judgments of Bramwell B and Cleasby B are unanswerable:

> "No doubt the clerk did not intend to [...] give to Middleton what did not belong to him, yet he intended to do the act he did. What he did he did not do involuntarily nor accidentally, but on purpose."[163]

> "The clerk did not the less intend to make the payment which he deliberately made, because he was at the time under the influence of a mistake; he would not have intended to make the payment but for the mistake. Mistakes are constantly occurring, and few people can say that they have not acted under their influence, but their acts remain as acts done at the time, though their effects may be afterwards corrected. No doubt there was no intention to overpay the prisoner, that is, to produce the effect of overpayment; but the intention was to do the act of paying the larger sum, because it

161 See also Swadling, Unjust Delivery, 292–94; Turner, Kenny's Outlines of Criminal Law, 286–87; Turner, Russell on Crime, vol 2, 970–74.

162 Since the mistake had been self-induced, the bank would not even have had a power in rem to revest property, at least at common law but arguably also in equity; see Zogg, Proprietary Consequences, Chapter 5 section 7. It would thus have been limited to a personal restitutionary claim in unjust enrichment.

163 *R v Middleton* [1873] LR 2 CCR 38, 55–56 (Bramwell B).

was thought to be a proper one. [...] The clerk intended A to receive what he ought to have intended B to receive, but it was not the less his intention that A should receive what he handed over to him."[164]

2.2.2.4. Conclusions

It is concluded that a transferor's mistake as to the transferee's identity may – in quite narrow boundaries – be proprietarily fundamental and prevent the passage of property. The true reason for this, however, is not actually rooted in the fact that the transferor is mistaken about some features relating to the defendant's person but rather in the fact that the latter is not duly identified as the transferee of the transfer in question. Hence, this is rather a problem of *identification* than of *mistake*.

The identification of the addressee of a proprietary transfer operates on similar lines as the identification of an addressee of a contractual offer or acceptance. This is not to suggest that these are one and the same thing. Quite to the contrary, contract and proprietary transfer are distinct and independent from each other. But the question of *to whom* an intention to transfer property is addressed is governed by rules analogous to those which govern the question of *to whom* an offer to contract is addressed.

It follows that the addressee of a proprietary transfer is determined by an application of the objective principle, i.e. by an objective construction of the words and conduct of the transferor, unless either the transferor subjectively intends to transfer ownership to the defendant,[165] in which case property still passes to the latter, or unless the defendant knows that the transferor does not subjectively intend to transfer property to him, in which case property does not pass. If the parties have dealt with each other exclusively in writing, there is no additional problem (apart from the fact that one should recognise that extrinsic evidence is always admissible to determine the addressee of a transfer of property). By contrast, if the parties have dealt with each other face-to-face, the "face-to-face principle" as authoritatively established in the law of contract should equally apply on the proprietary level. There is accordingly a rule or at least a very strong presumption that a transferor, who has identified the transferee *by sight*, objectively *and* subjectively intends to transfer property to the person physically present. In such a case, a mistake about that person's name, address, date of birth or other details may not prevent the passage of property.[166] Hence, a mistake as to the transferee's person may not generally – or indeed

[164] Ibid, 73 (Cleasby B).

[165] Or to "the writer of the letters" or to "whomever he is dealing with", the transferee's identity simply being irrelevant to the transferor.

[166] In face-to-face cases, such a mistake may only render a proprietary transfer voidable.

never – be proprietarily fundamental if the transferor has physically identified the transferee by sight.

With regard to the scope of the face-to-face principle, reference may be made to the remarks made in relation to the contractual position.[167] It appears that this principle applies *only* but *always* if the transferor has – at some point – identified the transferee *by sight*. Whether or not the parties have been physically present within the same room is arguably irrelevant. The principle arguably also applies to an identification by video link. However, an identification *by hearing* or *by touching* is not equivalent. The face-to-face principle does not accordingly apply if the transferor is blind or if the transfer is made in the dark or by telephone. Finally, it will be recalled that there is a general agency exception which applies if the transferor, though having identified the other person by sight, does not intend – according to the objective or the subjective principle – to deal with that person as a principal but only as an agent.[168]

2.3. MISTAKES AS TO THE TRANSFERRED PROPERTY'S IDENTITY

A second category of proprietarily fundamental mistakes are mistakes as to the transferred property's identity.[169] These are not merely motivational mistakes relating to the *why* a certain transfer shall be made but rather mistakes which relate to the very transfer itself where the transferor is mistaken about the fact *that* he is carrying out the transfer in question at all. In the following sub-sections, it will be argued that this type of mistake similarly concerns – just as mistakes as to the transferee's identity do – an issue of *identification* rather than *mistake*, casually speaking, and that the identification of the object of a proprietary transfer (the transferred property) is governed by similar principles as those which govern the identification of its subject (the transferee). Furthermore, it is argued that there is again a close parallel between the proprietary and the contractual positions.

2.3.1. Contractual Level

2.3.1.1. Five Ways How a Mistake as to the Contract Goods May be Relevant

Suppose that A (seller) and B (buyer) are negotiating about the sale of a cow. A or B or both may in some way be mistaken about what exactly shall be the

[167] See Chapter 4 section 2.2.1.3.
[168] See text to fn 118–122.
[169] See the references in fn 4.

object of the contract or about some facts relating to that object. For example, A might believe that they are negotiating about cow 1, whereas B might think that he is buying cow 2 (or "a milk cow", in generic terms). Alternatively, if both have "cow 1" in mind, A or B or both might believe that cow 1 is in calf or sound whereas it is, in fact, barren or unsound. Conceptually, there are basically five different ways how a mistake in relation to the contract goods might operate on the contractual level:

(1) Analytically, the first question always is whether the parties are sufficiently *ad idem* with regard to the contract goods, namely as to what shall be the object of their sale or similar contract. This may be called the *identification issue*.[170] If the contract goods are insufficiently identified by the relevant offer or acceptance, the parties are not *ad idem* and their mistake negatives their apparent consent. The contract is then void *ab initio*.
(2) If the parties have sufficiently identified the contract goods and are thus *ad idem*, there might still be – within very narrow confines – a contractually fundamental mistake with regard to the true substance and nature of the so identified goods. Such a mistake, however, is only relevant if it is shared by both parties (common mistake).[171] If operative, a common mistake nullifies the otherwise existing consent and renders the contract void.
(3) If the contract is not void according to (1) or (2), a mistake in relation to the contract goods' nature or attributes might still entitle the mistaken party to rescind the contract if the mistake has been induced by the other party. The contract is then voidable.
(4) If the contract is neither void according to (1) or (2) nor voidable according to (3), one or both of the parties might still be mistaken about the terms of the contract relating to the identified contract goods, for example about whether a warranty that the contract goods have certain attributes or qualities is included. In such a case, one must apply the general amalgam of the objective and the subjective principle as provided by general contract law.[172] This will either lead to the result that the term in question is included into the contract or that it is not included, and that the mistake is thus inoperative, or perhaps – if the term in question is an essential one – that the entire contract is void for lack of consent.
(5) If neither of (1)–(4) affects the contract, a party might still be mistaken about some factual features – as opposed to the terms of the contract – of the identified contract goods, particularly their quality. Such a mistake may not – if neither (2) nor (3) applies – affect the contract. However, it

170 Cf Montrose, Canadian Bar Review 1937, 763–67, distinguishing between "definition" and "description".

171 See Chapter 4 sections 1.2. and 2.1.2.

172 See Chapter 4 section 1.1.

may indirectly be remedied if the existence of the believed state of affairs (quality, attributes or the like) has been made a term of the contract (breach of contract).

We are here exclusively concerned with issue (1), the identification issue, since only this kind of mistake may be proprietarily fundamental. It has already been pointed out that common mistakes (2) may not prevent the passage of property[173] and it is quite obvious that mistakes of categories (3)–(5) may neither.[174]

2.3.1.2. Identification of the Contract Goods

A mistake which relates to the object of the contract, the contract goods, and which puts the parties at cross-purposes in that regard completely negatives their apparent consent and renders the apparent contract void. The question whether the parties are *ad idem* in relation to the contract goods – and the question of what the contract goods are – is, as any other term of the contract, determined by the general amalgam of the objective and the subjective principle.[175] Hence, the question whether A offers or accepts to sell "cow 1", "cow 2, "a cow" or "a milk cow" and whether B accepts or offers to buy the same thing, in which case the parties are *ad idem*, or a different thing, in which case the contract is void for lack of consent, is generally determined by the objective principle, unless the parties are in fact subjectively *ad idem* or unless one of the parties knows of the other party's divergent subjective intention. It follows that a mistake relating to the contract goods only negatives the parties' consent if (i) they are not in fact subjectively *ad idem*, (ii) if neither of them knows of the other party's divergent subjective intention[176] *and* (iii) if an unambiguous objective interpretation is unavailable.[177]

It turns out that mistakes as to the contract goods' identity may only render the parties' apparent contract void in a narrower range of circumstances than mistakes as to the other party's identity. The reason relates to a problem of authority: If A deals with B and if A's offer or acceptance is objectively or subjectively addressed to C, B has no authority to bind C. The apparent contract between A and B is void for lack of consent and the apparent contract between A and C is void for lack of authority (and for lack of consent). By contrast, if B intends to buy cow 1 but if A's offer objectively or – if B has knowledge of this – subjectively relates to cow 2, there might still perfectly be a contract for cow 2

[173] See Chapter 4 section 2.1.2.
[174] Cf Chapter 4 section 2.1.1. (esp text to fn 44–48) and Chapter 4 section 2.5.
[175] See Chapter 4 section 1.1.
[176] See fn 14.
[177] See fn 15.

if B accepts A's offer, since B of course has the authority to bind himself to buy cow 1, cow 2 or any other cow.

(a) Specific and generic contract goods

The contract goods as initially identified may be specific or generic (unascertained).[178] They are specific if the very items to be transferred are unequivocally and fully identified at the time of conclusion of the contract,[179] for example if A and B agree on the sale of cow 1. In this case, A can only discharge his contractual duty by delivering cow 1 but not by delivering any other cow, even if of better quality. By contrast, the contract goods are generic (or quasi-specific) if the parties merely define the genus (or the source) from which A might effectively perform,[180] for example if A and B agree on the sale of "a cow" or "a milk cow". In such a case, A is free to choose any item from the respective genus (or source) to discharge his contractual obligation.[181]

For the sake of simplicity, we shall here focus on contracts, particularly contracts of sale, where specific goods are initially identified (or purportedly identified). But the principles applying with regard to agreements to sell generic (or quasi-specific) goods are quite similar if the act of appropriation is included into the analysis.

As far as a sale of specific goods is concerned, the only issue is whether the parties have contractually agreed on "cow 1" or on "cow 2" or whether they were not *ad idem* at all, and it will be argued that similar principles ought to apply with regard to the question whether property in cow 1, in cow 2 or in none of them has passed.

As far as an agreement to sell generic or quasi-specific goods is concerned, the analysis basically involves two steps on the contractual level. First, the question arises of what is the genus or source from which the seller might perform. This is a question of the terms of the contract which is determined by the general amalgam of the objective and the subjective principle. Second, the seller must choose one item from that genus or source and *unconditionally appropriate* it to the contract. This is basically a two-sided process. The buyer must – subsequently or in advance – assent to the seller's appropriation (or vice versa).[182] Once appropriation has been made, the appropriated specific item is identified as the ascertained contract goods. The seller might then no longer perform by tendering any other item. On the proprietary level, it is clear that property might only pass once appropriation has been made.[183] It is arguable that the

178 They may also be quasi-specific, namely if A and B agree that A shall perform from a specifically defined source, for example a certain bulk, but if the quantity purchased from that source is less than that contained in that source; see Goode, Commercial Law, 8.10–17.
179 See s 61(1) of the SGA 1979; Goode, Commercial Law, 8.5–7.
180 Goode, Commercial Law, 8.10–13.
181 If the goods are wholly unascertained, A might choose from any present or future source; if they are quasi-specific, the source(s) from which he might choose are limited.
182 See Goode, Commercial Law, 8.19–22; Bridge et al, Benjamin's Sale of Goods, 5.67–108.
183 Section 16 of the SGA 1979; see Chapter 2 section 2.1.

process of appropriation, i.e. the subsequent bilateral identification of the specific (ascertained) contract goods, should operate – on the contractual *and* the proprietary level – on similar lines as a specific identification at the time of conclusion. In other words, whether and which specific item is *appropriated* (subsequently identified) by an act of the parties should be similarly determined by an application of the general amalgam of the objective and the subjective principle, coupled with a "face-to-property principle" as set out below.

(b) Identification (or appropriation) of specific contract goods

We may now turn to the question of how goods are identified as the contract goods, either specifically at the time of conclusion or by a subsequent act of appropriation. This issue may be illustrated by the following five examples which shall be discussed in the following sub-sections: (1) B, intending to buy "one ton of oranges" from A, by some clerical error sends an order to the latter mistakenly stating "one ton of mandarins". A accepts the offer. (2) B goes to the warehouse of A, inspects a bulk of mandarins, points his finger at this bulk and offers to buy "this entire bulk" which he, however, for some reason mistakenly believes to be a bulk of oranges. A accepts the offer. (3) The same as (2) but B offers to buy "this entire bulk of oranges". (4) A and B negotiate at B's premises and A offers to sell "the entire bulk of oranges which is located at my warehouse X in spot Y". B accepts the offer but the bulk at the agreed place is not one of oranges but one of mandarins. (5) One night in the dark, A takes out a mandarin from his pocket which he believes to be an orange and offers to sell "this orange" to B. B accepts the offer.

Is there a contract in those cases and, if so, for oranges or mandarins? We may easily dispose of case (1) which is a simple case of an agreement to sell generic goods. The buyer's offer must objectively be construed as being for mandarins and the natural meaning of his words is binding, unless A has either known that B actually intended to buy oranges or unless A has also subjectively intended to sell oranges.

(aa) Identification by sight: Cases (2) and (3)

Case (2) concerns a bare sale of specific goods without either a description nor any explicit warranty, whereas case (3) concerns a sale of specific goods by description.[184] In both cases, the goods are specifically identified (earmarked) by sight.

---

184 A sale by description is not an antithesis to a sale of specific goods; rather, even specifically identified goods may be sold by description; see s 13(3) of the SGA 1979; *Grant v Australian Knitting Mills Ltd* [1936] AC 85 (PC), 100 (Lord Wright); Montrose, Canadian Bar Review 1937, esp 764; Goode, Commercial Law, 11.34–44; Bridge et al, Benjamin's Sale of Goods, 11.7–10; but cf still *Varley v Whipp* [1900] 1 QB 513 (QBD). In such a case, the description does not – as in an agreement to sell generic goods – delimit the potential objects in the world (genus) from which the seller might choose to perform; neither does it – if the identification has been effected by sight – *identify* the specific contract goods. It rather simply defines a fundamental obligation of the seller (condition) that the identified chattels correspond with the description. If they do not, the contract is still valid but the buyer might reject the goods

An answer to those cases might to some extent be derived from *Smith v Hughes*,[185] though this case actually concerned an unproblematic identification at a distance by description (case (4)). The seller asked the buyer whether he was willing to buy "oats" and provided a sample of new oats. He explained that he had a bulk of forty or fifty quarters of such oats at his premises (he had apparently no other oats) and that he would be willing to sell them. The buyer inspected the sample and accepted to buy all oats which the seller had. Cockburn J held that this was a sale of specific goods, namely of the entire bulk of oats located at the seller's premises.

The identification issue (issue 1 as defined above[186]) was not really a problem in that case since the parties had unequivocally identified the contract goods by description ("all oats at the seller's premises"). The dispute solely turned on what we have described as issues (4) and (5): The buyer had believed that the sample oats were old oats and refused to take delivery when he discovered that they were in fact new oats (the sample corresponding with the bulk). The seller sued for the price. The question was whether the contract contained a term that the oats are old oats and whether the buyer was accordingly entitled to reject the goods as non-conforming. Supposedly, nothing had been said in the negotiations about the sample oats being old or new but the seller had been aware that the buyer had believed that the sample oats were old oats.[187] Applying the principle of *caveat emptor*,[188] it was held – and this has since remained a crucial distinction in English contract law[189] – that the relevant question[190] was whether the seller had only been aware that the buyer had believed that the oats were – *as a matter of fact* – old or whether, first, the buyer had actually believed that the *contract terms* would include a warranty or a condition that the oats are old oats and whether, second, the seller had (also) been aware of this. In the former case (mistake as to the factual condition of the goods), the buyer would not have had any remedy. In the latter case (mistake as to the contract terms known by the other party), however, the subjective principle would have displaced the objective principle and a term that the oats are old oats would have been included into the contract.[191]

for non-conformity; the seller might, if at all, only cure the defect by *repairing* the specifically identified goods but not by retendering *other* goods; see Goode, Commercial Law, 11.34–44, 12.19–22.

185 *Smith v Hughes* [1871] LR 6 QB 597.

186 See Chapter 4 section 2.3.1.1.

187 The buyer's mistake was self-induced and the seller was under no duty to correct it; therefore, the contract was not voidable.

188 Cockburn J (603, 605–6) not only held that this was a sale of specific goods but also that the buyer had inspected the goods (inspection of the sample amounting to an inspection of the bulk); consequently, no warranty as to quality was implied; see today s 14(2C)(b) and (c) of the SGA 1979.

189 See (e.g.) *The Harriette N* [2008] EWHC 2257 (Comm), [87]–[96] (Aikens J).

190 This question was to be determined by the jury in a new trial.

191 See fn 14.

Smith v Hughes itself concerned an identification at a distance by description (case (4)) and it will be argued in the next sub-section that this actually involves quite different principles as where goods are identified by sight (cases (2) and (3)). Yet, *Smith v Hughes* still brings out a clear distinction between the issue of identification of the contract goods as such and the issue of a mistake as to the so identified contract goods, whether factually and/or in relation to the contract terms:

> "It only remains to deal with an argument which was pressed upon us, that the defendant in the present case intended to buy old oats, and the plaintiff to sell new, so the two minds were not ad idem; and that consequently there was no contract. This argument proceeds on the fallacy of confounding what was merely a motive operating on the buyer to induce him to buy with one of the essential conditions of the contract. Both parties were agreed as to the sale and purchase of *this particular parcel of oats*. The defendant believed the oats to be old, and was thus induced to agree to buy them, but he omitted to make their age a condition of the contract. All that can be said is, that the two minds were not ad idem as to the age of the oats; they certainly were ad idem as to the sale and purchase of *them*."[192]

It follows that a mistake as to the *identified* contract goods – even if most serious in nature – does not call into question an unequivocal identification of the contract goods as such. If we slightly adapt the facts of *Smith v Hughes*, supposing that the buyer had not only inspected the sample but also the purchased bulk at the seller's premises itself, this would have been all the more obvious. In this case, the parties would have physically identified the contract goods *by sight*, agreeing to sell and buy "this particular parcel", and any mistake as to the so identified contract goods' quality or, it is submitted, identity[193] would still not have affected their unequivocal identification.

If we further change the facts of *Smith v Hughes*, replacing old oats with oranges and new oats with mandarins, we arrive at our case (2): If A and B stand in front of a bulk of mandarins, the buyer for some reason mistakenly believes that the mandarins are oranges, and if both parties point their fingers at the bulk and agree to sell and buy "this bulk" for a certain price, the contract goods are specifically and unequivocally identified by sight.[194] The seller owes delivery of

---

192 *Smith v Hughes* [1871] LR 6 QB 597, 606 (Cockburn J) (emphases added).

193 By contrast, it will be argued that a mistake as to the goods' identity is relevant if the goods have only been identified *by description*, i.e. otherwise than by sight, as in *Smith v Hughes* itself. Hence, the bulk of oats located at the seller's premises would not have been identified as the contract goods in *Smith v Hughes* had the contract *terms* identified as the contract goods "all rye at the seller's premises". However, a mere *factual* mistake of the buyer as to the goods' identity would, even in such a case, still not have affected the identification and the contract's validity.

194 But the contract might still be void for common mistake (if the seller equally believes that these are oranges) or voidable for misrepresentation (if the seller induced the buyer's mistake).

"this bulk". Generally, the *caveat emptor* principle applies. But even if – as in case (3) – the parties have included a term (description[195]) that this bulk contains oranges, the parties would still have been *ad idem* about "this bulk" being the contract goods. The seller could then only perform by delivering "this bulk" but not by delivering any other bulk. Yet, the specific contract goods ("this bulk") would be non-conforming and the buyer would have a right to reject them.

The underlying reason for this arguably lies in what may be called a "*face-to-property principle*" which is a logical consequence of the face-to-face principle as established in *Shogun Finance v Hudson*.[196] According to the latter principle, an identification of a person by sight very generally – if not indeed always – prevails over an inconsistent identification by description, for example by providing a name, address, date of birth or other descriptive details of a person. If A has identified B by sight, his contractual offer or acceptance is objectively and subjectively addressed to B and not to the party identified by description. That principle ought to apply by analogy with regard to an identification of contract goods: If A has identified the contract goods by sight, his offer or acceptance must objectively and subjectively relate to the physically identified goods. Identification by sight should not only prevail with regard to the *subject* of an offer (addressee) but also with regard to its *object* (contract goods). If B enters the store of A and says that he wants to buy "this orange", unequivocally pointing with his fingers at a fruit which is a mandarin, the identification by sight must prevail objectively and subjectively. In this case, B subjectively intends – or is taken to intend – to buy "this item physically present" rather than "an orange". Therefore, "this item" is identified as the contract goods even if A knows that B believes that this item is an orange. The face-to-property principle does not set down an artificial fiction inconsistent with B's actual subjective intention; rather, it resolves a difficult conundrum:[197] In the mentioned case, B has generally two things in mind, namely "I want to buy this item" and "I want to buy an orange". Since he believes, at the time of conclusion, that these are one and the same things, one would never, in a retrospective assessment, get a proper answer by asking of what he *really* intended; he simply intended *both*. In *Shogun Finance v Hudson*, their Lordships have provided a simple and convenient solution to this impasse in favour of the physical identification by sight. Though this case only related to mistakes as to the other *party's* identity, there is no reason why this principle should not be extended by analogy to mistakes as to the transferred *property's* identity.

If this is correct, it follows that a mistake as to the contract goods' identity may not generally – if not indeed never – negative the parties' consent if the

---

195 See fn 184.

196 *Shogun Finance v Hudson* [2003] UKHL 62; see Chapter 4 section 2.2.1.2.

197 Cf *Shogun Finance v Hudson* [2003] UKHL 62, [138], [153], [170] (Lord Phillips) and text to fn 108–109.

goods have been unequivocally identified by sight. A good example is *Sherwood v Walker*[198] which concerned the sale of a cow which had been specifically and unequivocally identified by sight and which was, in fact, in calf whereas both parties had believed that it was barren. Though it is arguable that the contract was void for common mistake and that the features "in calf" or "barren" went to the goods' identity, the cow had still been specifically identified by sight and the parties had still been *ad idem* that "this cow" should be the object of the contract. Assuming that one of the parties had known that the cow was in calf, there being no *common* mistake, there would plainly have been a valid contract for the sale of "this cow".[199]

Finally, it may be added that the face-to-property principle does not refer to the fact that the *parties* have communicated with each other face-to-face but to the fact that the parties have identified the *goods* by sight. Since the object of identification is not here the other party, but the goods, and because one cannot communicate with goods, it becomes apparent that the face-to-face and the face-to-property principles are not actually linked to the mode of communication but to the mode of identification.

(bb) Identification by description (at a distance): Case (4)

The contract goods may also be specifically identified at a distance if the parties (one or both of them) have never seen them physically, namely by description, particularly by providing their current location. This occurred in *Smith v Hughes*[200] where the parties have specifically identified as their contract goods "all oats at the seller's premises". This is the subject of case (4).

Two problems must be strictly distinguished: First, if the seller in case (4) actually intends to sell his oranges in "spot Z" but mistakenly states "spot Y" or if he actually means "mandarins" but states "oranges", the question of what his offer refers to must be determined by the general amalgam of the objective and the subjective principle. A second, much more difficult problem occurs if the parties have – according to those rules – agreed to sell and buy "the bulk of oranges in warehouse X, spot Y" but if there are, as a matter of fact, only mandarins in that spot. Are those mandarins still the parties' specifically identified contract goods or are the contract goods actually non-existent? In this particular case, the latter appears to be the correct answer.[201]

---

198 *Sherwood v Walker* [1887] 66 Mich 568; for further examples, see fn 69.

199 If one party had induced the other party's mistake, however, the contract would have been voidable.

200 *Smith v Hughes* [1871] LR 6 QB 597.

201 Non-existence of the contract goods does not by itself mean that the contract is inevitably void. The parties' consent may be nullified by the doctrine of common mistake (see also s 6 of the SGA 1979) but this need not be so, for example if the seller has warranted the goods' existence or if their non-existence has been caused by the seller's fault; see *Bell v Lever Bros* [1932] AC 161, 217–18 (Lord Atkin); *McRae v Commonwealth Disposals Commission* [1951]

Certainly, the contract goods would be non-existent in such a case if there are no goods at all in spot Y. The seller could not then perform by tendering other oranges since other oranges would not be the specifically identified contract goods. A similar example is provided by *McRae v Commonwealth Disposals Commission*[202] where an oil tanker was sold by describing its location ("wrecked on Jourmaund Reef approximately 100 miles north of Samarai"). Yet, there was no such tanker in this area. Since the seller had warranted the goods' existence, the contract was not void for common mistake. Still, the seller could not have performed the contract by tendering another tanker, even if of better quality, since any tanker not located within this area would not have been the specifically identified contract goods.

The contract goods must also be regarded as non-existent if there happen to be some chattel in spot Y which is entirely different from the chattel envisaged by the parties' description. It would be absurd to suggest that even a car, a horse or a bulk of gold bullions which – coincidentally or not – happen to be in spot Y at the time of conclusion would be regarded as the specifically identified contract goods in case (4). In fact, the parties have identified their contract goods *by description*, i.e. by the use of words, and, though the description of their location ("warehouse X, spot Y") was *one* aspect of the identifying description, the goods' kind or identity ("oranges") was *another*. In some cases, goods might even be specifically identified by description (at a distance) without mentioning their current location at all, for example if A and B agree to sell and buy "all of A's oranges", i.e. all oranges to which A has title at the time of conclusion.

The solution of the problem of specifically identifying goods at a distance arguably lies in an application of the amalgam of the objective and the subjective principle, similarly as with regard to mistakes as to a person's identity where the parties have dealt with each other at a distance and where the question arises of to whom an offer has been addressed (*Cundy v Lindsay*-type of case). The crucial issue is whether the goods in question have been objectively or subjectively addressed by the offer or acceptance. Such an identification of goods is, however, even more difficult than an identification of persons since it is still much less evident which features of goods go to their *identity* and which go merely to their *attributes*:[203] It appears that mandarins factually located in spot Y would be caught by a descriptive identification with the words "fruits in spot Y" but not if the term "oranges in spot Y" is used. It is even possible that the parties agree on "whatever chattels located in spot Y at the time of conclusion", the buyer effectively buying a chance. In this case, fruits, cars, horses, gold bullions

84 CLR 377 (HC of Australia); Treitel, Contract, 8.8–10. Apart from that, the contract may be voidable if the mistake of one party has been induced by the other.

202 *McRae v Commonwealth Disposals Commission* [1951] 84 CLR 377; see also *Couturier v Hastie* [1852] 8 Ex 40, 155 ER 1250.

203 A similar – almost philosophical – problem exists in relation to persons; see fn 109.

and diamond rings would be identified as contract goods if only located within spot Y at the time of conclusion.

This evidently raises the question whether *all* features or characteristics used by the parties to describe the goods are inevitably relevant to the identification of the contract goods at a distance or, if not, *which* of them are and which of them are not. For example, what is the position if the parties agree on "the bulk of oranges from Brazil in spot Y" or on "the bulk of navel oranges from Brazil in spot Y" but if there are, in fact, only oranges from Mexico or pera oranges in that spot? It appears that this was one of the problems with which Channell J was confronted in the difficult case of *Varley v Whipp*.[204] A sold a reaping machine to B which B had never seen before and which was described to be "at Upton" and as a "second-hand self-binder reaping machine" which was "new the previous year" and which had been "used to cut only fifty or sixty acres". Channell J held that this was not a sale of specific goods at all and that rule 1 of s 18 of the SGA 1893 was not therefore applicable. The judge apparently supposed that it was a logical impossibility that a sale was specific *and* by description. However, it has since been rightly pointed out that this is inaccurate and that even sales of specific goods might well contain a description.[205] Besides that, it seems that Channell J struggled with a difficult identification problem. Since the buyer had never seen the goods, they could only have been specifically identified by description. If the parties had actually intended to sell a *specific* machine, the terms "at Upton" and "reaping machine" would probably have been features which served to *identify* the very contract goods. A reaping machine located at Huddersfield at the time of conclusion or a plough being at Upton would not then have been identified as the contract goods. But what if there had been a reaping machine at Upton which had not been a self-binder or which had been third-hand, older than one year or which had been used to cut one hundred acres? In this context, Channell J said this:

> "The case turns on a fine point, namely, whether the words used by the seller with regard to the machine were part of the description, or merely amounted to a collateral warranty. [...] The machine which was to be sold had never been seen by the buyer [...]. It was described as being at Upton, as being a self-binder, as being nearly new, and as having been used to cut only about fifty or sixty acres. All these statements were made with regard to the machine, and we have to consider how much of these statements was *identification* of the machine, and how much was *mere collateral warranty*. If a man says that he will sell the black horse in the last stall in his stable, and the stall is empty, or there is no horse in it, but only a cow, no property could pass. Again, if he says he will sell a four-year old horse in the last stall, and there is a horse in the stall, but it is not

204 *Varley v Whipp* [1900] 1 QB 513 (QBD); cf also Montrose, Canadian Bar Review 1937, 763–67.

205 See fn 184.

> a four-year old, the property would not pass. But if he says he will sell a four-year old horse, and there is a four-year old horse in the stall, and he says that the horse is sound, this last statement would only be a collateral warranty."[206]

This issue evidently resembles the difficult distinction between *identity* (substance) and *attributes* (quality) which delineates, in agreements to sell generic goods, the contractual genus from which the seller might choose to make an effective appropriation of a specific item to the contract.[207] Whether a certain feature is identification-relevant, going to the goods' identity, or whether it merely defines the required quality, going to the goods' attributes, is not determined by some philosophical or metaphysical approach but by a "broader, more commonsense, test of a mercantile character".[208] Those principles might arguably also be adopted to determine whether, in a sale of specific[209] goods, the goods in question are sufficiently identified by the identifying description used in the contract. At any rate, however, it appears that the question whether a certain feature is identification-relevant or not is, ultimately, a question of the parties' intention, as determined by the objective and the subjective principle.[210]

(cc) Identification by touching or by other means: Case (5)

It may be concluded that a mistake as to the goods' identity (for example mandarins instead of oranges, rye instead of oats, a plough instead of a reaping machine or a cow in calf instead of a barren cow) is in any case irrelevant – as far as the question of a consensus *ad idem* is concerned[211] – if the identity has not been made part of the contractual terms. But even if and as far as the identity was part of the terms, it may still not negative the parties' consent if the parties have physically identified the goods by sight. Identification by sight prevails over an inconsistent identification by description (*face-to-property principle*).

---

206 *Varley v Whipp* [1900] 1 QB 513, 515–16 (Channell J) (emphases added). There is some conflict between the judge's view that a non-four-year-old horse in the last stall would not have been identified had the parties agreed on "the four-year-old horse in the last stall" and the case of *Smith v Hughes* [1871] LR 6 QB 597. In the latter case, the parties had agreed on "all oats at the seller's premises" and it appears that the (new) oats in fact located at the seller's premises would have been identified as the contract goods even if the parties had included a term that the oats had been "old oats".

207 See Goode, Commercial Law, 11.36–44; cf also Montrose, Canadian Bar Review 1937, 763–67.

208 *Ashington Piggeries Ltd v Christopher Hill Ltd* [1972] AC 441 (HL), 489 (Lord Wilberforce).

209 Whether the contract goods are specific, i.e. specifically identified at the time of conclusion, is apparently not only a matter of the parties' intention and contractual formulation but also a matter of fact: If the contract is for "the black horse in the last stall" and there are, in fact, two black horses in that stall, the goods are unascertained (quasi-specific). On the other hand, if the contract is for "one of the two black horses in the last stall" but there is merely one, the goods are specific; Goode, Commercial Law, 8.5–7.

210 Cf Montrose, Canadian Bar Review 1937, 763–67.

211 However, the contract may still be void for common mistake, if shared by the other party, or voidable, if induced by the other party.

The description then only constitutes – even as far as going to the goods' substance – a fundamental obligation of the seller that the specifically identified goods do correspond with that description. By contrast, if the parties have only identified the contract goods at a distance and by description, the goods in question must meet that description in order to be specifically identified as the contract goods. They must then be of the kind (identity) as specified by the contract terms.

This leaves the question of the exact scope of the face-to-property principle. If, as in case (5), A and B have not identified the goods in question by sight but for example by touching them in the dark, does such an identification still prevail over an inconsistent identification by description ("this orange")? Does the face-to-property principle apply to blind persons? This issue has already been raised in relation to the face-to-face principle and it will later, in connection with the difficult case of *R v Ashwell*,[212] be argued that neither the face-to-face nor the face-to-property principle should apply if the parties have contracted or executed a proprietary transfer in the dark or if the mistaken party is – at least if to the knowledge of the other – blind. It is only an identification *by sight* which ought to prevail over an identification by description. This should not be extended to other forms of physical identification, such as an identification by touching, by hearing or by smelling. It will be argued that in those latter cases, an identification by description should, if existing, still prevail. Accordingly, the mandarin in case (5), which A took out of his pocket in the dark, is not identified by the descriptive words "this orange". Hence, the contract goods should be regarded as non-existent in that case.

2.3.2. Proprietary Level

2.3.2.1. The Contract Analogy

We may now turn to the proprietary position: Does a mistake of the transferor about the transferred property's identity negative his intention to transfer legal ownership and, if so, in what circumstances? Pure motivational mistakes where the transferor is merely mistaken about the *why* he is carrying out a certain transfer may not prevent the passage of property.[213] Yet, the identity of the transferred property, i.e. *what* shall be transferred, is a parameter of the transfer itself. A mistake of the transferor about the object of the transfer affects his intention *that* a certain transfer shall be made at all. Evidently, a transferor's intention to transfer property in his bicycle is insufficient to transfer property in his car. But in what circumstances does a transferor indeed intend – or must be taken to intend – to transfer his bicycle and when his car?

212 *R v Ashwell* [1885] 16 QBD 190; see Chapter 4 section 2.3.2.4.
213 See Chapter 4 section 2.1.

Similarly, as with regard to mistakes as to the transferee's identity, it is argued that a close parallel should be drawn between the contractual and the proprietary position. It is helpful to compare the transferor's intention to transfer property with an offer to transfer property and the transferee's intention to receive it with a corresponding acceptance.[214] Both, the question of *to whom* an offer to transfer property is addressed (transferee) and the question of *what is its object* (transferred property) should be determined by analogous principles as those which determine the questions of to whom an offer to conclude a contract is addressed (offeree) and of what that offer's object is (contract goods). Yet, this contract analogy must not disguise the fact that the contract and the proprietary transfer are still distinct and independent from each other. Mistakes as to the goods' identity are, as far as operative, *dual defects* which not only render a contract void but which also – independently of that – negative a transferor's intention to transfer property.

It follows that a mistake as to the goods' identity is only operative to prevent the passage of property if it leads to the conclusion that an offer to transfer property was in fact made in relation to goods other than those in question or in relation to non-existent goods. The issue of *what is the object* of an offer to transfer property is – in accordance with the rules derived from the contractual position – primarily determined by an identification *by sight* (face-to-property principle). If A has seen the goods which he purports to transfer to B, the identification by sight is generally conclusive to unequivocally identify those goods as the object of the transfer, even if A has given an inconsistent description as to what he believed those goods to be. By contrast, if A has never seen the goods in question, they are generally identified *by description*. In this case, one must carefully analyse – according to the objective and the subjective principle – whether the descriptive words used by the parties went to the goods' identity or merely to their quality. For property to pass, the goods in question must meet the identification-relevant features, particularly as to their location and identity. Alternatively, the goods might also be identified *by touching* (or by smelling or by hearing). It will be argued that such a mode of identification does not prevail over a concomitant identification by description.

2.3.2.2. Identification by Description (at a Distance)

There are not many cases concerned with a (potential) mistake as to the goods' identity where the goods have only been identified at a distance by description and where the passage of property has been an issue. An exception is *Varley v Whipp*.[215] Concerned with an action for price, Channell J held that property in the reaping machine in question had not passed to the buyer. Though the judge

---

214 See text to fn 127–129.

215 *Varley v Whipp* [1900] 1 QB 513; see text to fn 204–209.

might have been misled by the inaccurate assumption that a sale by description might never be specific, his judgment might still be (re)interpreted on the basis of a lack of specific identification: The machine was sold as a "reaping machine, at Upton, self-binder, second-hand, new the previous year, used to cut only fifty to sixty acres". The buyer rejected the machine because it was older than one year. Channell J indicated that he would have thought that a "one-year-old reaping machine" was not of the same kind as a "non-one-year-old reaping machine" and that the age went to the goods' identity.[216] If that were correct, the seller's old reaping machine at Upton would indeed not have been identified by this description and property in it would not have passed at the time of conclusion.[217] However, it is at least debatable whether the age of the machine has indeed been an identification-relevant feature in *Varley v Whipp*. Arguably, the features "old" or "new" do not generally go to the goods' identity, as is demonstrated by *Smith v Hughes*[218] where the parties have similarly identified the contract goods specifically at a distance by description ("all oats at the seller's premises") and where that identification would apparently still have been valid had the parties agreed on "old oats". Yet, the question whether a certain feature is identification-relevant or not appears to be, ultimately, a question of the parties' intention construed according to the objective and the subjective principle.

2.3.2.3. Identification by Sight

Suppose that A and B stand in front of a bulk of mandarins and agree to sell and buy "this entire bulk" while pointing at it (case (2) as described above[219]). Does property in that bulk of mandarins pass to B if A mistakenly believes that this is a bulk of oranges? It has been argued above that a so concluded *contract* would be valid,[220] providing for "this bulk" as the specifically identified contract goods, and that this would be so even if the parties included a term into their contract that this bulk consists of "oranges" (case (3)). If this is correct, logic dictates that such a mistake might neither – *a fortiori* – be operative to prevent the passage of *property* in "this bulk".[221] In both of those cases, the parties have unequivocally

216 This appears from what he said about a "four-year old horse in the last stall" (516).

217 The seller later sent the machine to the buyer and thereby unequivocally identified it as the object of his transfer of property. But the buyer rejected delivery and thereby expressed his rejection to receive ownership; there was thus neither delivery nor a real agreement. Property did not, accordingly, pass by delivery.

218 *Smith v Hughes* [1871] LR 6 QB 597.

219 See Chapter 4 section 2.3.1.2.(c).

220 The contract might, however, be void for common mistake (if the buyer equally believes that these are oranges) or voidable (if the buyer induced the seller's mistake). But those would not be grounds preventing the (initial) passage of property.

221 This follows from the principle that a defect (mistake), which is not even capable of avoiding a contract, cannot still render a proprietary transfer void ("indirect curing effect"); see Chapter 1 section 2.1.1.2.

identified the goods *by sight* which ought to prevail on the contractual *and* the proprietary level over any other mode of identification (face-to-property principle).

If a mistake as to the property's identity may not – if the goods have been identified by sight – prevent ownership from passing in cases where an accompanying contract was concluded, such a mistake may neither prevent the passage of property where it merely occurred in the performance stage or where no contract has been concluded at all, as in cases of mistaken deliveries. This follows from the abstract nature of the transfer of property. An illuminating example was provided by Bramwell B in *R v Middleton*:

> "A tells B he has ordered a wine merchant to give B a dozen of wine, B goes to the wine merchant, bona fide receives, and drinks a dozen of wine. After it is consumed, the wine merchant discovers he gave B the wrong dozen, and demands it of B, who, having consumed it, cannot return it. It is clear the wine merchant can maintain no action against B, as B could plead the wine merchant's leave and licence."[222]

Bramwell B rightly assumed that property would have passed in this case. Unfortunately, however, the majority in *R v Middleton* gave an alternative example and apparently suggested that property would not have passed in such a case:

> "[L]et us suppose that a purchaser of beans goes to the warehouse of a merchant with a genuine order for so many bushels of beans, to be selected from the bulk and so become the property of the vendee, and that by some strange blunder the merchant delivers to him an equal bulk of coffee. If that coffee was sold (not in market overt) by the recipient to a third person, could he retain it against the merchant, on the ground that he had bought it from one who had the property in the coffee, though subject to be divested? […] [T]here can be no doubt he could not."[223]

This mirrors the judges' disagreement with regard to the "cabman case", another hypothetical example considered in *R v Middleton*: A passenger hands over a sovereign to a cabman, which he mistakenly believed to have been a shilling. Bramwell B[224] assumed that property in the sovereign would have passed in such

222 *R v Middleton* [1873] LR 2 CCR 38, 56 (Bramwell B). This must mean that ownership in the wrong dozen of wine had passed to B and that the wine merchant could not, therefore, have claimed in conversion. Furthermore, though the merchant (or perhaps A) might have had a personal claim in unjust enrichment, B could, once he had consumed the wine in good faith, have invoked the change of position defence.

223 Ibid, 44–45.

224 Ibid, 57.

a case whereas the majority[225] suggested that it would not. The former view is preferable. The wine merchant in the wine example, the merchant in the bean/coffee example and the passenger in the cabman example have all unequivocally identified the goods *by sight* which must mean that their intentions to transfer property could only have related to those physically identified goods. Property in the wrong dozen of wine, in the coffee and in the sovereign must accordingly have passed in each of those examples. The mistaken transferors should have been limited to a personal claim in unjust enrichment.

The same result was apparently reached by a majority in *R v Hehir*.[226] Leech owed £2, 8 s., 9d. to Hehir for work done by the latter. Intending to discharge this debt, Leech handed over to Hehir nine shillings in silver and two bank notes, each of which both believed to have been a £1-note but one of which was, in fact, a £10-note. Hehir later discovered the mistake and decided to appropriate the £10-note. He was charged of larceny but a bare majority in the Court for Crown Cases Reserved quashed the conviction. Though the reasons provided by the majority judges are not entirely clear with regard to the question whether property in the £10-note had passed, their judgments are – the one of Andrews J apart – apparently not inconsistent with such a view.[227] Arguably, this is at least how the case should be (re)interpreted today. Though Leech had been mistaken about the value of one of those notes, he had still unequivocally identified the two notes *by sight* as the objects of his proprietary transfer. He objectively and subjectively intended to transfer "these two notes" to Hehir. Hence, the mistake was insufficient to negative his intention to transfer property in them. Leech should have been limited to a personal claim in unjust enrichment for the value of £9.

It is concluded that a mistake as to the goods' identity or quality – for example as to their kind (beans or coffee; oranges or mandarins), their chemical composition (silver or white gold) or their value (£1-note or £10-note) – is insufficient to prevent the passage of ownership if the relevant goods have been identified by sight (face-to-property principle). This applies irrespective of the mistake's gravity. Such mistakes are, in other words, merely motivational in

225 Ibid, 45; see also J. Smith, Crim LR 1972, 587; Pollock/Wright, Possession, 102–3 (with the example of ancient coins, transferred as specific chattels).

226 *R v Hehir* [1895] 18 Cox 267 (Ct for Crown Cases Reserved (Ireland)); see similarly *R v Jacobs* [1872] 12 Cox 151.

227 Johnson J seemed to assume that property had passed, whereas Andrews J (who wrongly assumed that the question of "property in the note [was] immaterial in this case") suggested that property had not passed but that Leech had still intended to transfer possession. The tenor of the other majority judges appeared to have been that Leech had a valid (though vitiated) intention to transfer at least possession to Hehir and that the mistake could not have negatived that intention. By contrast, the minority judges (Madden, Gibson, Holmes, Murphy JJ) assumed that property had not passed to Hehir.

nature, relating to the reason *why* a transferor *does* intend to transfer the relevant item of property. The face-to-property principle is an indirect consequence of the face-to-face principle as established in *Shogun Finance v Hudson*[228] and, to some extent, also of the *caveat emptor* principle as established in *Smith v Hughes*.[229]

2.3.2.4. Identification by Touching

We shall now turn to the difficult question of the exact scope of the face-to-property (and the face-to-face) principle: Does this principle equally apply if the transferor has identified the goods only by touching but not by sight, as for example where the transferor is blind or where the transfer was made in the dark? This question underlay the difficult case of *R v Ashwell*.[230] Keogh and Ashwell met in a public-house on a January evening. When they went out into the yard, Ashwell asked Keogh to lend him a shilling which he would pay back the next day. Keogh agreed and – in the dark – put his hand into his pocket and pulled out what he believed to have been a shilling but which was, in fact, a sovereign. He handed over that coin to Ashwell who, at that time, equally believed that this was a shilling. About one hour later, when Ashwell had discovered the mistake, he decided to appropriate the coin. He was convicted for larceny of the sovereign in the first instance. Upon appeal, the Court of Crown Cases Reserved was, very unfortunately, equally divided (seven to seven), which meant that the conviction stood. It is, accordingly, impossible to extract a proper ratio of this case. The analysis is further complicated by the fact that a conviction for larceny required various things and that the passage of property was only one of several issues. Larceny could not have been upheld if either property in the sovereign had passed to Ashwell, if Keogh had consented to the transfer of possession of the sovereign (there would then have been no trespassory taking) or if – whether or not Keogh had consented to the transfer of property or possession – Ashwell had not had a felonious intent at the time of taking, i.e. at the time when he had obtained possession.

The seven judges who upheld the conviction, namely Cave J (with whom Hawkins J agreed), Lord Coleridge CJ (with whom Grave, Pollock and Huddleston JJ agreed) and Denman J, gave quite similar reasons for their judgments. On the one hand, they assumed – though without proper discussion – that property in the sovereign had not passed to Ashwell and that Keogh had not consented to the transfer of possession. Both of those findings were apparently based on the fact that Keogh had been unaware that he was handing over a sovereign. On the other hand, they held that Ashwell had not obtained possession of the coin

228 *Shogun Finance v Hudson* [2003] UKHL 62.
229 *Smith v Hughes* [1871] LR 6 QB 597.
230 *R v Ashwell* [1885] 16 QBD 190.

when he had taken it from Keogh but only when he had realised that the coin was a sovereign rather than a shilling. This was based on the assumption that there could not have been an intention to possess a chattel unless one was aware of the kind (or quality or value) of that chattel. Hence, those judges treated the case as one of finding – Ashwell "found" the sovereign when he had discovered the mistake – which meant that Ashwell had had a felonious intent at the time of taking.

Smith J, one of the seven judges who would have quashed the conviction, based his judgment on two grounds, namely that, on the one hand, the taking of the sovereign had not been against the will of Keogh and that, on the other hand, Ashwell had not had a felonious intent at the time of taking. It is uncertain whether Smith J thought that property had passed to Ashwell in this case. Though he expressed his consent with the majority's view on the "cabman example" in *R v Middleton*, his basic reasons were that Keogh had formed a plain intention to deliver "the coin" to Ashwell and that Ashwell had formed a plain intention to receive "the coin". This meant that their mistakes as to the coin's value had not negatived their intention to transfer and receive "the coin". The judgment of Stephen J (with whom Day and Wills JJ agreed) is to a similar effect. Mathew and Manisty JJ rather clearly assumed that property in the sovereign had passed to Ashwell. They both suggested that Ashwell plainly had a right to change the sovereign for 20s. and to return to Keogh the *value* of 19s. as money had and received and the *value* of 1s. as money lent. This meant that Keogh merely had a personal claim in unjust enrichment (for the value of 19s.) and a personal claim in contract (for the value of 1s.). Field J agreed with Smith, Stephen, Mathew and Manisty JJ without expressing his own reasons.

Notwithstanding its uncertain status, *R v Ashwell* has since been regarded as a case concerned with a proprietarily fundamental mistake and as the principal authority for the proposition that a mistake as to the goods' identity – as opposed to their quality – prevents the passage of property.[231] According to the view adopted in this book, the result in *R v Ashwell* (of the seven judges upholding the conviction) is at least questionable. Yet, if it is indeed correct that Keogh had retained property in that case, this finding should be explained on the basis that the transfer had been made in the dark and that neither of the parties had identified the object of the transfer by sight. There can be little doubt that property would have passed had the transfer been made in daylight and had Keogh identified the coin, i.e. the object of the transfer, by sight.[232]

[231] *Ilich v R* [1987] 162 CLR 110, 126–27 (Wilson, Dawson JJ); Fox, Property Rights, 4.129–31; Virgo, Restitution, 574–75; Williams, Crim LR 1958, 222; Williams, Criminal Law, 32.133–34 (fn 351); Ormerod/Williams, Smith's Law of Theft, 2.251–52; critically: *R v Potisk* [1973] 6 SASR 389, 394–98 (Bray CJ); Turner, Russell on Crime, vol 2, 978–80, 1553–74; Turner, Kenny's Outlines of Criminal Law, 314–18; Swadling, Unjust Delivery, 294–96 (but cf still Swadling, LQR 2005, 152).

[232] But cf Williams, CLJ 1977, 64–65.

In such a case, the face-to-property principle would have applied and property would have passed just as it apparently did in *R v Hehir*[233] and as it would have passed in the mandarin/orange, the wine, the coffee/bean and the cabman example.[234] Keogh would then have been limited to a personal claim in unjust enrichment.

It is not an easy question whether the face-to-property (and the face-to-face) principle ought to apply if a transfer has been made in the dark or if a transferor is blind.[235] After all, Keogh had physically identified the coin by taking it out of his pocket and by handing it over to Ashwell. At that time, he – objectively and subjectively – intended two inconsistent things: "I want to transfer property in this item/coin which I physically hold in my hand" and "I want to transfer property in this shilling". Since Keogh had in fact believed that these were one and the same things, we cannot – in a retrospective assessment – get a proper answer by asking of what he *really* or *rather* intended. There is a conundrum in this case just as where a transferor identifies the transferee or the transferred property by sight. The relevant question is whether there should be a legal rule or at least a strong presumption which equally resolves this conundrum in favour of the physical element (the touching) rather than the identification by description ("shilling").

It could be argued that a transferor who takes the risk of transferring an item, which he has never actually seen, cannot complain if the transferred item is in fact the "wrong" item. This would effectively mean that blind persons would always have to bear the risk of mistakenly transferring wrong items and that they would always be limited to personal unjust enrichment claims or, if the mistake was induced by the transferee, to powers in rem. This would not seem right.[236] A transfer by a blind or a transfer made in the dark should rather be compared with a transfer at a distance where the property is identified by description. This is all the more obvious if the transferor has not even actually touched the item in question but if he merely pointed at it. Suppose that Keogh had a shilling in his right pocket and a sovereign in his left one and that he instructed Ashwell to "take out the shilling of my left pocket". Arguably, such a case should be governed by the same principles as those applying to cases where the transferred property has been identified at a distance by description, as for example where A agrees to transfer "my horse in my last stall" but where there is only a cow in that last stall.

If this is correct, the identification of the object of the proprietary transfer is, in cases like *R v Ashwell*, governed by a two-step analysis: First, one has to

233 *R v Hehir* [1895] 18 Cox 267.

234 See text to fn 222–229.

235 This was explicitly left open by Lord Walker in *Shogun Finance v Hudson* [2003] UKHL 62, [187]; his Lordship gave the biblical example of Jacob who impersonated his elder twin brother Esau to deceive his blind father Isaac (Genesis, ch 27).

236 See also GOODHART, LQR 1941, 240–41 (who, however, denied any face-to-face principle).

determine the actual description of the transferred goods by an objective or – if known to the transferee – a subjective interpretation of the words and conduct of the transferor. Second, one has to determine whether the goods in question (here: the sovereign) are indeed identified by this description. This particularly requires that they meet all identification-relevant features. If A transfers "the horse in my last stall" but if there is no horse in that last stall or if there is only a cow or a bulk of gold bullions, nothing would pass since no existing item of property would be identified as the object of the proprietary transfer. By contrast, if A transfers "the sound horse in my last stall" and if there is an unsound horse in that stall, that horse would generally still be identified as the object of the proprietary transfer; property in it would pass since "soundness" is not generally an identification-relevant feature.

Arguably, *R v Ashwell* should be explained on this basis. Keogh had effectively described the object of his transfer as "this shilling in my hand". Hence, the relevant question was whether "shilling" was an identification-relevant feature or merely a feature going to the goods' quality. It seems that this question – amongst others – divided the judges. Is a sovereign a thing of a different kind than a shilling or are they both simply "money" or "coins" with different values? The preferable view seems to be that the denomination (and perhaps even the currency) of money is not – at least where money is transferred as currency – generally going to the identity of the chattel but merely to its quality or value.[237] But the question whether a certain feature is identification-relevant or not should, ultimately, be a question of the parties' intentions as objectively and subjectively construed and it is not impossible to explain the judgments of the seven judges favouring Ashwell's conviction on those lines.

2.3.2.5. Chattels Contained within Other Chattels

Quite similar as transfers in the dark or transfers by blinds is the case where a chattel is transferred which contains, unbeknown to the transferor, another chattel or a chattel different from that envisaged by him. Take the case that a shopkeeper, who has received an order for a watch from B, puts such a watch into a box which he prepares for delivery. For some reason, whether fraudulent or not, some other person (without authority) opens the box, takes out the watch and puts a diamond ring of the shop into it. The shopkeeper, without knowledge and without reopening the box, hands it over to B when the latter enters the

[237] See Fox, Property Rights, 4.132; Fox, RLR 1996, 66; Turner, Russell on Crime, vol 2, 980, 1553–74; Turner, Kenny's Outlines of Criminal Law, 314–18; Swadling, Unjust Delivery, 294–96 (but cf still Swadling, LQR 2005, 152); *R v Potisk* [1973] 6 SASR 389, 395–98 (Bray CJ); *Ilich v R* [1987] 162 CLR 110, 140 (Brennan J) (but cf 126 (Wilson and Dawson JJ)); contra: Virgo, Restitution, 574–75 (fn 120); Williams, CLJ 1977, 64–65; Williams, Criminal Law, 32.133–34; Ormerod/Williams, Smith's Law of Theft, 2.251–52.

store to pick up the watch; B appropriates the ring when he later discovers the mistake. This is a much clearer case than that of *R v Ashwell*. Quite obviously, the shopkeeper has no intention at all to transfer property in the diamond ring.[238]

The face-to-property principle should – *a fortiori* – be inapplicable where the purportedly transferred chattel is contained within another chattel and where it has not as such been identified by sight. The question whether property in a chattel, which is concealed within a container, passes together with the container should arguably be determined by the same principles as those which govern the transfer of goods identified at a distance and by description: First, one must establish – according to the objective and the subjective principle – the description used by the transferor to identify the object(s) of his transfer. Second, one has to determine whether the chattel in question (the concealed one) meets the identification-relevant features of this description.

This is plainly consistent with the result of *Merry v Green*.[239] A bureau was sold at a public auction. Unbeknown to the seller and the buyer, the bureau contained a purse and money in a secret drawer. The buyer appropriated the money and the purse when he later found them. The seller caused the buyer's detention by the police and the buyer sued in trespass (assault and false imprisonment). This action depended on the question whether he had committed larceny. Parke B ordered a new trial on the basis that the jury had to determine whether the buyer had "reasonable ground for believing that he bought the bureau with its contents." Though Parke B apparently expressed this under the head of *mens rea*, it appears that the very same criterion was equally decisive for the question whether property in the money and the purse had passed to the buyer.[240]

If the contract goods were contractually described as "the bureau with (whatever) contents", the seller's proprietary intention to transfer property would have similarly related to "the bureau with (whatever) contents". The face-to-property principle does not apply in such a case since the purse and the money were hidden within the bureau. Hence, the money and the purse could only have been identified *by description* as the objects of the transfer. There was no clear evidence whether the seller had, as a matter of fact, subjectively intended to only transfer "the bureau alone, without its contents" and, if so, whether the buyer had knowledge of this. Unless this was proved, one had to apply the objective principle, asking whether a reasonable person in the buyer's position would have understood that the object(s) of the sale and the object(s) of the proprietary transfer was "the bureau with (whatever) contents" or "the bureau

---

238 Cf also Turner, Kenny's Outlines of Criminal Law, 286.

239 *Merry v Green* [1841] 7 M&W 623, 151 ER 916; cf also the similar case of *Cartwright v Green* [1803] 8 Ves Jr 405, 32 ER 412, where, however, the bureau (containing the money) had not been sold but merely handed over for reparation. Accordingly, there had not even been an intention to pass property in the bureau itself (container).

240 Cf also Pollock/Wright, Possession, 109 (with regard to possession).

alone, without contents". If the former, property in the purse and the money would have passed; if the latter, property would have remained with the seller. Similarly, if the seller had – objectively or subjectively – intended to transfer "the bureau with the purse and the money", only the purse and the money would have been caught by the descriptive identification but not, for example, a diamond ring or a watch contained within the bureau.

In *R v Ashwell*, the seven judges favouring Ashwell's conviction based their decisions particularly on *Merry v Green* (and *Cartwright v Green*). Lord Coleridge CJ, for example, said this:

> "I can see no sensible or intelligible distinction between the delivery of a bureau not known to contain a sum of money or a purse and the delivery of a piece of metal not known to contain in it 20 s."[241]

However, it is respectfully submitted that there is quite an obvious difference between those two cases since a sovereign does not actually "contain" 20 shillings but merely has the value of 20 shillings. Anything else would be to "[confuse] the physical and the metaphysical."[242] *R v Ashwell* was not a case of a transfer of a chattel contained (hidden) within another chattel. But it is submitted that there is still a close parallel between those two cases since the chattels in question – the sovereign in *R v Ashwell* and the purse and the money in *Merry v Green* – were respectively *concealed* and were not, as such, identified by sight. In one case, the chattel was hidden in the dark; in the other case, it was hidden within another chattel. Had Keogh handed over the coin in daylight, *R v Ashwell* would have had nothing in common with *Merry v Green*.

2.4. MISTAKES AS TO THE TRANSFERRED PROPERTY'S QUANTITY

The third category of proprietarily fundamental mistakes are mistakes as to the transferred property's quantity.[243] It will be seen that the applicable principles are – at least from a conceptual point of view – broadly similar to those elaborated in the previous section relating to mistakes as to the property's identity. Yet, there is one crucial antecedent question, namely whether the bulk of goods in question is sold as *one specific item* – of which its weight, volume or number of components are merely attributes – or whether only a *certain amount* (quantity) out of this bulk is sold (as quasi-specific goods). Furthermore, there is an additional complication by s 30 of the SGA 1979.

---

241 *R v Ashwell* [1885] 16 QBD 190, 225 (Lord Coleridge CJ).

242 Swadling, Unjust Delivery, 295.

243 See the references in fn 4.

2.4.1. *Contractual Level*

2.4.1.1. Sale of Generic, Quasi-Specific or Specific Goods?

The identification of the quantity of the contract goods is part of the identification of the contract goods as such. It is therefore governed by principles similar to those set out in the previous section.[244]

Suppose that A intends to sell "100 tons of satsuma mandarins, Brazil, price X" but that by some clerical error he sends an offer to B which mistakenly states "200 tons of satsuma mandarins, Brazil, price X" and that B accepts the offer. This is an agreement to sell generic goods. The analysis on the contractual level involves two steps:[245] First, one has to determine the precise contractual terms with regard to the quantity agreed. If B knows that A merely intends to sell 100 tons or if B also only intends to buy 100 tons, the contract is for 100 tons. Otherwise, the objective principle applies and A is bound by the natural meaning of his words (200 tons). Second, once the contracted quantity has been determined, the seller must make an effective appropriation, which means in principle that he must appropriate the correct quantity of specific items from the defined genus to the contract. This issue will be discussed in the next sub-section.

By contrast, take the case that A and B stand in front of a bulk of satsuma mandarins, which in fact weighs 200 tons, and that they agree to sell and buy "this entire bulk of mandarins". This is a sale of specific goods. The object of the contract (the contract goods) is "this entire bulk" and the quantity is *one* bulk. The weight or the number of components (mandarins) of the bulk is not even made a term of the contract in this case. If A or B is mistaken about the true weight of the bulk, he is still not mistaken about *how much* he sold or bought – namely one bulk – but merely about an attribute or the quality of the contract goods (their weight) and perhaps about the reason *why* he intends to sell or buy "this bulk" for this price. The position is just the same as where A or B believes that the bulk consists of oranges instead of mandarins. The contract is perfectly valid for "this bulk";[246] this follows from the *caveat emptor* principle as established in *Smith v Hughes*.[247]

The position is less straightforward if A and B stand in front of a bulk of mandarins weighing 200 tons and if they agree to sell and buy "this bulk of mandarins; weight: 100 tons". Is this a contract for the sale of *specific* goods ("this bulk"), which contains a term, usually a condition, as to those goods' (this bulk's)

---

244 Chapter 4 section 2.3.1.

245 See Chapter 4 section 2.3.1.2.(a).

246 However, the contract might be void for common mistake (if both parties are mistaken about the true weight) or voidable for misrepresentation (if one party's mistake was induced by the other party).

247 *Smith v Hughes* [1871] LR 6 QB 597.

weight, or is this an agreement to sell *quasi-specific* goods ("100 tons out of this bulk"), which merely defines the source (this bulk) from which the seller might perform? If the former, the seller would – even though the bulk weighs 200 tons – still be obliged to transfer the *entire* bulk. If the latter, he would only be obliged to appropriate 100 tons out of this bulk to the buyer. Similarly, if the bulk only weighs 50 tons, that bulk would in the former case still be the entire contract goods but the seller would be in breach for non-conformity. In the latter case, the contract goods would be partially non-existent.

It appears that the question whether the sale is for "100 tons out of this bulk" (quasi-specific goods[248]) or for "this entire bulk, warranted to be 100 tons" (specific goods) is a question of construction of the contract which is determined by the ordinary amalgam of the objective and the subjective principle. Certainly, in an example as the one above, the parties will most usually have agreed on the former but there is no reason why the latter should not be possible, at least in theory. The case would then be similar as where A for example sells his "second-hand car, warranted to be no older than one year, to be in good condition and to weigh 900 kilograms". Obviously, "one car" and not "900 kilograms" would then be the relevant quantity of the contract goods.

There is accordingly a difference between this case (quantity mistake) and the case where A and B, standing in front of a bulk of mandarins, agree on "this bulk of oranges" (identity mistake). Why is A, if he has identified the bulk by sight, generally bound to sell the bulk of mandarins even if they have agreed on "this bulk of oranges" but not usually to sell the entire bulk if they agreed on "this bulk; weight: 100 tons"? Why does the answer in the latter but not in the former case depend on a construction of the descriptive words used by the parties? The reason arguably lies in the fact that a face-to-property or some "face-to-quantity" principle does not generally apply in quantity mistake cases. In the above case, A had two things in mind: "I want to sell this bulk" and "I want to sell 100 tons of mandarins". As in cases of identity mistakes, it is impossible to get a proper answer by asking what A *really* or *rather* intended since he simply intended both. It could be argued that the element of physical identification – the pointing at the bulk – should equally prevail over an identification by description in quantity mistake cases. However, it will be seen that an analogy should rather be drawn with the cases of *Merry v Green*[249] and *Cartwright v Green*[250] where the quite obvious rule was effectively laid down that the face-to-property principle does not apply if the chattel in question has been hidden within another chattel.

---

248 The contract goods are only quasi-specific if they are not in fact fully identified at the time of conclusion. If the bulk only contains 100 tons or less, the sale is – even if the contract formulation is worded in quasi-specific terms – still for specific goods; Goode, Commercial Law, 8.5–7; see fn 209.

249 *Merry v Green* [1841] 7 M&W 623.

250 *Cartwright v Green* [1803] 8 Ves Jr 405.

This rule, which should equally apply to transfers made by blinds and transfers made in the dark, might be extended to quantity mistake cases where the chattel(s) in question, i.e. the excess, is generally[251] hidden amongst other chattels. Though the transferor might perhaps visually perceive the *entirety* of all chattels, he will still not usually have noticed – or counted – each of those chattels *individually*.

For that reason, there is – as far as quantity mistakes are concerned – generally no difference between cases where the goods (quantity) have been identified by sight and cases where they have been identified at a distance by description. If the parties agree on "the bulk of mandarins at warehouse X in spot Y; weight: 100 tons" but if that bulk weighs more than 100 tons, one must construe the contract and ask whether the parties have objectively or subjectively intended to contract for "100 tons out of that bulk" (quasi-specific goods) or for "that bulk, warranted to be 100 tons" (specific goods).

2.4.1.2. Appropriation and the Problem of s 30 of the SGA 1979

If the parties agree on *specific* contract goods in the above sense, as for example where A and B agree to transfer "this bulk, warranted to be 100 tons", property in the entire bulk might – if so agreed – immediately pass (ss 16–19 of the SGA 1979) and any mistake as to the bulk's weight would only be motivational in nature. If the bulk weighs more or less than 100 tons, s 30 of the SGA 1979 would not apply since the seller in fact delivers the correct quantity (one bulk) if he delivers that bulk. But the buyer might then have a right (but no duty) to reject the non-conforming goods.

By contrast, if the contract goods are *quasi-specific* or *generic*, the seller must make an effective appropriation and property might not pass prior to that (s 16 of the SGA 1979[252]). Arguably, a mistake occurring in the stage of appropriation (execution) is generally governed by principles similar to those applying where the parties have initially agreed on specific goods and where the mistake has already occurred in the formation stage.[253] However, s 30 of the SGA 1979 contains a specific rule in this context which deviates from the general principles to some extent.

If the seller appropriates and delivers a quantity less than agreed (short delivery), there is no issue of a quantity mistake. The buyer might – unless sub-section 2A applies – reject the short delivery or accept it and pay at the

[251] An exception should perhaps be made – if this is ever going to happen in practice – where only a very small quantity of granular goods is transferred under a quantity mistake, as for example if A transfers a quantity of four oranges in an open basket to B which he mistakenly believes to be only three.

[252] An exception applies for quasi-specific goods if the requirements of s 20A are met.

[253] See text to fn 182–183. In fact, the act of appropriation is a two-sided contractual act by which the exact contract goods are specifically identified.

contract rate (s 30(1)).[254] If the seller appropriates and delivers a quantity larger than contracted for (excessive delivery), s 30(2) and s 30(3) provide that the buyer may (i) reject the whole, unless sub-section 2A applies, or (ii) take out the correct quantity and reject the excess or (iii) accept the whole quantity and pay for the excess at the contract rate.

This latter rule that the buyer might accept an excessive delivery and pay at the contract rate gives rise to some uncertainty: It is generally accepted that the underlying basis of this rule is that a seller's excessive delivery is to be regarded as an offer to alter (extend) the existing contract with regard to the quantity and that the buyer's acceptance of the goods is an acceptance of that offer.[255] Evidently, *if* and *as far as* this section is effective to create a contractual basis for the excessive delivery, property must – quantity mistake or not – inevitably pass in the excess too.[256,257] However, the exact scope and effect of s 30(2) and s 30(3) is quite uncertain.[258] Do those sub-sections also apply if the seller acts under a genuine quantity mistake? If yes, do they even apply if the buyer knows that the excessive delivery was caused by such a mistake? Do those sub-sections merely restate the general rules of offer and acceptance or do they lay down a statutory rule going beyond that?

Section 30 only applies to "contracts of sale" as defined by s 2 of the SGA 1979 but not to other types of contracts, such as barters or loans, and it only applies to deliveries of goods (but not money) of the wrong quantity of the same kind.[259] Arguably, there is no good reason why s 30 should inevitably be regarded as

---

254 Property passes according to the ordinary rules of ss 16–19 and, if the buyer rejects the short delivery, revests according to principles similar to those applying where he rejects the goods for non-conformity; see Chapter 2 fn 133.

255 *Cunliffe v Harrison* [1851] 6 Ex 903, 155 ER 813, 814: "The delivery of more than [the contracted quantity] is a proposal for a new contract"; Williams, Crim LR 1958, 229–32; Williams, CLJ 1977, 74–78; Bridge et al, Benjamin's Sale of Goods, 8.43; Twigg-Flesner et al, Atiyah and Adams' Sale of Goods, 114–15.

256 This follows from the principle that a defect (mistake), which is not even capable of avoiding a contract, cannot still render a proprietary transfer void ("indirect curing effect"); see Chapter 1 section 2.1.1.2. If there is a valid contract for the excess, the seller has not even a personal claim in unjust enrichment, even if the market value has risen in the meantime.

257 Prior to delivery and prior to the buyer's contractual acceptance, property might only pass in relation to the agreed quantity (but see Chapter 4 section 2.4.2.2. for the "identification and mixture problem"; see also s 20A of the SGA 1979). In relation to the excess, property might only pass upon and by delivery since there is, prior to the alteration of the contract, no consideration in that regard. In gratuitous transactions, mistaken payments or over-deliveries, legal title may only pass by delivery; see Chapter 2 section 3. Upon delivery, however, property does pass if the seller so intended, even if the buyer has not yet finally accepted ownership. If the buyer later rejects the excess, property will revest retroactively; see Chapter 2 section 1.3.; but cf somewhat differently *Karlshamns Oljefabriker v Eastport Navigation Co (The Elafi)* [1982] 1 All ER 208 (QBD), 212–13 (Mustill J); Ulph, LMCLQ 1998, 5–6; Goode, Commercial Law, 8.19–22.

258 See esp Williams, Crim LR 1958, 229–32; Williams, CLJ 1977, 74–78.

259 Williams, CLJ 1977, 77.

stipulating an invariable rule of law – or a fiction – that a seller is in any case whatsoever *deemed* to have contractually offered the excess.[260] That provision should rather be interpreted as broadly restating the general rules of offer and acceptance and as merely providing a *presumption* that a seller's excessive delivery is to be regarded as an offer.[261] If the buyer has no knowledge that the seller has made a mistake, for example if he believes that the seller has intentionally sent an excessive quantity, the seller is generally bound by his apparent offer. In so far, s 30 concretises the objective principle by laying down a presumption that the buyer is entitled to rely on this being an offer. By contrast, if there is evidence, for which the seller bears the burden of proof, that the buyer knew or ought to have known (i) that the seller had made a mistake and that he had not in fact meant to make an offer for the surplus[262] and (ii) that the seller would still not now – that he had already shipped the goods to the buyer – have made an offer for the excess at the contract rate, the subjective principle must prevail and the buyer should not be entitled to snap up the offer. Arguably, however, the buyer might still accept the apparent offer if he only knew (i) but not (ii) and if it was reasonable for him to assume that the seller would now rather offer the surplus at the contract rate than demanding re-delivery at his expense. In so far, s 30 indeed deviates – to that limited extent – from the ordinary rules of offer and acceptance since there is not generally room to snap up a *hypothetical offer* if the apparent offeree knows that the offer, as objectively understood, does not correspond with the offeror's actual subjective intention.

2.4.2. Proprietary Level

Does a mistake of the transferor about the quantity of the transferred goods negative his intention to transfer property and, if so, in what circumstances? Two kinds of cases must be distinguished: First, cases where the transferor exactly knows *what* and *how much* he is transferring but where he is mistaken about the reason *why* he is doing so, particularly if his mistake relates to the existence or the extent of a corresponding liability. Such a mistake is merely motivational in nature and does not prevent the passage of property.[263] Second, cases where the transferor knows that he is transferring *some* property but where he is genuinely mistaken about *how much* he is in fact handing over to the transferee.[264]

260 This was, though with some reluctance, apparently assumed by Williams, Crim LR 1958, 229–32; Williams, CLJ 1977, 74–78.

261 See Ulph, LMCLQ 1998, 6–7.

262 Twigg-Flesner et al, Atiyah and Adams' Sale of Goods, 114–15, assume that s 30(2) and s 30(3) are never applicable if the buyer knows that the seller has not meant to make an offer.

263 To this category belong cases such as *Moynes v Coopper* [1956] 1 QB 439; *Lacis v Cashmarts* [1969] 2 QB 400; *R v Potisk* [1973] 6 SASR 389; see Chapter 4 section 2.1.

264 The case of *Russell v Smith* [1958] 1 QB 27 (QBD) arguably belongs to this category; see text to fn 288–289.

It is only this latter kind of mistake with which we are concerned here since only this type of mistake may prevent property from passing. However, it will be seen that this distinction is sometimes an extremely difficult one to draw.[265]

Genuine quantity mistakes must further be distinguished from the category of mistakes as to the property's identity or quality.[266] If the parties agree on the transfer of specific goods, for example "this bulk" or "this car", and if one of the parties is mistaken about the weight, the volume or the number of components of that specific item of property, the mistake is not one as to *quantity* but one as to *identity* or *quality*.

If the parties agree to sell and buy generic or quasi-specific goods, for example "100 tons out of this bulk", property may not – s 20A of the SGA 1979 apart – pass unless and until an effective appropriation has been made (s 16). If the seller appropriates and delivers a quantity larger than the contracted amount, that might be taken as an offer to sell the surplus (s 30). If so, property in the excess inevitably passes if the buyer accepts the offer.[267] But as far as s 30 does not apply – by reason of the seller's mistake and because the buyer has knowledge of this[268] – the question arises whether the seller's quantity mistake prevents the passage of ownership.

Since the transfer of the excess is, in the latter case, a *non-contractual* one, property might only pass upon and by delivery. Hence, the position is just the same as where the transferor for example intends to make a gift of ten tennis balls but mistakenly includes an eleventh or where a contract of sale of 50 watches is void for some reason and where the transferor – in the belief that it is valid – mistakenly delivers 51 watches. In such cases, the relevant question is whether the transferor's offer to transfer ownership identifies "this bulk" or, for example, "50 items out of this bulk" as its object. It will be argued that the face-to-property or a face-to-quantity principle does not generally apply in such cases and that the quantity as such may generally only be identified by description but not by sight. It will furthermore be argued that this issue may, in a sense, be compared with the question whether the parties regard the quantity of the transferred mass as a mere *attribute* (quality) or as a feature going to the *identity* of the mass.

2.4.2.1. Lack of Clear Authority

The case most frequently cited in the context of quantity mistakes is *Ilich v R*.[269] Brighton owed $1,176 to Ilich for work done by the latter. On the assumed facts, Brighton handed over to Ilich (or rather threw at him since he was upset)

[265] See esp Chapter 4 section 2.4.2.3.
[266] See Chapter 4 section 2.4.2.4.
[267] See fn 256 and 257.
[268] See text to fn 260–263.
[269] *Ilich v R* [1987] 162 CLR 110 (HC of Australia).

three bundles of notes containing $1,706 in discharge of this debt; one of the bundles was contained within an envelope. Ilich took the money and discovered the excess only some hours later. It was assumed that Brighton was mistaken about the amount which he was actually handing over to Ilich and that he believed that the bundles only contained $1,176. Ilich was accused of stealing which, under the relevant Western Australian statute, required that ownership in the bundles had not passed to him. Wilson and Dawson JJ held that a fundamental mistake as to the transferred quantity may, in principle, prevent the passage of property. However, they apparently left open whether there had been such a mistake in the present case. They rather seemed to assume that even if there had been such a mistake, Ilich would still have acquired ownership in the money by reason of the bona fide purchase defence.[270] Deane J substantially agreed with Wilson and Dawson JJ on this point.[271] Brennan J equally appeared to assume that the bona fide purchase defence might, in principle, even be available in two-party-cases as the present one but held that the defence does not apply if the transferor lacks an intention to transfer property to the transferee. He then held that Brighton's mistake had not been fundamental but merely motivational in nature and that property in all of the notes had therefore passed to Ilich.[272] In his dissenting judgment, Gibbs CJ held that the *nemo dat* exception did not apply[273] and that there had been a fundamental quantity mistake which prevented ownership from passing in the surplus of $530.[274]

An application of the bona fide purchase defence in this case was, with all due respect, flawed. Such a defence – whether the *Miller v Race* exception for money

---

270 Ibid, 126–28 (Wilson and Dawson JJ): "In the present case there was no mistake as to the identity of the person to whom the money was delivered. There was no mistake as to the identity of the thing delivered, which was money. If there was any mistake it was as to the quantity of money delivered and it is therefore necessary to turn to the qualification of that category of fundamental mistake which we think must be made in the case of money"; this "qualification" was said to be the *nemo dat* exception for money as established in *Miller v Race* [1758] 1 Burr 452, 97 ER 398.

271 *Ilich v R* [1987] 162 CLR 110, 142–43 (Deane J) ("honest receipt of currency").

272 Ibid, 138–41 (Brennan J): "[T]here was no fundamental mistake in this case. Brighton simply handed notes to the applicant in payment of what he owed. There was no evidence of Brighton being mistaken as to what he was doing, or what he was handing to the applicant or who the applicant was. The only mistake was as to the number or value of the notes needed to discharge the debt owed to the applicant. That was not a fundamental mistake: it did not vitiate Brighton's intention that the applicant should have as his own the notes which Brighton put on the table in payment."

273 It is uncertain whether he assumed (rightly) that the bona fide purchase defence could *a priori* not apply since the case concerned a two-party-dispute, i.e. a transfer from the true owner, or whether he only (but also rightly) assumed that there was no consideration for the excess.

274 Ibid, 117–18 (Gibbs CJ): "[Brighton] made no mistake as to the amount of money which he was bound to pay to [Ilich] but [...] he was mistaken as to the quantity of money which he in fact paid over. Mr Brighton had no intention to transfer to the applicant the property in any amount greater than $1,176 and in my opinion he did not do so."

or a statutory *nemo dat* exception – can *a priori* only ever apply in relation to (otherwise effective) transfers by *non-owners* to third parties but not with regard to an (ineffective) transfer by the true owner himself. It is the sole function of the bona fide purchase defence to heal a defect in title of the transferor. It may not cure any other defect in the transfer in question, such as the absence of an intention of the transferor to transfer title. The bona fide purchase defence only ever applies to title conflicts in three-party disputes.[275]

Ilich v R concerned a simple two-party-dispute where the true owner (Brighton) purportedly made a transfer of property. If he acted under a proprietarily fundamental mistake, property could not pass. There was no title conflict in that case; Brighton had been the beneficial legal owner of the notes at the beginning of the story. The only question was whether he had – by a sufficient intention to do so – transferred ownership to Ilich. In so far, the assumption of Wilson, Dawson and Deane JJ that Ilich could successfully invoke the bona fide purchase defence and acquire property on that basis cannot be correct. To make things worse, they even suggested that Brighton would still have had a personal claim in unjust enrichment for the surplus.[276] This apparently suggests that the bona fide purchase defence, if applicable, is only effective on the proprietary level but that it is not a defence against personal claims in unjust enrichment. With respect, this is unconvincing and certainly not the law in England.[277] If a thief transfers stolen money for consideration – even if at an undervalue – to a good faith purchaser, the former owner is certainly not only precluded from suing the good faith purchaser in conversion (based on title) but also from suing him in unjust enrichment.[278] Otherwise, the rationale of *Miller v Race* and the fungibility and free circulation of money as currency would be seriously thwarted.[279] Applicability of the bona fide purchase defence in two-party-cases would also have meant that this defence would – had it been invoked – also have helped Ashwell against his conviction for larceny in *R v Ashwell*.[280] The prisoner

---

275 Convincingly Swadling, Unjust Delivery, 296–97; see also *Barclays Bank plc v Boulter* [1999] 1 WLR 1919 (HL), 1924 (Lord Hoffmann); Barker, Change of Position, 193, 198–205; Burrows, Restitution, 580; contra: Fox, Property Rights, esp 4.144–46, 3.17–18, 3.68–71, 4.50, who assumes without argument that the *nemo dat* exception for money might apply even in two-party-disputes and that it might even cure the absence of an intention of the true owner to transfer title; see also Fox, RLR 1996, 61–62, 67; Grantham/Rickett, RLR 1997, 88–89; Virgo, Restitution, 575 (fn 125); Williams, Criminal Law, 32.133–35.

276 *Ilich v R* [1987] 162 CLR 110, 129 (Wilson, Dawson JJ), 143 (Deane J).

277 See *Lipkin Gorman v Karpnale Ltd* [1991] 2 AC 548 (HL); Burrows, Restitution, 573–80; Birks, Unjust Enrichment, 240–45; Goff/Jones, Unjust Enrichment, ch 29; Barker, Change of Position, 194, 211–12.

278 The change of position defence would not be sufficient; see the examples provided by Burrows, Restitution, 576.

279 Birks, Unjust Enrichment, 242.

280 *R v Ashwell* [1885] 16 QBD 190.

had received the sovereign as currency in good faith and he had promised to repay the loan; this promise may well be seen as sufficient consideration.[281]

Assuming that the bona fide purchase defence was a priori unavailable in *Ilich v R* and that at least the judgments of Wilson, Dawson and Deane JJ were flawed in that regard, what is left of this case? Those three judges effectively left open the question whether Brighton's mistake was proprietarily fundamental or not. Brennan J assumed that it was not, whereas Gibbs CJ held that it was. In this regard, no proper ratio may be extracted from this case which may not accordingly – even apart from the fact that it would not be binding in England – provide any clear guidance on the issue of quantity mistakes. It will later be argued that Brighton's mistake was not, on the facts of the case, proprietarily fundamental.[282] Brighton had the intention to transfer "those three bundles of notes" and he was simply mistaken about the monetary *value* of those bundles. He was neither mistaken, nor did he care, about the exact *number* of notes. Probably, he had not even an idea of how many notes were contained within those bundles.

Another case, concerned with similar facts, is *Brochu v R*.[283] Brochu presented a cheque for $1,500 to a bank clerk who mistakenly handed over $2,500, namely one bundle of fifty $10-notes, which he had just taken out of his cage, counted and bundled together, and one bundle of one hundred $20-notes, which was a fresh bundle received from and pre-bundled by the head office earlier in the day and which the clerk had neither taken apart nor counted. The Quebec Court of King's Bench (Appeal Side) upheld a conviction for theft of $1,000 which, according to the relevant statute, required that property in those $1,000 had not passed to Brochu. The court assumed that the bank had retained property in the surplus as a result of the clerk's mistake. No reasons were expressed for this conclusion nor did the court figure out what exactly had been the clerk's mistake. The clerk was probably not mistaken about the number or denomination of the notes contained in the bundle which he had just prepared himself. But it is uncertain whether (i) he mistakenly believed that the other bundle merely contained fifty notes (although all fresh bundles usually contained one hundred notes), whether (ii) he mistakenly believed that the other bundle was made up of $10-notes (although even a witness waiting in the queue behind Brochu was able to see that the first note of that bundle was a $20-note) or whether (iii) he was – which is most realistic – simply mistaken about the total value of the two bundles by some miscalculation. Only (i) could be regarded as a genuine

---

281 Executory consideration is apparently sufficient (at least at law); see Fox, Property Rights, 8.33–38; Goff/Jones, Unjust Enrichment, 29.7.

282 See Chapter 4 section 2.4.2.4.

283 *Brochu v R* [1950] 10 CR 183 (Quebec Ct of KB).

quantity mistake,[284] whereas (ii) and (iii) would rather have been mistakes as to the goods' identity or quality.[285]

Owing to this lack of reasoning, *Brochu v R* may not be regarded as a (persuasive) authority for the proposition that a mistake as to the *amount* of money transferred, i.e. as to the total *value* of all notes and coins contained within a mass, is inevitably a fundamental quantity mistake which prevents the passage of property in the surplus. In fact, a mistake which only relates to the total monetary value of a mass or a bundle of notes can at most be a mistake as to the identity or quality of that mass or bundle. By contrast, a genuine quantity mistake must inevitably relate to the *quantity (number) of items* contained within a mass. It follows that there must be evidence that the transferor had a clear – but wrongful – idea about that quantity (number of items).[286] It will later be argued that a transferor of a bulk of corporeal money (notes and coins) most usually objectively and subjectively intends to transfer "this bulk of money", rather than a specific number of notes or coins, and that such mistakes accordingly almost always merely relate to the bulk's total value rather than the number of components.[287]

There is apparently only one case from England which has in fact concerned a genuine quantity mistake, namely *Russell v Smith*.[288] J bought one ton of pig

---

284 But see Chapter 4 section 2.4.2.4.

285 Applying the face-to-property principle, this mistake would not have been proprietarily fundamental.

286 It would certainly be wrong to suggest that a £10-note for example "contains" ten pounds sterling or (even worse) that it contains two £5-notes or ten £1-coins. This fallacy of confusing the physical with the metaphysical regrettably underlay the judgment of Lord Coleridge CJ in *R v Ashwell* [1885] 16 QBD 190, 225; see text to fn 241–242.

287 See Chapter 4 section 2.4.2.4.

288 *Russell v Smith* [1958] 1 QB 27. There are three other English cases which deserve mentioning but which have all concerned mere motivational (liability) mistakes: In *Moynes v Coopper* [1956] 1 QB 439, a wages clerk put more money than due into a pay packet which he handed over to an employee. The clerk exactly knew how much he was putting into the packet but he was mistaken about the amount due; see text to fn 49–52. In *R v Flowers* [1886] 16 QBD 643 (Crown Cases Reserved), an employee received a pay bag which was 3d. short. He took out the money and gave the empty bag to an accountant in charge of correcting errors. Another employee was equally complaining and returned his pay bag with the money. The accountant mistakenly handed over the other employee's (full) bag with an additional 3d. Quite evidently, property in that bag and the money in it had remained with the other employee; the accountant simply handed over someone else's money without authority. But even if the money had (again) become the employer's, there would still have been no mistake about the amount handed over (the amount contained in the bag was correctly written on its face) but only as to the motivational fact that the employee was still owed such an amount. In *R v Webster* [2006] EWCA Crim 2894, the Crown mistakenly sent a second (duplicate) medal as a gift to a member of forces. How the mistake had exactly come about is unclear but it had certainly not been a quantity mistake (the medals were not sent together) but a simple motivational mistake, for example relating to the fact that the recipient had not yet received

meal from C. The prisoner, Smith, was the lorry driver who had to deliver the cargo from C to J. The pig meal was packaged in half hundredweight sacks and Smith stood by when C's employees (with authority) took the sacks from C's warehouse and loaded them onto the lorry by dropping them through a chute. By some mistake ("probably in counting"), the employees loaded 48 instead of the ordered 40 sacks onto the lorry. Smith had neither counted the sacks nor had he noticed that too many sacks had been loaded onto his lorry. He only realised the mistake when the correct amount was discharged at J's premises. He then decided to appropriate the excess. The court convicted him for larceny and, applying *R v Ashwell*, held that there had been no taking (possession) until Smith had knowledge of the excess and that there had accordingly been a felonious intent at the time of taking. The conviction for larceny presupposed that property in the excess had not passed to Smith. Though the judgment might perhaps be read to suggest that C had retained property in the excess (also) by reason of the quantity mistake,[289] the fact that property had not passed to Smith – in any of the 48 sacks! – was actually very obvious in that case. Smith was merely a bailee (carrier) and C had never intended to transfer ownership in any of the sacks to him but only to J. The interesting question would rather have been whether property in the excess would have passed to J had Smith delivered all sacks to him. In so far, Lord Goddard CJ's dictum was strictly obiter. However, it will later be suggested that, had Smith delivered all 48 sacks to J, C's mistake would indeed have been a genuine quantity mistake which would have prevented the passage of ownership in the excess.

2.4.2.2. The Problem of Identification and Mixture: Co-Ownership Rights and the Rules of Following

In light of this, there is apparently no clear authority on the issue of quantity mistakes, at least none which would be binding in England. Considering the matter on the basis of principle, we must first dispose of a difficult preliminary issue of mixture and identification: If we for now assume, contrary to the argument made later in this section, that there had indeed been a genuine fundamental quantity mistake in *Ilich v R*, one might be troubled by the problem that it was impossible to exactly identify one or several notes – as specific items

---

such a medal. The case was decided under the Theft Act 1968 and it was apparently held that *equitable* (not legal) ownership had been retained by the Crown; cf critically on that point Zogg, Proprietary Consequences, Chapter 5 sections 3–5.

[289] *Russell v Smith* [1958] 1 QB 27, 35 (Lord Goddard CJ): "In the present case these eight sacks were not intended to be put into [Smith's] lorry; they were not intended to be delivered to [J] when the rest of the property was delivered. I think it is very much akin to a finding. If a person by inadvertence places sacks in a lorry, it is not very much different from having lost the sacks."

of property – contained within the three bundles in relation to which Brighton's mistake would have related and property in which would have been retained. This identification problem apparently worried Brennan and Deane JJ who assumed that this was an insuperable obstacle to the contention that property had not passed in the excess.[290,291] Gibbs CJ, by contrast, was unimpressed by this argument.[292] Similarly, this identification problem led Virgo to draw a distinction between overpayments and double payments. With regard to the former, he concluded that property must inevitably pass in the *entire* mass.[293]

This conclusion, however, is difficult to accept. Take the admittedly extreme example that A owes B £10 but that he delivers by some genuine quantity mistake £1,000 or that he owes 10 sacks of pig meal but delivers 1,000 sacks. It could scarcely be right to suggest that property passes in the *entire* mass (100%) solely because one cannot exactly say in relation to which of the particular items the mistake (affecting 99% of the mass) has related. This would, in a sense, turn on its head the basic rule that property may not – s 20A of the SGA 1979 apart – pass in *any* of the unascertained goods unless and until a sufficient appropriation has been made.[294] If A sells (in generic terms) "10 sacks of pig meal" to B but appropriates 1,000 sacks, property may not generally pass in *any* of the sacks, and it would be difficult to see why property should still all at once pass in the *entire* mass if A later delivers – under a supposedly genuine quantity mistake – possession of the 1,000 sacks to B. Suppose for example that s 20A applies prior to delivery and that A and B both acquire proportionate co-ownership in the bulk. If A then delivers the entire mass without a proper intention to do so, i.e. under a genuine quantity mistake, it would be difficult to understand why he would still lose his existing co-ownership rights in the mass based on an argument that an identification is (now) impossible.

It rather appears that the identification problem would, if at all, lead to the opposite conclusion, namely that no property passes in *any* of the items

290 *Ilich v R* [1987] 162 CLR 110, 140 (Brennan J), 142 (Deane J).

291 Indeed, as far as the *criminal law* is concerned, there might – depending on the applicable statute – be some difficulty in that regard. Prior to the advent of the Theft Act 1968, a conviction for larceny was only possible if there was evidence that all of the required elements (esp the taking, the carrying away, the lack of the owner's consent and the absence of a claim of right) were present in respect of one and the same particular item of property; see Williams, Crim LR 1958, esp 223–25. There is, however, no corresponding problem as far as *private law* (the law of property) is concerned. If a specific identification is impossible, there is still the option of co-ownership in the mass.

292 *Ilich v R* [1987] 162 CLR 110, 118–19 (Gibbs CJ).

293 Virgo, Restitution, 575–76; see similarly Swadling, Unjust Delivery, 297. Virgo's conclusions regarding double payments are less clear; he seems to assume that there was a genuine quantity mistake in *Chase Manhattan Bank NA v Israel-British Bank (London) Ltd* [1981] Ch 105 (ChD) – a conclusion which is not shared in this book (see fn 302).

294 Section 16 of the SGA 1979; see (e.g.) *Re Wait* [1927] 1 Ch 606 (CA); *Re Goldcorp Exchange* [1995] 1 AC 74.

(owing to lack of appropriation).[295] But this would be equally unacceptable.[296] Suppose that A, a watch retailer, intends to transfer a watch (watch 1) to B which he puts into a box awaiting delivery, that someone else (without authority) then puts a second identical[297] watch of A (watch 2) into that box and that A, without knowledge of this and without reopening the box, delivers the box to B. *In theory*, it would be perfectly possible to say in relation to which of the watches A has formed an intention to transfer property (watch 1) and in relation to which he has not formed such an intention (watch 2). Yet, as a matter of evidence, it is now impossible to identify the very watch which he had himself put into the box. This evidentiary impasse is just the type of problem which is conveniently coped with by the rules of following.[298] Though these rules usually apply to cases where the mixture occurs *subsequent to* the defective transfer in question – for example where B, having purchased watch 1 from A, steals watch 2 and mixes them together –, there is no reason in principle why the rules of following might not equally apply where the mixture has occurred *prior to* the defective transfer in question. If a third party mixes the watches together and if A, without knowledge of this, transfers possession in the entire mass to B, property must pass only in watch 1 but not in watch 2. As a result, A and B should – since the two watches are now contained in a mixture of indistinguishable items – each get a 50% co-ownership share in the mass.[299]

If this is correct, there should neither be a difference between cases, where one could at least *theoretically* say in relation to which of the particular items the transferor's mistake has actually related, and cases where this is impossible even in theory. Suppose that A, the watch retailer, routinely receives boxes from his supplier each of which usually contains one watch (and which are said to contain one watch). Suppose further that the supplier in one instance, by some non-fundamental mistake, puts two watches into a box and that A – in the fundamentally mistaken belief that the box only contains one watch – delivers that box to B without opening it. In such a case, it is simply impossible to say, even in theory, in relation to which of the two watches A's quantity mistake has related. But it would be very difficult to explain why there should be any difference in principle between this case and the case where some unauthorised

295 Cf Williams, Crim LR 1958, 228–29.

296 Cf *Ilich v R* [1987] 162 CLR 110, 142 (Deane J): "It could scarcely be (and has not been) suggested that the property in none of the notes passed with the result that [Ilich] was bound to return all of them to Mr Brighton."

297 Suppose further that the watches do not have a serial number or the like or that A does not remember them.

298 See esp L. Smith, Tracing, 70–89; broadly endorsed in *Foskett v McKeown* [2001] 1 AC 102 (HL), esp 132 (Lord Millett); see also Zogg, Proprietary Consequences, Chapter 1 section 3.2.4.1.

299 This legal co-ownership right in the mixture is a form of *mutated co-ownership* which confers a unilateral right of partition on the co-owners; see Zogg, Proprietary Consequences, Chapter 1 section 3.2.4.2(a); L. Smith, Tracing, 71–77.

third party has subsequently put a second watch into the box or where a second watch has subsequently come into the box by some other accident. Arguably, A should retain (or obtain) a 50% co-ownership share in the mass (mutated tenancy in common), subject to the rules of following, in any of those cases, whether the mixture has occurred after or prior to the transaction in question and whether an identification of the mistakenly transferred item(s) would be possible in theory or not.[300]

2.4.2.3. The Difficult Distinction between Genuine Quantity Mistakes and Mere Motivational Mistakes

Having concluded that the issue of mixture and identification is not generally an obstacle, even in overpayment or over-delivery cases, a clear distinction must be drawn between genuine quantity mistakes, where the transferor is actually mistaken about the exact *number* of items transferred, and mere motivational mistakes, where he is only mistaken about the reason *why* he is carrying out a transfer of a certain number of items. The passage of property may only be prevented by a mistake of the former but not of the latter category. However, this distinction may sometimes be a very fine and difficult one. We shall first consider three straightforward examples and then turn to more delicate cases:[301]

(1) Take the case that A, a watch wholesaler, receives an order for 50 watches from B and sends a box containing 50 watches to the latter. The next day, having forgotten that he has already performed the contract, he sends another box containing 50 watches to B. This is a straightforward example of a purely motivational liability mistake. A is not, when he despatches the second consignment, mistaken about what he is (now) doing and about how many watches he is (now) sending to B. His mistake merely relates to his liability to do so. Property in the second consignment plainly passes to B and A is limited to a personal claim in unjust enrichment.[302] The case is no

300 Cf also Williams, Crim LR 1958, 228–29, who, however, assumes that s 16 of the SGA might be an obstacle even after delivery.

301 The examples offered in this sub-section are inspired by the examples provided by Williams, Crim LR 1958 (in the context of criminal law).

302 This was the result in *Moynes v Coopper* [1956] 1 QB 439; *Lacis v Cashmarts* [1969] 2 QB 400; *R v Potisk* [1973] 6 SASR 389 and it should have been the result in *R v Gilks* [1972] 1 WLR 1341; see Chapter 4 section 2.1.1. Such a purely motivational mistake equally underlay *R v Flowers* [1886] 16 QBD 643 (if the transferred money had been the property of the transferor at all; see fn 288). Furthermore, and contrary to an argument made by Virgo, Restitution, 575–76, there was no more than such a motivational liability mistake in *Chase Manhattan Bank v Israel-British Bank* [1981] Ch 105: Bank A paid some $2 million (incorporeal money) to bank B and, later in the day, made a second payment of an equal sum. The error occurred because employee 1 had mistakenly believed that there had been a new instruction. This mistake was discovered in due time by employee 2 who gave instructions

different if A, for whatever reason, mistakenly believes that he has only sent 49 watches the day before and therefore sends one extra watch to B. In this case, A is still perfectly aware of what he is (now) doing, namely sending one watch to B. His mistake again only relates to his liability (motivation) to do so.

(2) By contrast, suppose that A, having received an order for 50 watches from B, takes a box which contains some straw at the bottom, puts 50 watches into it and delivers it to B. If there was, unbeknown to him, a diamond ring or another watch buried in the straw, property in that diamond ring or watch would certainly not pass to B. This follows from *Merry v Green*[303] where a seller sold a bureau which contained, unbeknown to both parties, a purse and money in a secret drawer. It has been concluded, on the one hand, that the face-to-property principle does not apply in such a case since the property in question has never been identified by sight. On the other hand, it has been argued that the question whether property in the purse and the money had passed to the buyer depended on whether the object of the seller's offer to transfer property – as identified by description – had been "the bureau with (whatever) contents" or "the bureau alone, without its contents" and that this was to be determined by the general amalgam of the objective and the subjective principle.[304] The position must be exactly the same in our diamond ring and watch example. The first relevant question accordingly is whether A has *subjectively* intended to transfer (i) "this box with (whatever) contents", (ii) "this box with all (however many) watches" or (iii) "this box with 50 watches". If A subjectively intended (i), property would pass even in a buried diamond ring.[305] If he intended (ii) or (iii), one must ask how A's offer to transfer property was to be *objectively* construed, i.e. how a reasonable person in the position of B would have understood it: In the sense of (i), (ii), (iii) or something else? If this differs from A's actual subjective intention, the objective principle would prevail unless B had knowledge of this. In practice, A will most usually have intended (iii) and

---

to cancel the payment. Yet, employee 3 overlooked those instructions and eventually executed the second payment. Certainly, employee 3 has known what he was doing, namely effecting a payment of $2 million to bank B, and he has done so because he had mistakenly believed that the bank had been liable to make such a payment. Similarly, there was only a non-fundamental liability mistake (double payment) in *R v Milne* [1990] ABCA 323 (CanLII) (revd on other grounds in [1992] 1 SCR 696).

303 *Merry v Green* [1841] 7 M&W 623.

304 See Chapter 4 section 2.3.2.5.

305 This is so whether A's offer to transfer property must objectively be understood in the same way or not (cf fn 129 and text to it). Since the transferee's acceptance of ownership is not, upon delivery, an initially constitutive requirement (see Chapter 2 section 1.3.), property may apparently pass provisionally in accordance with the transferor's unilateral *subjective* intention. If the transferee later subjectively accepts the transfer, their "subjective consent" prevails over the objective outward appearance.

B will, if he has ordered 50 watches and then finds a diamond ring or a 51st watch buried in straw, almost always have known (or should have known) that A has subjectively intended (iii). But even if not, this would only rarely, if ever, be objectively taken as an offer for (i) or (ii) in such circumstances. It follows that property in the diamond ring or in the 51st watch would not generally pass in such a case.

(3) Those principles – which may conveniently be called the *Merry v Green* principles – should equally apply in a case where A puts 50 watches into an empty box, preparing it for delivery, and where someone else (without authority) puts an identical extra watch of A into it before A, without reopening it, transfers the box to B.

(4) What is the position if A, in the last example, briefly reopens the box prior to delivery and prima facie convinces himself that it (solely) contains the watches which he has put into it? Would the *Merry v Green* principles still apply in such a case, with the result that property in the 51st watch would not pass to B and that A would obtain a ¹⁄₅₁ co-ownership share in the mass? Or should – by an analogy to the rationale of *Shogun Finance v Hudson*[306] – a face-to-property or a face-to-quantity principle apply, with the result that A would be taken to have intended to transfer "this entire mass of watches"?

It would be unconvincing to suggest that case (4) should be treated fundamentally different from case (3) and that A's act of physical identification by briefly opening the box and by looking at the bulk of watches as a whole should prevail over his identification by description ("this box with 50 watches"). In fact, the rationale of *Shogun Finance v Hudson* cannot apply here since there is not actually a proper identification by sight of each of the individual items of property in question. Some of the watches might not be readily visible at all if A merely looks at the mass as a whole, for example because they are piled up in multiple tiers. But even if the watches are all visible at one sight, one can still not usually identify a *quantity* (number of items) by a simple sight. It is not generally possible to determine whether a mass contains 50, 49 or 51 watches, unless they are counted one by one.[307]

This case is certainly different from an identification by sight of *one* person or *one* item of property and from an error about that person's or property's identity (or attributes). It is rather comparable with the case

306 *Shogun Finance v Hudson* [2003] UKHL 62.

307 An exception must perhaps be made for the uncommon case that a very small quantity of items is misconceived, for example if four watches are taken to be three. In such a case, an actual identification of the quantity *by sight* does not seem impossible and should arguably prevail, unless the extra item is for example buried in straw or otherwise hidden; cf the example of two crisp new banknotes sticking together given by Coté J in *R v Milne* [1990] ABCA 323 (CanLII), [23] (revd on other grounds in [1992] 1 SCR 696).

of *Merry v Green* where a chattel has been hidden within another chattel. Metaphorically, it may be said that in case (4) the 51st watch (or any one of the 51 watches) is hidden amongst the other watches and that very generally in quantity mistake cases one (or more) chattel(s) is (or are) hidden amongst other chattels. For those reasons, it is generally preferable to apply the *Merry v Green* principles, rather than a face-to-quantity principle, in quantity mistake cases even if the quantity as such, i.e. the bulk in its entirety, is visually perceptible. It would for example be unconvincing to suggest that Brighton's mistake in *Ilich v R* relating to the enveloped (hidden) bundle should – at least if he had not himself put the notes into the envelope – be governed by principles different from those governing his mistake in relation to the two non-enveloped (visible) bundles.

(5) Now suppose that A, having received an order for 50 watches from B, takes an empty box and puts into it – one by another – watch 1, watch 2, watch 3, up to watch 50, and then, since he has lost count, puts watch 51 on top. Is there any relevant difference between this case (or any case where A has indeed *counted* the watches) and case (4) where A has merely looked at the mass of the watches *as a whole*? Would it be correct to say that A, when he put watch 1 into the box, has formed an intention to transfer property in that watch to B, that he has similarly formed such an intention in relation to watch 2, watch 3, watch 4 and so on when he respectively put those watches into the box and that, when he put the last one (watch 51) on top of the mass, he has equally formed such an intention in relation to that last watch?[308]

Certainly, if A sends 51 times a box to B, for example one per day, each of which contains one watch, he has – at the time when he despatches the last watch – a plain intention to transfer property in that very watch to B. This is case (1). A is not at that time mistaken about what he is doing, namely that he is transferring one watch to B, but merely about the reason *why* he is doing so, namely because he believes that he has until now only sent 49 consignments to B and that he is still liable to send one more. Such a mistake about past facts does not, even if relating to quantity, constitute a genuine quantity mistake. The position is the same as in any double payment or double delivery case where A has simply forgotten (or never realised) that he had already discharged the relevant debt.

But what applies if A despatches the 51 watches in one single consignment which he has himself prepared? Is this more like the *Chase Manhattan*[309] or *Moynes v Coopper*[310] type of case, i.e. a mere liability mistake (case (1)

---

[308] Williams, Crim LR 1958, 225–26, has argued (in the context of criminal law) that A's intention is vitiated in relation to the last watch.

[309] *Chase Manhattan* [1981] Ch 105.

[310] *Moynes v Coopper* [1956] 1 QB 439.

as described above), or is it more like *Merry v Green*,[311] where a hidden chattel was delivered (cases (2)–(4))? The latter view is preferable. On the one hand, a distinction between the case where A has merely looked at the mass *as a whole* and a case where he *(mis)counted* the items would be difficult to sustain. On the other hand, the transferor's intention to transfer property must be examined at the time of conveyance (delivery). As long as A is merely preparing the box for delivery, he has not yet formed an unconditional intention to transfer property in the last watch (for which no consideration is provided). Yet, when he later delivers the box to B, he has not any more a *specific* intention to transfer the 51st watch but merely a *general* intention to transfer "this box with 50 watches" (if this is his relevant intention according to the *Merry v Green* principles).

This brings us back to the case of *Russell v Smith*[312] where C's employees (with authority) took one sack of pig meal after another out of C's warehouse and put them, one by one, onto Smith's lorry by dropping them through a chute. Smith was merely the carrier which meant that there had in any case been no intention to transfer property to him. Yet, would property in the excessive eight sacks have passed to J had Smith delivered all 48 sacks to him (assuming that s 30 of the SGA would not have applied[313]) or would C have obtained a ⅙ co-ownership share in the mass by reason of his mistake? Arguably, the latter would have been preferable. This is basically the same case as where C takes an empty box (here: the lorry), puts one watch after another into it (here: the sacks) and then despatches it to J. At the time when C – acting through his employees – sends away the lorry, he has not 48 separate intentions to transfer 48 sacks but only one general intention to transfer property in "40 sacks out of this lorry"; C does not generally intend to transfer "this bulk of (however many) sacks". It is furthermore unlikely that J would not have been aware of that actual subjective intention and that this would not also have been the objective understanding of C's proprietary offer.

(6) Finally, suppose that J comes himself with his own lorry to C's premises in order to pick up the sacks or that he sends one of his employees to do so. This is perhaps the most difficult of the cases discussed so far. It could be argued that C, acting through his employees, would in such a case have formed an intention to transfer property in each of the 48 sacks since he would then have 48 times delivered one sack to J by putting them – one by one – onto the latter's lorry and that he would – at the time when he was delivering the last eight sacks onto the lorry – merely have been unaware of

311 *Merry v Green* [1841] 7 M&W 623.
312 *Russell v Smith* [1958] 1 QB 27; see text to fn 288–289.
313 See Chapter 4 section 2.4.1.2.

the fact that he had already discharged the debt (liability mistake). Whether this analysis is correct apparently depends on the question whether this way of loading the transferee's lorry involves 48 separate deliveries (or 48 separate acts of appropriation) or whether this must still be regarded as one single act of delivery (or act of appropriation). The latter seems preferable. C should still be regarded as having merely one general intention to transfer "40 sacks out of this mass". Hence, there would arguably still have been a genuine quantity mistake in such a case.

2.4.2.4. The Difficult Distinction between Genuine Quantity Mistakes and Mistakes as to the Transferred Property's Identity or Quality

In the previous sub-section, we have discussed the difficult distinction between genuine quantity mistakes and mistakes which merely relate to the motive of a transfer, for example liability mistakes. As far as one is concerned with a genuine quantity mistake, the *Merry v Green* principles, rather than a face-to-quantity principle, should generally apply. According to those principles, the decisive question is whether the transferor has – subjectively or objectively – intended to transfer "this entire bulk with however many items" (as one single item of property) or for example "50 items out of this bulk". This issue closely relates to, or even entails, the distinction between quantity mistakes and mistakes as to the transferred property's identity or quality: If the transferor – subjectively or objectively – intends to transfer the bulk as a single item of property, the number of that bulk's components, its weight or its volume are no more than attributes of that bulk. By contrast, if the focus lies on the component parts of the bulk, there might be a mistake as to the quantity of those components.

If the relevant transfer for example concerned a specific number of watches or similar goods, the conclusion will generally be that the transferor subjectively and objectively intends to transfer such a number of items out of the delivered bulk. However, that need not necessarily be so if the transfer relates to a mass of small granular items (such as corn or mandarins), a liquid mass or a mass of corporeal money (notes and coins).

Ilich v R concerned a transfer of three bundles of notes; one was enveloped, the others were not. The total value of all three bundles in fact amounted to $1,706 but the transferor (Brighton) believed that it was only $1,176. The relevant question arguably was whether Brighton had – subjectively or objectively – intended to transfer (i) "this bulk of notes (however many and of whatever denomination)" or, for example, (ii) "thirty $20-notes, forty $10-notes, thirty-four $5-notes and six $1-notes out of this bulk of money" or, with regard to the envelope, (iii) "this envelope with whatever contents". Option (iii) seems unrealistic. A diamond ring mistakenly contained within the envelope would certainly not have been part of the proprietary transfer. Option (ii) seems equally unrealistic. Brighton (probably) had neither an idea nor did he care about the exact *number* of notes contained within the mass. Without such an idea, however, there can be no mistake about the number of *items* transferred. All that Brighton had in mind and all that he had cared about was the *total value* of the mass and his mistake solely related to that value. But that cannot be a genuine quantity mistake.

Crucially, a $10-note does not "contain" ten dollars and it does neither "contain" the value of ten dollars or ten $1-notes or ten $1-coins. This would be to confuse physics with metaphysics.[314] A $10-note is simply *one* indivisible piece of paper which has the *value* of ten dollars. One cannot be mistaken about the quantity of *one* $10-note (unless one is concerned with a case like *Merry v Green* where the note is hidden). One may only be mistaken about that item's value. Yet, the value of an item is merely an *attribute* of that item; and as far as money is concerned, the value or denomination is generally only going to the chattel's quality rather than its identity.[315] The same must apply if a bulk of notes and coins is transferred. A mistake about the mass' *total value*, rather than the exact *number* of its component items (notes and coins), is not a genuine quantity mistake but a mistake about an attribute of the bulk. The fact that Brighton (probably) had no clear idea about the exact number of notes contained within the mass should have been sufficient evidence that his mistake had not been one as to quantity but merely one as to the bulk's attributes (qualities).

In *Brochu v R*, the bank clerk handed over to the customer one bundle of fifty $10-notes and one bundle of one hundred $20-notes.[316] The clerk believed that the total value of the mass was $1,500 but it is uncertain how exactly his mistake came about. Most likely, he simply miscalculated the total value of the notes. As in *Ilich v R*, this would not have been a genuine quantity mistake but merely a mistake as to the mass' attributes (quality). The same would apply if the clerk believed that the second bundle contained one hundred $10-notes instead of one hundred $20-notes. A mistake as to the value of a note or the value of a bundle of notes is merely a mistake as to that note's or bundle's quality. Eventually, the clerk might have believed that the second bundle merely contained fifty instead of one hundred $20-notes. Now this might have been a genuine quantity mistake. Applying the *Merry v Green* principles, the question would then have been whether the clerk had – subjectively or objectively – intended to transfer "this bulk of money" (as one single item) or, with regard to the second bundle, "fifty notes out of this bundle". It appears that a transfer of money as currency generally objectively and subjectively refers to "this mass of corporeal money" and that a mistake as to the *amount* of money contained in a bulk of notes and coins almost always, in fact, merely amounts to a mistake as to the bulk's *value* rather than its *number of component items* (notes or coins).

---

314 This fallacy regrettably underlay the judgment of Lord Coleridge CJ in *R v Ashwell* [1885] 16 QBD 190, 225; see text to fn 241–242.

315 See fn 237 and text to it.

316 *Brochu v R* [1950] 10 CR 183; see text to fn 283–287.

Finally, what is the position if A transfers a liquid mass or a bulk of granular items, such as wheat or oats, and if he is mistaken about that bulk's weight or volume? May this still be a genuine quantity mistake as in the watch cases set out in the previous sub-section or is this rather a mistake as to an attribute (quality) of the transferred bulk as in the money cases, such as *Ilich v R* or *Brochu v R*? Suppose that in *Russell v Smith*[317] C had not packaged the pig meal (for example soybeans) into sacks but that he had simply loaded the cargo onto the lorry or that he had put the entire bulk into one container and that C was accordingly not mistaken about the number of sacks but about the weight of the bulk delivered to the transferee (1,200 kg instead of 1,000 kg). If the transferor's mistake only relates to the *weight* of the bulk, rather than the (countless) *number* of granular items (soybeans) contained therein, may this still be a genuine quantity mistake rather than merely a mistake as to an attribute of the bulk? The answer seems to be "yes". This is not to confuse physics with metaphysics and to commit the same error which underlies the assumption that a $10-note "contains" ten dollars. A $10-note is an *indivisible* chattel, whereas a bulk of soybeans is a *divisible* mass of countless components. Since the weight of the bulk directly corresponds with the number of constituent parts contained therein, a mistake about the bulk's weight might arguably be compared with a mistake about the number of component items. Though perhaps less evidently, the same should apply with regard to liquid masses.

This does not suggest that a mistake about the weight or volume of a granular or liquid mass does *necessarily* amount to an operative quantity mistake; it only means that this *may* be so. Arguably, the *Merry v Green* principles, rather than a face-to-quantity principle, should equally apply here. If this is correct, the relevant question still is whether the object of the proprietary transfer is – subjectively or objectively – "this entire bulk" (as one single item) or for example "one ton out of this bulk". It appears that the latter is perhaps a little less frequently the case in relation to transfers of bulks of small granular items (such as wheat or oats) or liquid bulks than for example in relation to transfers of bulks of watches, but certainly much more often than with regard to transfers of bulks of corporeal money (notes and coins).

2.5. MISTAKES AS TO THE NATURE OF THE UNDERLYING TRANSACTION: FUNDAMENTAL IF RELATING TO THE LEGAL INTEREST TO BE TRANSFERRED

Courts and commentators generally only refer to three categories of proprietarily fundamental mistakes, namely mistakes as to the transferee's identity, mistakes

317 *Russell v Smith* [1958] 1 QB 27.

as to the transferred property's identity and quantity mistakes.[318] However, there is actually a fourth category of mistakes which equally negatives a party's intention to transfer or receive property, namely mistakes as to the type of legal interest (ownership or possession) to be transferred.[319]

On the *contractual* level, any operative mistake relating to an essential term of the contract renders the contract void, i.e. negatives the parties' apparent consent. Whether such a mistake is operative or not is determined by the general amalgam of the objective and the subjective principle.[320] Briefly summarised, there is no contract if the parties are not subjectively *ad idem* in respect of an essential term, if neither of the parties has known (or ought to have known) the other party's actual subjective intention and if an unambiguous objective interpretation of the parties' words and conduct is unavailable. For example, a contract is void if A and B are – objectively and subjectively – in disagreement about the question whether there should be consideration for the transfer of a chattel at all, namely if A subjectively intends to sell a certain chattel to B, if B intends to receive it as a gift, if neither of the parties knows (or should know) of the other party's divergent subjective intention *and* if an unambiguous objective interpretation of the transaction being a sale or a gift is unavailable. The same applies if A and B are – objectively and subjectively – in disagreement about the kind of B's counter-performance (for example whether the transaction should be a sale or a barter), about its amount (particularly of the purchase price)[321] or about the interest to be transferred from A to B (for example whether the transaction should be a sale or a bailment on terms of deposit, hire or the like).

By contrast, on the *proprietary* level it is clear that not every mistake, which negatives the parties' contractual consent, may also negative their abstract real agreement. Property passes if the transferor intends to transfer ownership and if the transferee (sooner or later) accepts its receipt. There is no requirement of an effective contract. Property might pass – at least by delivery – even if a contract is inexistent or void (principle of abstraction). It follows that a strict distinction must be drawn between cases where the parties are in disagreement about the *type of legal interest to be transferred* and cases where they are merely in disagreement about the transferee's *counter-performance* or some other essential term of the underlying transaction. It is only the former type of mistake which is proprietarily fundamental and which prevents the passage of property, whereas

318 See the references in fn 4.

319 See only Pollock/Wright, Possession, 101–2.

320 See generally Chapter 4 section 1.1.

321 See (e.g.) *Felthouse v Bindley* [1862] 11 CBNS 869; *Hartog v Colin & Shields* [1939] 3 All ER 566; *South East Windscreens v Jamshidi* [2005] All ER (D) 317 (Dec); Treitel, Contract, 8.44; cf also *Woodhouse AC Israel Cocoa v Nigerian Produce Marketing* [1972] AC 741, 767–68 (Lord Cross).

the latter is, in fact, a merely motivational liability mistake as to the underlying transaction's existence:

(1) If A intends to transfer no more than *possession* to B (for example on bailment for loan, hire or deposit) but if B intends to receive *ownership* in the chattel (for example on terms of a gift, sale or barter), there is – subject to what will be said about the objective principle – a lack of intention of the transferor to transfer ownership and thus no real agreement. Property does not pass. In the converse case, where A intends to transfer ownership but where B merely intends to receive possession, there is in principle similarly a lack of intention to receive ownership by the transferee. However, it has already been explained that property may pass provisionally by delivery if the transferor has intended to transfer ownership and if the transferee has at least formed an intention to possess, whereby the latter may – as soon as he realises that ownership has actually been transferred to him – unequivocally repudiate the transfer of ownership with the effect that property revests retroactively.[322] The mere fact that the transferee has received the chattel with no more than an intention to possess as bailee does not by itself amount to an unequivocal repudiation. He might rather still accept property upon acquiring knowledge that the transferor has actually intended to transfer ownership rather than mere possession.

 The question whether A intends to transfer ownership or merely possession and the question whether B intends to receive ownership or only possession (and, if the latter, whether B effectively repudiates a transfer of property) should be determined by the general amalgam of the objective and the subjective principle. This follows from the broad contract analogy, which has been drawn in the previous sections in respect of the transferor's offer to transfer property. If A subjectively intends to merely transfer possession, for example on bailment for a loan, but if his words and conduct must objectively be understood as constituting an offer to transfer ownership, for example on terms of an outright gift, A is bound by the objective appearance of his words and conduct and may not be heard to say the contrary, unless B knows (or should know) that this is not A's actual subjective intention.[323] If A subjectively intends to transfer ownership, however, his subjective intention is – in some contrast to the contractual position – alone sufficient to transfer ownership to B, subject to the

322 See Chapter 2 section 1.3. and the references in Chapter 2 fn 42.

323 See Pollock/Wright, Possession, 101: "If the receiver reasonably believes the giver to intend to pass the property, it must be (unless in some very abnormal case) that the giver has entitled him so to believe, and therefore cannot be heard to say the contrary."

latter's repudiation. This is a result of the combined facts that the parties' actual subjective consent prevails over an objective outward appearance and that the transferor's intention to transfer ownership is, subject to the transferee's repudiation, sufficient to provisionally pass ownership.

(2) By contrast, if the parties are only in disagreement (i.e. mistaken) about the terms of the underlying transaction, for example about whether the transaction concerns a sale, barter or gift or about the amount of the purchase price, but not about the fact that ownership shall be transferred from A to B, the mistake is not proprietarily fundamental and property may still pass upon and by delivery.[324] Though such a mistake negatives the parties' contractual agreement, it is a merely motivational liability mistake on the proprietary level. Neither the transferor nor the transferee is actually mistaken about the fact *that* he is transferring or receiving ownership but only about the reason *why* he is doing so, namely because an underlying contract or other legal basis is supposed to validly exist.

An illuminating example is *Hill v Wilson*.[325] W sent a cheque for £500 to H which he subjectively intended to be a gift (and this was apparently also how his offer was to be objectively understood). H, however, rejected the offer and wrote back that he would only (but still) take the cheque as a loan and that he would later repay the money. H apparently cashed the cheque before W has accepted or rejected the loan offer and it was one of the issues whether W has, in fact, later accepted it or not. Though it was eventually held that the parties had – after the cashing of the cheque – agreed on a loan, it was apparently still assumed that property in the cheque had anyway passed to H, even prior to and without W's acceptance of the loan:

> "[I]n order to make out a gift, it must be shewn, not only that the cheque was sent as a gift, but that it was received as a gift. It requires the assent of both minds to make a gift as it does to make a contract. […] It appears to me that if within a reasonable time […] the party who receives the money says, 'I would rather receive it as a loan than as a gift,' then, *although he has used the money*, still, if his answer is acquiesced in by the person who has sent the money, the transaction would be a loan and not

---

[324] See also Fox, Property Rights, 3.57; Häcker, Impaired Consent, 196 (fn 154); apparently contra: van Vliet, Transfer of movables, 130–31.

[325] *Hill v Wilson* [1873] LR 8 Ch App 888 (CA in Chancery). See also *Dewar v Dewar* [1975] 1 WLR 1532 (ChD), 1538–39 (Goff J), where A transferred money as a gift to B but where B received it as a loan. It was apparently held (in somewhat ambiguous language) that full legal and beneficial ownership had passed to B: "[W]here a person intends to make a gift and the donee receives the thing given, knows that he has got it and takes it, the fact that he says: 'Well, I will only accept it as a loan, and you can have it back when you want it' does not prevent it from being an effective gift."

a gift. *The using the money does not appear to me to be inconsistent with that; for whether it be a loan or a gift, he is to have it and use it*, and until the two minds come to an agreement that it shall be a gift, or to an agreement that it shall be a loan, the matter, as it appears to me, remains open [...]."[326]

That must be right. W intended to transfer ownership in the cheque to H, on terms of a gift, and delivered it to H who equally intended to receive ownership, though on terms of a loan. By cashing the cheque, H had unequivocally accepted the transfer of ownership. The fact that there had been no underlying transaction at that time (yet) is immaterial since transfers by delivery are abstract. Had the parties not subsequently reached an agreement, property in the cheque would still have passed and W would only have been entitled to a personal claim in unjust enrichment (based on failure of consideration).

The same result must be reached – if delivery has been made[327] – in cases where the parties are in agreement that ownership shall be transferred, for example on terms of a sale or a barter, but where they are – subjectively and objectively – in disagreement about the price or the kind of counter-performance. An example is *Lacis v Cashmarts*.[328] The defendant selected various goods in a supermarket, put them on the counter and the manager (having full authority) asked for £85 8s. instead of £185 8s. since the till had turned back to zero when it had reached £100. In a questionable analysis, Lord Parker CJ held that there was only a contract for the last couple of goods but not for the previous ones. Alternatively, however, it could be argued that – because the defendant must have known that the manager's objective offer to sell the goods for £85 8s. had not corresponded with his actual subjective intention – there was either no contract at all (disagreement as to the price) or, preferably, that there was for that reason a binding contract for all of the delivered goods for a price of £185 8s., the defendant still owing the balance.[329] But in any of those contractual analyses, property would – on the assumption that the manager had not (objectively or subjectively) intended to reserve a right of disposal[330] – still have passed in *all* of the goods since the manager's mistake was in any case

326 *Hill v Wilson* [1873] LR 8 Ch App 888, 896–97 (Mellish LJ) (emphases added).

327 If the parties' contractual consent is *negatived*, there is no consideration – not even if counter-performance has been made since any nexus of reciprocity is then destroyed (see text to Chapter 2 fn 213–217) – and property may therefore only pass by delivery, just as in gift cases.

328 *Lacis v Cashmarts* [1969] 2 QB 400; see text to fn 53–55.

329 See fn 14 and 54.

330 But cf fn 55.

merely motivational in nature, relating to the contract's valid existence or the fact that the defendant has fully paid the price.[331]

Felthouse v Bindley[332] is not an authority to the contrary. N and P reached an apparent agreement about the sale of a specific horse by the former to the latter but it turned out that they had been in disagreement about the price (£30 or 30 guineas) and that this mistake had negatived their apparent consent. P then made a new offer to buy for £30 15s. which was, however, never accepted or rejected by N until he had sold the horse through the defendant auctioneer. P sued the latter in conversion and the question arose whether property in the horse had passed to him. Willes J (Byles and Keating JJ agreeing) held that there had never been a complete contract of sale between N and P prior to the sale by auction and that "[n]othing, therefore, had been done to vest the property in the horse in [P]" until the auction had taken place. The actual reason, however, why ownership had not passed to P was because *delivery* had never been made to him. The fact that the parties' apparent agreement had been negatived by their mistake about the price meant that there had been no consideration[333] and that property could not have passed by mere consent but only upon and by delivery. But if delivery had been made to P prior to the sale by auction, property in the horse would plainly have passed to him since both, N and P, had in fact intended to transfer and receive ownership in the horse. They were merely in disagreement about P's counter-promise.

---

331 This was also Lord Parker CJ's analysis in relation to the last couple of goods; see equally *R v Dawood* [1975] 27 CCC (2d) 300 (SC of Alberta) where a customer had removed the price tag from a blouse and put the blouse on a hanger with a jumper. The cashier (with authority) only asked for the price of the jumper. McDermid JA and Allen JA (Clement JA dissenting) held that property had passed in both items since there had been an intention of the cashier to transfer property in both of them; affd in *R v Milne* [1990] ABCA 323 (CanLII), [15] (Coté J) (revd on other grounds in [1992] 1 SCR 696).

332 *Felthouse v Bindley* [1862] 11 CBNS 869.

333 Even if P had already paid the £30, which he had believed to be the contract price, that would still not have been consideration since the parties' disagreement about the price had destroyed any apparent nexus of reciprocity between the two promises or performances; see Chapter 2 fn 217 and text to it.

CHAPTER 5
CONCLUSION

We have analysed, on the one hand, the mechanics of how exactly legal ownership is transferred consensually from one person to another and, on the other hand, the effects of various kinds of defects, particularly mistakes, on the passage of property. It is essential to strictly distinguish between three different levels at which any particular kind of defect might operate, namely property, contract and unjust enrichment. Defects which render contracts void (obligatory defects) are not necessarily sufficient to equally render transfers of property void (real defects). Defects which – in the absence of a justifying legal basis – give rise to a personal restitutionary claim in unjust enrichment (unjust factors) are not necessarily sufficient to affect a contract or even a transfer of property. Conversely, mistakes which are not even capable of rendering contracts void or of giving rise to a claim in unjust enrichment cannot – *a fortiori* – prevent the passage of property.

There are basically three different *modes* of how legal ownership in tangible movable property may be transferred, namely delivery, sale (or mere intention) and deed. As far as the scope of those modes of transfer is concerned, it has been argued that delivery or a deed is only but always required if the transfer is gratuitous, i.e. for no consideration, or if the transferred chattel is corporeal money. It has furthermore been argued that each of those three modes of transfer is governed by a *principle of separation*, in the sense that real conveyance is notionally distinct and separate from an underlying obligatory transaction, for example a contract, and by a *principle of abstraction*, which means that the conveyance's effectiveness is not dependent on the existence or validity of such an underlying contract or other obligatory transaction. To convey legal title, it is – again with regard to each of those three modes of transfer – basically required that the transferor sufficiently intends to transfer legal ownership and that the transferee (sooner or later) sufficiently intends to receive it. The combination of those two intentions may be called a *real agreement*.

If this real agreement – i.e. the transferor's intention to transfer property and/or the transferee's intention to receive it – is sufficiently affected (rendered void) by a certain defect, legal ownership does not pass to the transferee *ab initio*. This is evidently the case if the transferor has not at all intended to transfer ownership, as in cases of theft, loss or misappropriation, or if a corresponding intention of another person is not attributable to the legal owner (lack of authority). Furthermore, the transferor's consent must be equally treated as virtually inexistent in cases of fundamental duress, where such a "consent" has been procured by serious violence against the person or by threats of such violence.

By contrast, mistakes are only very rarely sufficient to prevent the passage of legal ownership. In fact, title passes unless the transferor's mistake is so fundamental that his intention to convey ownership – in certain property to a certain person – must be regarded as virtually absent altogether. This is only the case if the mistake relates to the fact *that* a certain transfer shall be made, namely (i) that legal ownership (as opposed to mere possession) shall be transferred at all, (ii) that property shall be transferred to the transferee in question, (iii) that property shall be transferred in the chattel(s) in question or (iv) that property shall be transferred in all of the chattels in question. Motivational mistakes, which merely relate to the reason *why* a certain transfer shall be carried out, for example if a corresponding contract or other liability is erroneously supposed to exist, are invariably insufficient to prevent the passage of property. This applies regardless of the gravity of such a mistake.

The distinction between proprietarily fundamental mistakes and mere motivational mistakes may be a very fine and delicate one. It has been argued that the proprietary position should – with regard to the four mentioned types of fundamental mistakes – be broadly analogous to its contractual counterpart. In this context, it is helpful to compare the transferor's intention to transfer property with an *offer to transfer ownership* and the transferee's intention to receive property with an *acceptance*. A transfer of ownership is effective if the transferor's proprietary offer must objectively be understood as an offer (i) to transfer ownership (ii) to the transferee in question (iii) in each of the chattels in question, unless – if this is not also the transferor's actual subjective intention – the transferee knows (or should know) of the transferor's divergent subjective intention. If the transferor in fact subjectively intends to execute the very transfer in question, albeit perhaps under a motivational mistake, his subjective intention is – by some contrast to the contractual position – *alone* sufficient to transfer ownership to the transferee, subject to repudiation by the latter. This is a result of the combined facts that the parties' actual subjective consent prevails over an objective outward appearance and that the transferor's unilateral intention to transfer ownership is, subject to the transferee's repudiation, sufficient to provisionally pass ownership (at least if delivery has been made).

It has furthermore been argued that the so-called face-to-face principle, as authoritatively established in the contractual context,[1] according to which

1 *Shogun Finance Ltd v Hudson* [2003] UKHL 62, [2004] 1 AC 919. The rationale of this case has been criticised on the basis of policy reasons and regret has been expressed that their Lordships have missed an opportunity to bring more coherence into the law of

an identification of the addressee of a contractual offer *by sight* prevails over an inconsistent identification *by description*, should equally apply on the proprietary level. Moreover, this principle should be extended by analogy to a "face-to-property principle", according to which an identification of the chattel to be transferred – as the object of the contractual and/or the proprietary offer – by sight should equally prevail over an inconsistent identification by description. As a result, any mistake as to the transferee's name, address, date of birth or the like and any mistake as to a feature of the transferred chattel will, if identified by sight, inevitably be reduced to a mistake as to a mere attribute or quality, rather than identity.

By contrast, the face-to-face or the face-to-property principle does not apply if the transferee or the chattel in question has not actually been identified by sight but only at a distance by description. Arguably, such principle neither applies if the transfer has been made in the dark or by a blind or if the chattel in question has been hidden within another chattel or amongst other chattels.[2] It follows that a face-to-property or a "face-to-quantity" principle does not generally apply with regard to quantity mistakes.

In cases where the face-to-face or the face-to-property principle is inapplicable, one must determine – by an application of the general amalgam of the objective and the subjective principle – whether the transferee and the chattel(s) in question have been effectively identified by the relevant description in the respective proprietary offer. As far as this is the case, the mistake is inoperative and may not prevent the passage of property. As far as this is not

---

identity mistakes; see (e.g.) Hare, MLR 2004; MacMillan, CLJ 2005; Thomas, LMCLQ 2008; Treitel, Contract, 8.39. It must be noted that it is very unlikely that the Supreme Court will, in light of the fact that the House of Lords has offered its fullest attention to it, reconsider this issue in the nearer future. Apart from that, however, the face-to-face principle and the distinction between dealings *inter praesentes* and dealings at a distance is neither arbitrary nor unprincipled. Arguably, this is rather based on a general preponderance of an identification by sight over an inconsistent identification by description. This is not to introduce an unnecessary fiction; rather, there is inevitably a conundrum which must be resolved. A person who identifies the other party by sight *and* by description has generally (subjectively) two things in mind: "I want to contract with this person physically present" and "I want to contract with X, living in Y". In a retrospective assessment, it is impossible to get a proper answer by asking what such a person *really* intended; he simply intended *both*. Giving preference to the physical element (identification by sight) seems perfectly natural. By contrast, the view of the minority in *Shogun Finance* that an offer should always – even in cases where the other party has not been identified by sight – be regarded as addressed to the person, with whom the mistaken party has *in fact been dealing*, would effectively mean that an offer is generally addressed to *whomever might in fact receive it*, even if by pure chance. This seems artificial and motivated by the fact that this is generally the only way of protecting bona fide purchasers. It cannot be correct to manipulate one area of the law (the law of mistakes) in order to correct the perceived shortcomings of another (the law on title conflicts). If at all, the legislator would have to introduce a more general *nemo dat* exception.

2 As far as the identification of the transferee is concerned, the face-to-face principle arguably does apply if the parties have communicated by video link but not if merely by telephone.

the case, the mistake is operative and negatives the transferor's intention to transfer ownership.

Finally, it must be recalled that the scope of this book has been limited. We have merely analysed the question whether – in a case where A transfers tangible movable property to B by mistake or some other defect – *legal* ownership passes to B or whether A retains it *ab initio*. However, even if legal title does pass to B (in a first step), A might still acquire other rights – proprietary or personal – which entitle him to remedy the defective transaction, i.e. to recover the transferred chattel itself or to claim at least its value. In particular, the proprietary transfer, though being effective to transfer legal and equitable ownership in a first instance, might still be *voidable*, which means that the transferor acquires a power in rem to revest legal or equitable ownership in a second instance. Similarly, the proprietary transfer might be *void in equity*, in the sense that equity imposes – by reason of the defect in question – an immediate resulting or constructive trust or some other proprietary right in favour of the transferor.

The ambit and the doctrinal analysis of such proprietary rights and remedies arising in the context of defective transfers of ownership – particularly of what is known as *equitable proprietary restitution* – is very controversial and by no means settled in the case law. This difficult subject is discussed by the author in depth elsewhere.[3]

[3] Zogg, Proprietary Consequences.

BIBLIOGRAPHY

Secondary literature is respectively cited in an abbreviated form [as indicated in square brackets].

Atiyah, P.S., Judicial Techniques and the English Law of Contract, Ottawa LR 1968, 337–62 [Atiyah, Ottawa LR 1968]

—— The Infants Relief Act, 1874 – A Reply, LQR 1958, 97–104 [Atiyah, LQR 1958]

Baker, John, An Introduction to English Legal History, 4th edn, Butterworths, London 2002 [Baker, English Legal History]

—— The Oxford History of the Laws of England, vol 6, 1483–1558, OUP, Oxford 2003 [Baker, Oxford History, vol 6]

Bant, Elise, Reconsidering the Role of Election in Rescission, OJLS 2012, 467–86 [Bant, OJLS 2012]

Barker, Kit, After Change of Position: Good Faith Exchange in the Modern Law of Restitution, in: P. Birks (ed), Laundering and Tracing, Clarendon Press, Oxford 1995 [Barker, Change of Position]

Beatson, Jack/Burrows, Andrew/Cartwright, John, Anson's Law of Contract, 30th edn, OUP, Oxford 2016 [Beatson et al, Anson's Law of Contract]

Bell, Andrew, Modern Law of Personal Property in England and Ireland, Butterworths, London/Edinburgh 1989 [Bell, Personal Property]

Birks, Peter, An introduction to the law of restitution, revised edn, OUP, Oxford 1989 [Birks, Introduction]

—— No Consideration: Restitution after Void Contracts, UWALR 1993, 195–234 [Birks, UWALR 1993]

—— Property and Unjust Enrichment: Categorical Truths, NZ L Rev 1997, 623–667 [Birks, NZ L Rev 1997]

—— Property, Unjust Enrichment, and Tracing, CLP 2001, 231–54 [Birks, CLP 2001]

—— Restitution and Resulting Trusts, in: S. Goldstein (ed), Equity and Contemporary Legal Developments, Hamaccabi Press, Jerusalem 1992 [Birks, Restitution and Resulting Trusts]

—— Retrieving Tied Money, in: W. Swadling (ed), The *Quistclose* Trust: Critical Essays, Hart Publishing, Oxford 2004 [Birks, Tied Money]

—— The Law of Restitution at the End of an Epoch, UWALR 1999, 13–64 [Birks, UWALR 1999]

—— Trusts Raised to Reverse Unjust Enrichment: The *Westdeutsche* Case, RLR 1996, 3–26 [Birks, RLR 1996]

—— Unjust Enrichment, 2nd edn, OUP, Oxford 2005 [Birks, Unjust Enrichment]

Bowstead, William/Reynolds, F.M.B. (edited by P. Watts/F.M.B. Reynolds), Bowstead and Reynolds on Agency, 20th edn, Sweet & Maxwell, London 2014 [Bowstead/Reynolds, Agency]

BRIDGE, MICHAEL, Personal Property Law, 4th edn, OUP, Oxford 2015 [BRIDGE, Property Law]

—— The Sale of Goods, 3rd edn, OUP, Oxford 2014 [BRIDGE, Sale of Goods]

BRIDGE, MICHAEL (general editor), Benjamin's Sale of Goods, 10th edn, Sweet & Maxwell, London 2017 [BRIDGE et al, Benjamin's Sale of Goods]

BRIDGE, MICHAEL/GULLIFER, LOUISE/MCMEEL, GERARD/WORTHINGTON, SARAH, The Law of Personal Property, Sweet & Maxwell, London 2013 [BRIDGE et al, Personal Property]

BURN, E.H./CARTWRIGHT, J., Cheshire and Burn's Modern Law of Real Property, 18th edn, OUP, Oxford 2011 [BURN/CARTWRIGHT, Cheshire and Burn's Modern Law of Real Property]

BURROWS, ANDREW, Absence of Basis: The New Birksian Scheme, in: A. Burrows/A. Rodger (eds), Mapping the Law: Essays in Memory of Peter Birks, OUP, Oxford 2006 [BURROWS, Absence of Basis]

—— A Restatement of the English Law of Unjust Enrichment, OUP, Oxford 2012 [BURROWS, Restatement]

—— (ed), English Private Law, 3rd edn, OUP, Oxford 2013 [CONTRIBUTOR, English Private Law]

—— The Law of Restitution, 3rd edn, OUP, Oxford 2011 [BURROWS, Restitution]

CANTON, CLARE, Sale of Goods and Barter, MLR 1976, 589–92 [CANTON, MLR 1976]

CARTWRIGHT, JOHN, Misrepresentation, Mistake and Non-Disclosure, 4th edn, Sweet & Maxwell, London 2017 [CARTWRIGHT, Misrepresentation]

CHAMBERS, ROBERT, Constructive Trusts in Canada, AlbLR 1999, 173–220 [CHAMBERS, AlbLR 1999]

—— Resulting Trusts, Clarendon Press, Oxford 1997 [CHAMBERS, Resulting Trusts]

—— Resulting Trusts, in: A. Burrows/A. Rodger (eds), Mapping the Law: Essays in Memory of Peter Birks, OUP, Oxford 2006 [CHAMBERS, Mapping the Law]

—— Resulting Trusts in Canada, AlbLR 2000, 378–414 [CHAMBERS, AlbLR 2000]

CHITTY JOSEPH JUNIOR (general editor: H. Beale), Chitty on Contracts, vol 1, General Principles, 33rd edn, Sweet & Maxwell, London 2018 [EDITOR, Chitty on Contracts, vol 1]

—— (general editor: H. Beale), Chitty on Contracts, vol 2, Specific Contracts, 33rd edn, Sweet & Maxwell, London 2018 [EDITOR, Chitty on Contracts, vol 2]

COOTE, BRIAN, Another look at *Bowmakers v. Barnet Instruments*, MLR 1972, 38–51 [COOTE, MLR 1972]

CRAGO, NEVILLE, Principles of Disclaimer of Gifts, UWALR 1999, 65–83 [CRAGO, UWALR 1999]

DAVIES, PAUL/WORTHINGTON, SARAH, Gower's Principles of Modern Company Law, 10th edn, Sweet & Maxwell, London 2016 [DAVIES/WORTHINGTON, Gower's Principles of Modern Company Law]

DIAMOND, AUBREY L., The Effect of an Illegal Contract, MLR 1960, 451–454 [DIAMOND, MLR 1960]

DROBNIG, ULRICH, Transfer of Property, in: A.S. Hartkamp et al (eds), Towards a European Civil Code, 4th edn, Kluwer Law International, Alphen aan den Rijn 2011 [DROBNIG, Transfer of Property]

ENONCHONG, NELSON, Title claims and illegal transactions, LQR 1995, 135–157 [ENONCHONG, LQR 1995]

Enright, Sean (consultant editor), Personal Property, in: Lord Mackay (editor in chief), Halsbury's Laws of England, vol 80(3), 5th edn, LexisNexis, London 2013 [Enright, Halsbury's Laws of England, vol 80(3)]

Etherton, Terence, The role of equity in mistaken transactions, TruLI 2013, 159–71 [Etherton, TruLI 2013]

Fox, David, Property Rights in Money, OUP, Oxford 2008 [Fox, Property Rights]

—— The Transfer of Legal Title to Money, RLR 1996, 60–70 [Fox, RLR 1996]

Friedmann, Daniel, The objective principle and mistake and involuntariness in contract and restitution, LQR 2003, 68–93 [Friedmann, LQR 2003]

Furmston, Michael, Cheshire, Fifoot & Furmston's Law of Contract, 17th edn, OUP, Oxford 2017 [Furmston, Cheshire, Fifoot & Furmston's Law of Contract]

Goff, Robert/Jones, Gareth (edited by C. Mitchell/P. Mitchell/S. Watterson), The Law of Unjust Enrichment, 9th edn, Sweet & Maxwell, London 2016 [Goff/Jones, Unjust Enrichment]

—— The Law of Unjust Enrichment, 8th edn, Sweet & Maxwell, London 2011 [Goff/Jones, Unjust Enrichment (8th edn)]

Goode, Roy (edited by E. McKendrick), Goode on Commercial Law, 5th edn, Penguin Books, London 2016 [Goode, Commercial Law]

Goodhart, A.L., Mistake as to Identity in the Law of Contract, LQR 1941, 228–44 [Goodhart, LQR 1941]

Goodwin, James, Failure of Basis in the Contractual Context, RLR 2013, 24–45 [Goodwin, RLR 2013]

Grantham, Ross/Rickett, Charles, Restitution, Property and Mistaken Payments, RLR 1997, 83–89 [Grantham/Rickett, RLR 1997]

Häcker, Birke, Causality and abstraction in the common law, in: E. Bant/M. Harding (eds), Exploring Private Law, CUP, Cambridge 2010 [Häcker, Causality and abstraction]

—— Consequences of Impaired Consent Transfers: A Structural Comparison of English and German Law, Mohr Siebeck, Tübingen 2009 [Häcker, Impaired Consent]

—— Das Trennungs- und Abstraktionsprinzip im englischen Recht – dargestellt anhand der Übereignung, Zeitschrift für europäisches Privatrecht (ZEuP) 2011, 335–65 [Häcker, ZEuP 2011]

—— Proprietary Restitution after Impaired Consent Transfers: A Generalised Power Model, CLJ 2009, 324–60 [Häcker, CLJ 2009]

—— Rescission and Third Party Rights, RLR 2006, 21–40 [Häcker, Third Party Rights]

—— Rescission of Contract and Revesting of Title: A Reply to Mr Swadling, RLR 2006, 106–111 [Häcker, Reply]

—— The effect of rescission on bona fide purchase, LQR 2012, 493–97 [Häcker, LQR 2012]

Hackney, Jeffrey, Understanding Equity and Trusts, Fontana Press, London 1987 [Hackney, Trusts]

Hamson, C.J., Contract – Illegality – in pari delicto, CLJ 1964, 20–23 [Hamson, CLJ 1964]

—— Illegal contracts and limited interests, CLJ 1949, 249–59 [Hamson, CLJ 1949]

Hare, Christopher, Identity Mistakes: A Missed Opportunity?, MLR 2004, 993–1007 [Hare, MLR 2004]

Harpum, Charles, Registered Land – A Law Unto Itself?, in: J. Getzler (ed), Rationalizing Property, Equity and Trusts: Essays in Honour of Edward Burn, LexisNexis, 2003 [Harpum, Registered Land]

HARPUM, CHARLES/BRIDGE, STUART/DIXON, MARTIN, Megarry & Wade, The Law of Real Property, 8th edn, Sweet & Maxwell, London 2012 [HARPUM et al, Megarry & Wade, The Law of Real Property]

HICKEY, ROBIN, Property and the Law of Finders, Hart Publishing, Oxford 2010 [HICKEY, Finders]

HIGGINS, M.J., The Transfer of Property under Illegal Transactions, MLR 1962, 149–62 [HIGGINS, MLR 1962]

HILL, JONATHAN, The role of the donee's consent in the law of gift, LQR 2001, 127–49 [HILL, LQR 2001]

HILL-SMITH, ALEXANDER, Forgery and land registration: the decision in Malory Investments v Cheshire Homes, CPL 2009, 127–40 [HILL-SMITH, CPL 2009]

HOLDSWORTH, WILLIAM, A History of English Law, vol 3, 5th edn, Sweet & Maxwell, London 1942 (reprinted 1966) [HOLDSWORTH, History of English Law, vol 3]

—— A History of English Law, vol 7, 2nd edn, Sweet & Maxwell, London 1937 (reprinted 1966) [HOLDSWORTH, History of English Law, vol 7]

IBBETSON, DAVID, Sale of goods in the fourteenth century, LQR 1991, 480–99 [IBBETSON, LQR 1991]

KERSLEY, R.H., Goodeve's Modern Law of Personal Property, 9th edn, Sweet & Maxwell, London 1949 [KERSLEY, Goodeve's Modern Law of Personal Property]

KREBS, THOMAS, In defence of unjust factors, in: D. Johnston/R. Zimmermann (eds), Unjustified Enrichment: Key Issues in Comparative Perspective, CUP, Cambridge 2002 [KREBS, Unjust factors]

—— Restitution at the Crossroads: a comparative study, Cavendish Publishing, London 2001 [KREBS, Restitution]

LANHAM, D.J., Duress and void contracts, MLR 1966, 615–21 [LANHAM, MLR 1966]

LAWSON, F.H./RUDDEN, BERNARD, The Law of Property, 3rd edn, OUP, Oxford 2002 [LAWSON/RUDDEN, Law of Property]

MACMILLAN, CATHARINE, Rogues, swindlers and cheats: the development of mistake of identity in English contract law, CLJ 2005, 711–44 [MACMILLAN, CLJ 2005]

MAITLAND, F.W., Equity: A Course of Lectures, 2nd edn, CUP, Cambridge 1936 [MAITLAND, Equity]

MATTEI, UGO, Basic principles of property law: a comparative legal and economic introduction, Greenwood Press, Westport 2000 [MATTEI, Property law]

MCCORMACK, GERARD, Mistaken payments and proprietary claims, CPL 1996, 86–97 [MCCORMACK, CPL 1996]

—— Proprietary claims and insolvency in the wake of Westdeutsche, JBL 1997, 48–71 [MCCORMACK, JBL 1997]

MCLAUCHLAN, D.W., Parol evidence and contract formation, LQR 2005, 9–16 [MCLAUCHLAN, LQR 2005]

MEIER, SONJA, Irrtum und Zweckverfehlung: Die Rolle der unjust-Gründe bei rechtsgrundlosen Leistungen im englischen Recht, Mohr Siebeck, Tübingen 1999 [MEIER, Irrtum]

—— Restitution after Executed Void Contracts, in: P. Birks/F. Rose (eds), Lessons of the Swaps Litigation, Informa law, Abingdon 2000 [MEIER, Void Contracts]

—— Unjust factors and legal grounds, in: D. Johnston/R. Zimmermann (eds), Unjustified Enrichment: Key Issues in Comparative Perspective, CUP, Cambridge 2002 [MEIER, Unjust factors]

MEIER, SONJA/ZIMMERMANN, REINHARD, Judicial Development of the Law, *Error Iuris*, and the Law of Unjustified Enrichment – a View from Germany, LQR 1999, 556–65 [MEIER/ZIMMERMANN, LQR 1999]

MILLETT, PETER, Proprietary Restitution, in: S. Degeling/J. Edelman (eds), Equity in Commercial Law, Thomson Reuters, Sydney 2005 [MILLETT, Proprietary Restitution]

—— Restitution and Constructive Trusts, LQR 1998, 399–418 [MILLETT, LQR 1998]

MILSOM, S.F.C., Sale of Goods in the Fifteenth Century, LQR 1961, 257–84 [MILSOM, LQR 1961]

MONTROSE, J.L., The Operation of Description in a Contract of Sale of Goods, Canadian Bar Review 1937, 760–88 [MONTROSE, Canadian Bar Review 1937]

NEWMAN, GEORGE (consultant editor), Gifts, in: Lord Mackay (editor in chief), Halsbury's Laws of England, vol 52(2), 5th edn, LexisNexis, London 2009 [NEWMAN, Halsbury's Laws of England, vol 52(2)]

ORCHARD, G.F., The Borderland of Theft Revisited, NZLJ 1973, 110–16 [ORCHARD, NZLJ 1973]

ORMEROD, DAVID/WILLIAMS, DAVID HUW, Smith's Law of Theft, 9th edn, OUP, Oxford 2007 [ORMEROD/WILLIAMS, Smith's Law of Theft]

O'SULLIVAN, DOMINIC/ELLIOTT, STEVEN/ZAKRZEWSKI, RAFAL, The Law of Rescission, 2nd edn, OUP, Oxford 2014 [O'SULLIVAN et al, Rescission]

O'SULLIVAN, JANET, Rescission as a self-help remedy: A critical analysis, CLJ 2000, 509–543 [J. O'SULLIVAN, CLJ 2000]

PENNER, JAMES, Resulting Trusts and Unjust Enrichment: Three Controversies, in: C. Mitchell (ed), Constructive and Resulting Trusts, Hart Publishing, Oxford 2010 [PENNER, Resulting Trusts]

POLLOCK, FREDERICK, Gifts of Chattels Without Delivery, LQR 1890, 446–51 [POLLOCK, LQR 1890]

—— Principles of contract at law and in equity: being a treatise on the general principles concerning the validity of agreements, with a special view to the comparison of law and equity and with references to the Indian Contract Act, and occasionally to Roman, American and Continental law, 2nd edn, London 1878 [POLLOCK, Principles of contract]

POLLOCK, FREDERICK/WRIGHT, ROBERT, An Essay on Possession in the Common Law, Clarendon Press, Oxford 1888 [POLLOCK/WRIGHT, Possession]

RICKETT, CHARLES/GRANTHAM, ROSS, Resulting Trusts – A Rather Limited Doctrine, in: P. Birks/F. Rose (eds), Restitution and Equity, vol 1: Resulting Trusts and Equitable Compensation, Mansfield Press, London 2000 [RICKETT/GRANTHAM, Limited Doctrine]

SHEEHAN, DUNCAN, The Principles of Personal Property Law, 2nd edn, Hart Publishing, Oxford, 2017 [SHEEHAN, Personal Property]

SLADE, C.J., The Myth of Mistake in the English Law of Contract, LQR 1954, 385–408 [SLADE, LQR 1954]

SMITH, J.C., Civil Law Concepts in the Criminal Law, CLJ 1972B, 197–224 [J. SMITH, CLJ 1972B]

—— Theft (R v Gilks), Crim LR 1972, 584–90 [J. SMITH, Crim LR 1972]

SMITH, LIONEL, The Law of Tracing, Clarendon Press, Oxford 1997 [L. SMITH, Tracing]

—— Unjust Enrichment: Big or Small?, in: S. Degeling/J. Edelman (eds), Unjust Enrichment in Commercial Law, Thomson Reuters, Sydney 2008 [L. SMITH, Unjust Enrichment]

SMITH, ROGER, Property Law, 9th edn, Pearson, Harlow 2017 [R. SMITH, Property Law]

SMITH, STEPHEN A., Concurrent liability in contract and unjust enrichment: the fundamental breach requirement, LQR 1999, 245–64 [S. SMITH, LQR 1999]

SNELL, E.H.T. (general editor: J. McGhee), Snell's Equity, 33rd edn, Sweet & Maxwell, London 2015 [EDITOR, Snell's Equity]

STADLER, ASTRID, Gestaltungsfreiheit und Verkehrsschutz durch Abstraktion: Eine rechtsvergleichende Studie zur abstrakten und kausalen Gestaltung rechtsgeschäftlicher Zuwendungen anhand des deutschen, schweizerischen, österreichischen, französischen und US-amerikanischen Rechts, Mohr Siebeck, Tübingen 1996 [STADLER, Gestaltungsfreiheit]

STANNARD, JOHN E./CAPPER, DAVID, Termination for Breach of Contract, OUP, Oxford 2014 [STANNARD/CAPPER, Termination]

STEVENS, ROBERT, Is there a Law of Unjust Enrichment?, in: S. Degeling/J. Edelman (eds), Unjust Enrichment in Commercial Law, Thomson Reuters, Sydney 2008 [STEVENS, Unjust Enrichment]

—— Justified Enrichment, OUCLJ 2005, 141–49 [STEVENS, OUCLJ 2005]

SWADLING, WILLIAM, A new role for resulting trusts?, LS 1996, 110–131 [SWADLING, LS 1996]

—— Property and Unjust Enrichment, in: J.W. Harris (ed), Property Problems: From Genes to Pension Funds, Kluwer Law International, London/The Hague/Boston 1997 [SWADLING, Property and Unjust Enrichment]

—— Rescission, property, and the common law, LQR 2005, 123–53 [SWADLING, LQR 2005]

—— Restitution for no consideration, RLR 1994, 73–85 [SWADLING, RLR 1994]

—— The New Birksian Approach to Unjust Enrichment, RLR 2004, 279–83 [SWADLING, RLR 2004]

—— Unjust Delivery, in: A. Burrows/A. Rodger (eds), Mapping the Law: Essays in Memory of Peter Birks, OUP, Oxford 2006 [SWADLING, Unjust Delivery]

SWEET, CHARLES, 'A Song of Uses': Some Reflections and a Moral, LQR 1919, 127–32 [SWEET, LQR 1919]

TANG, HANG WU, Restitution for Mistaken Gifts, JCL 2004, 1–34 [TANG, JCL 2004]

—— Unjust Enrichment within a Valid Contract: A Close Look at Roxborough v Rothmans of Pall Mall Australia Ltd, JCL 2007, 201–227 [TANG, JCL 2007]

TETTENBORN, ANDREW, Subsisting contracts and failure of consideration - a little scepticism, RLR 2002, 1 [TETTENBRON, RLR 2002]

—— The Law of Restitution in England and Ireland, 3rd edn, Cavendish Publishing, London 2002 [TETTENBORN, Restitution]

THOMAS, SEAN, Mistake of identity: a comparative analysis, LMCLQ 2008, 188–213 [THOMAS, LMCLQ 2008]

THOMPSON, MARK (consultant editor), Deeds and other Instruments, in: Lord Mackay (editor in chief), Halsbury's Laws of England, vol 32(2), 5th edn, LexisNexis, London 2012 [THOMPSON, Halsbury's Laws of England, vol 32(2)]

TREITEL, G.H., Mutuality in contract, LQR 1961, 83–97 [TREITEL, LQR 1961]

—— (edited by E. Peel), The Law of Contract, 14th edn, Sweet & Maxwell, London 2015 [TREITEL, Contract]

—— The Infants Relief Act, 1874, LQR 1957, 194–211 [TREITEL, LQR 1957]

—— The Infants' Relief Act, 1874 - A Short Rebutter, LQR 1958, 104–7 [TREITEL, LQR 1958]

Turner, J.W. Cecil (ed), Kenny's Outlines of Criminal Law, 19th edn, CUP, Cambridge 1966 [Turner, Kenny's Outlines of Criminal Law]

—— (ed), Russell on Crime, vol 2, 12th edn, Stevens & Sons, London 1964 [Turner, Russell on Crime, vol 2]

Twigg-Flesner, Christian (consultant editor), Sale of Goods and Supply of Services, in: Lord Mackay (editor in chief), Halsbury's Laws of England, vol 91(1), 5th edn, LexisNexis, London 2012 [Twigg-Flesner, Halsbury's Laws of England, vol 91(1)]

Twigg-Flesner, Christian/Canavan, Rick/MacQueen, Hector, Atiyah and Adams' Sale of Goods, 13th edn, Pearson, Harlow 2016 [Twigg-Flesner et al, Atiyah and Adams' Sale of Goods]

Ulph, Janet, The Proprietary Consequences of an Excess Delivery, LMCLQ 1998, 4–9 [Ulph, LMCLQ 1998]

Unger, J., Intent to Create Legal Relations, Mutuality and Consideration, MLR 1956, 96–100 [Unger, MLR 1956]

van Vliet, Lars P.W., The Transfer of Moveables in Scotland and England, Edinburgh Law Review 2008, 173–99 [van Vliet, EdinLR 2008]

—— Transfer of movables in German, French, English and Dutch law, Ars Aequi Libri, Nijmegen 2000 [van Vliet, Transfer of movables]

Virgo, Graham, Restitution Through the Looking Glass: Restitution Within Equity and Equity Within Restitution, in: J. Getzler (ed), Rationalizing Property, Equity and Trusts: Essays in Honour of Edward Burn, LexisNexis, London 2003 [Virgo, Looking Glass]

—— The Principles of Equity & Trusts, 3rd edn, OUP, Oxford 2018 [Virgo, Equity]

—— The Principles of the Law of Restitution, 3rd edn, OUP, Oxford 2015 [Virgo, Restitution]

Watts, Peter, Restitution - A Property Principle and a Services Principle, RLR 1995, 49–82 [Watts, RLR 1995]

Williams, Glanville, Mistake and Rectification in Contract, MLR 1954, 154–55 [Williams, MLR 1954]

—— Mistake as to Quantity in the Law of Larceny, Crim LR 1958, 221–32 [Williams, Crim LR 1958]

—— Mistake in the Law of Theft, CLJ 1977, 62–85 [Williams, CLJ 1977]

—— (edited by D.J. Baker), Textbook of Criminal Law, 4th edn, Sweet & Maxwell, London 2015 [Williams, Criminal Law]

—— Theft, Consent and Illegality, Crim LR 1977, 127–38 (part 1), 205–9 (part 2) [Williams, Crim LR 1977]

Worthington, Sarah, Proprietary Interests in Commercial Transactions, Clarendon Press, Oxford 1996 (reprinted 2005) [Worthington, Commercial Transactions]

—— The Proprietary Consequences of Rescission, RLR 2002, 28–68 [Worthington, RLR 2002]

Zogg, Samuel, Proprietary Consequences in Defective Transfers of Ownership, Intersentia, Cambridge 2020 [Zogg, Proprietary Consequences]

Zwalve, Willem/Sirks, Boudewijn, Grundzüge der europäischen Privatrechtsgeschichte: Einführung und Sachenrecht, Böhlau Verlag, Vienna/Cologne/Weimar 2012 [Zwalve/Sirks, Privatrechtsgeschichte]

INDEX

ABOUT THE AUTHOR

Samuel Zogg is a senior lecturer for private law at the University of Zurich, Faculty of Law. He also works as a law clerk at the Court of Appeal, Zurich, and he is a deputy judge at the District Court of Meilen, Zurich. His research focusses on private law, in particular the law of property and obligations, and civil procedure law.

www.ingramcontent.com/pod-product-compliance
Ingram Content Group UK Ltd.
Pitfield, Milton Keynes, MK11 3LW, UK
UKHW051922100926
8556IPUK00021B/1325

9 781780 688312